THE MINISTRY OF THE HOLY SPIRIT

STELLA N BABUDOH

CTK PUBLISHING LTD

CTK Publishing Ltd

ISBN: 978-1-915971-00-5

Printed in the United Kingdom

CONTENTS

This book is dedicated to everyone that wants to know more about the ministry of the Holy Spirit.
My desire is that this book will both impact and enable you to get a deeper understanding of the Holy Spirit, whether you know Christ or are seeking to understand the Christian faith.
May you be richly blessed, as you get to know the Holy Spirit intimately in your life.

ACKNOWLEDGMENTS

Firstly, I would like to express my profound gratitude and appreciation to my husband, Alexander, and my four children – Tonye, Abigail, Jonathan and Jesse, for putting up with me whilst writing this book.

I would also like to thank my family, friends, and well-wishers for their support and encouragement.

And a special thank you goes to my publication team for their push, support, and encouragement, to ensure that all the relevant tasks were completed.

And, finally, most importantly, thank you to God the Father, God the Son, and God the Holy Spirit, for counting me worthy, for allowing me to write about the person of the Holy Spirit, and for making it possible for me to complete and publish this book.

PREFACE

I was born into the Christian faith and became a committed Christian in 1990. Shortly afterward, I had a feeling that I needed to write a book but had no idea of what the book title should be at the time. As I grew in my new Christian faith, I began to learn about the Holy Spirit and decided to put what I was learning to test or into practice.

I often ask the Holy Spirit daily questions like what to wear, cook or eat. I converse with the Holy Spirit all day long, about anything and everything. When going through any situation, I ask the Holy Spirit for directions, even when I lose my way while driving. When I lose something in the house, I ask the Holy Spirit to show me where it is. At one point, I thought I was overusing the Holy Spirit because I would consult Him on everything, from mundane to very complex issues. I realised that the truth is, we cannot exhaust or overuse the Holy Spirit. He is here as our

Helper, Advocate, Teacher, Friend, and a shoulder to lean on, the very present help in time of need.

As I realised how useful and helpful the Holy Spirit is to my day-to-day life, I thought I could not keep this to myself, and felt led to share my experiences and what I have learned about the Holy Spirit through a book.

The intention of this book is to shed some light on the person of the Holy Spirit. Most people know God the Father and God the Son, but God the Holy Spirit is somewhat oblivious to them. Through this book, I would like to introduce God the Holy Spirit, both to people that may not know Him and to those that may seldom refer to the ministry of the Holy Spirit or know the function and the purpose of the Holy Spirit in our lives today.

Prior to writing this book, I read the Bible and compiled many references about the Holy Spirit and Holy Ghost. I also listened to several teachings, read books on the subject, and made notes as I gained inspiration or heard something that I felt would help one's understanding of the Holy Spirit. Essentially, the Holy Spirit Himself also ministered to me through my experiences as I wrote this book.

For several years, I toyed with the idea that one day I would author a book, but it was more of lip service, which went on for a very long time. It got to a point where the thought of writing a book would not leave me day or night, and then I knew at some point that I had to start writing one to get those thoughts out of my mind. I knew the topic that I was going to write about at this stage, as it was imprinted very early on in my mind after I became a committed Christian.

The journey to birth this book was tedious; it took several years of starting and stopping. I started writing this book in 2007 and finished my first draft in 2009. It would then take thirteen years before I took the steps to get the book published, cumulating in a total of thirty-two years from when I first felt the call to write.

I juggled writing the book with being a wife, mother, and working full-time. My strategy was to first attend to the needs of my household after work, then go to bed as early as 8:00 p.m. I would set an alarm to wake up at 4:00 a.m. and then write until 7:00 a.m. or 7.30 a.m. Then, I would start my day by getting the children ready for school and then off to work. It was not easy, but I persisted.

Another hurdle I had to overcome was thinking that no one would be interested or want to read what I have to say or write. I thought, after completing the draft in 2009, that I had fulfilled the yearning and nagging feelings. I put the manuscript to one side and threw myself into full-time work, believing that I would get someone to edit and eventually publish the book someday.

Getting someone to edit the book was another challenge; I had spoken to several individuals who offered to help with that, but I was not yet ready to share my writing or progress to the next stage. It took a few more years before I eventually spoke to an editor and the result is the book that you are reading. I still cannot believe that I have now finally published it.

I pray that this book will truly impact your life, and benefit and bless you as you develop your walk and have a closer fellowship with the Holy Spirit.

1

WHO IS THE HOLY SPIRIT?

The Holy Spirit is the third person of the Godhead or the Trinity. The Trinity is made up of God the Father, God the Son, and God the Holy Spirit. The Holy Spirit is a person and not an 'it' or an impersonal force. An 'it' is a pronoun used when people are referring to an unspecified entity, an implied situation, or a feeling. The Holy Spirit is a specified person with specific roles, purposes, and responsibilities.

Both God the Father and God the Son sent The Holy Spirit, to dwell in and guide believers. Many people profess to believe or trust in the Holy Spirit, but they really believe and trust in God the Father and God the Son. They see the Holy Spirit as a less equal partner of the Godhead.

The Holy Spirit is equal to, and in no way inferior to the other members of the Godhead. Some, in their misconception, reduce the Holy Spirit to an inanimate force such as electricity, which is very powerful, but completely devoid of being a living person, much less God.

The Holy Spirit is the presence of God living inside of us. Think about it this way: God, the creator of the universe, living on the inside of us, in the person of the Holy Spirit. Jesus Christ, who is God the Son, also lives in us through the person of the Holy Spirit. The Holy Spirit is equal to the Father and the Son in every respect. As the Deity is Omnipotent, which means 'Almighty, All-Powerful', so is the Holy Spirit equally God Almighty and All-Powerful in the same regard. He is Omniscient, which means He is all knowing. He knows everything about us; our past, present, and future. He is also Omnipresent, which means that He is everywhere at the same time. We carry the presence of God in the person of the Holy Spirit, everywhere and anywhere we go.

The Father, Son, and Holy Spirit are intricate beings, inseparable, and yet have distinct functions. Most people see the functions of God the Father defined, and see the roles and functions of God the Son defined as well, but are unsure of how to place the Holy Spirit. In other words, His functions and purpose to them are not clearly defined.

The intention of this book is to unravel the puzzle and shed some light on the person of the Holy Spirit. What I have compiled in this book is by no means all His functionalities, because He is after all, God the Holy Spirit, and His ways are past finding out. He is an infinite being and no human being will ever comprehend everything about the Holy Spirit. I have put together an aspect of His personality, attributes, functions, roles, and responsibilities, so that we can begin to understand the Ministry of the Holy Spirit and His role in our lives. The Godhead, as we know, is multifaceted; if you were to carry out your own study and research about the Holy Spirit – I am sure that He will reveal Himself to you as He desires. Perhaps He will reveal Himself to you in another facet.

The Holy Spirit is not a spooky personality, as some would like to conjure in their minds. They hear the word, 'Spirit' and they immediately think of, 'freaky, weird, strange, creepy' and, "that cannot be a person". The Holy Spirit is very real, and He has been there from the beginning and will be there throughout all eternity. As the name implies, He is Holy and not a devilish or evil spirit. The Holy Spirit has been misrepresented as some commit so many atrocities and deceptions in His name. This may explain why some people have knowingly or unconsciously decided to shy away and have nothing to do with anything remotely connected to the Holy Spirit. The purpose of this book is to help shed some light on both the real purpose of the Holy Spirit and why He has been sent as our indwelling companion on earth.

IN THE BEGINNING

The Holy Spirit is a Divine Personality, who has a definite function in the world. The Bible depicts His functions, regarding the universe and the people on earth.

The Holy Spirit was there from the very beginning. In the creation story, from Genesis 1: 1-2, the Bible records that: "*In THE beginning, God created the heavens and the earth. The earth was without form, and void; and darkness was upon the face of the deep.*" In the latter part of verse two, it says: "*And the Spirit of God was hovering* (moving) *over the face of the waters...*", and verse three goes on to say: "*Then God said let there be... and there was...*"

You can read the whole chapter for the full creation story. What I would like to bring out here is in the latter part of verse two, where the Bible recorded that the Spirit of the Lord was moving over the face of the waters and then God spoke. From this account, we can see that the Holy Spirit was very instrumental in creation. You will notice that it was when the Spirit was moving that God spoke and the earth came to being, as we know it today. We can say it this way; if the Holy Spirit were not present, God would not have spoken. So, you can see that He had a definite role in the creation story. If we read further down in the same chapter of Genesis, in verse twenty-six, we will see that the Holy Spirit was present in human creation. The verse reads like this: "*...and God said, let **us** make man* (the human race) *in our image...*" The '**US**' here refers to the Godhead. We are made in the image and likeness of God the Father, God the Son, and God the Holy Spirit.

Carrying on with the creation story, in Genesis 2:7, which was still the sixth day of creation, the Bible recorded that man (humanity) was formed in the image and likeness of God, from the dust of the ground. Little wonder when people die, their body decays and they are put back to the ground. The most important aspect of the human composition is the human spirit. In the same verse, the Bible documented that God breathed into the nostrils of the created man, the breath of life, and man became a living soul. This breath of life was the breath of the Spirit of God. Without the Holy Spirit, man today will not be a living soul. This probably explains the ***God Vacuum*** on the inside of every man; the spiritual void that cannot be filled until we make that connection back to God, through the person of the Holy Spirit. When the Spirit of God is absent in our lives, we are restless, and nothing truly fully satisfies us. The whole of humanity, past, present, and no doubt in the future, have tried and will continue to try to fill the vacuum in any way, with no success. Until we reconnect with the Holy Spirit, all our attempts to bridge this gap will always be futile and remain an impossible mission to accomplish.

I am sure that we can already begin to see the roles and functions of the Holy Spirit: He was there from the very beginning, and HE is still very much present, here and now. He has a vital role and wants to be active in our everyday lives; He is here to help us fulfil our preordained destiny and purpose in life.

As He moved in Genesis 1:2, He is still moving today and wants to move every moment, every second, every minute, every hour, and every day in our lives. We need to believe, speak, receive, trust, and obey, to activate the presence and unleash the power of the Holy Spirit in our lives. This will become clearer, as you journey through this book.

In the Old Testament, the Holy Spirit did not dwell in people. The Holy Spirit had what I will describe as a touch-and-go ministry because He would come upon the people and then go, but since the day of Pentecost, His ministry has somewhat changed. Reference to this is seen in Acts 2:1-4, in which the passage describes when the Holy Spirit changed address and took up residence in us. He came to indwell, commune, build a relationship, and abide in us permanently. The Holy Spirit takes up this residency position by invitation only; He will neither intrude nor invade our space, and He will only move in our lives to the degree that we allow Him. The Holy Spirit was there from the beginning, and He was there when the world was created and when we were formed. He gave us the breath of life and will still be very much around when we are gone. He knows everything about us — our past, present, and future — and He knows what is best for our lives.

THE PRESENT-DAY MINISTRY OF THE HOLY SPIRIT

This age, in many respects, can be described as the ***Age of the Spirit***. It is an age in which the Spirit of God is working in a special way, to call out a company of believers from all over the world to form the body of Christ, which in effect, is the church as we know it today. The Holy Spirit in His present-day ministry is fundamentally a gift to the Church.

However, He also has a primary ministry aimed at two other groups of people — those who may not attend a church body and those who may not know Christ. He convicts them of sin (wrongdoing and not living rightly before God). This work of conviction prepares an individual to accept Christ's gift of salvation and by accepting this gift of salvation, the person is automatically placed in the body of Christ. This is a special work of grace (favour, mercy), which enlightens the mind of those who are not yet Christ's disciples. If this sounds like mumbo jumbo to you now, do not despair. As we delve deeper into the subject of the Holy Spirit, I pray that this will become clearer in the following chapters.

The ministry of God the Son, on the other hand, is a gift to the world at large. This gift is called ***Salvation***. Salvation means that our souls have been saved and delivered from sin and destruction. To fully benefit and enjoy the ministry of the Holy Spirit, one will have to accept God's gift of salvation to the world.

Some sit in church pews today and do not really know the person of the Holy Spirit. They have heard of His name being mentioned; He does not mean much to them, nor has He influenced their Christian walk. I do hope that those who resonate with this description will find change, a new perspective, and insight into the Ministry of the Holy Spirit. I believe that the Holy Spirit is the best thing that has ever happened to the church and Jesus is the best thing that has ever happened to humanity. This will become more apparent as you read further.

CHARACTERISTICS OF THE HOLY SPIRIT

Some do not believe that the Holy Spirit is a person. Scientists have characterised the qualities possessed by human beings, which make us different from the animal and plant kingdoms. They say a human being must possess intelligence, emotion, and will. Well, the Holy Spirit possesses qualities such as intellect, emotions, and will. Some have said that He is not a human Person because He does not possess a human body as we do. The Holy Spirit is a Divine Person. He can be approached, shunned, trusted, doubted, loved, hated, adored, or grieved just like us.

In fact, the Holy Spirit possesses personal characteristics and traits that we as humans can relate to, and some of these traits are:

1. Will power – The Holy Spirit has His will power and the sovereignty to make decisions. He moves

and flows as He wills, not according to our wish but according to His wish and will.

2. Intelligence – The Holy Spirit instructs; The Holy Spirit is our teacher, and He instructs us.
3. Knowledge – He was there from creation and will be with us all the way. The Holy Spirit has 'knowledge' and knows all things.
4. Power – The Holy Spirit is powerful and has the power to change us. The Holy Spirit powerfully changed many people in biblical times and is still changing lives now.
5. Presence – The Holy Spirit is the presence of God living inside of us and we carry His divine presence with us wherever we go.
6. Capacity to Love – The Holy Spirit is the love of God personified. He keeps believers in the bond and unity of love.
7. Capacity to Grieve – We can grieve the Holy Spirit by not reverencing Him, honouring Him, and giving Him the respect that is due to Him. Also, we can grieve Him by not acknowledging Him or by ignoring Him.

The Holy Spirit does not speak on behalf of Himself; He does not work in isolation; He is part of the Godhead, and they work in perfect harmony.

RELEVANCE OF THE HOLY SPIRIT

One of the burning questions some people might want to ask is, "What's the relevance of the Holy Spirit in my life today?"

My answer to this question is very simple. Just imagine for one moment that you know someone who knows everything about you and has the answers to all your problems and issues in life. Would you not want to know a person like this and make him your best friend, confidante, and your first point of call on all issues? I would like to add that this is not a make-believe friend; this is a very real friend. If you have a friend like this, I am sure he/she will be very relevant in your life. You might be saying to yourself, "Is this possible? Does such a friend or person exist anywhere?" Well, think no further because the Holy Spirit is the friend that I have just described, and He is very relevant in our lives, our time, our day, our age, and our generation.

I will use another analogy to further explain the relevance of the Holy Spirit in our lives. When parents give birth to a newborn baby, they love the baby unconditionally and they automatically take on the role and responsibilities of caring for the baby's needs (except in certain circumstances, when they are not physically, emotionally, or mentally able to). Babies and children are on the other hand, solely dependent on their parents/carers for basic needs in life. As the child gets older and becomes an adult, they grow independent and can then fend for their livelihood themselves and depend less on their parent/carers for sustenance.

Even as adults, people still ask their parents/carers for advice, help, and support. Their parents or carers feel obliged to support and assist their children as much and as far as they can, if it is within their power and means to do so. It is the joy of every parent to see that their children succeed, achieve, and make headway in life. All these sacrifices, feelings, and expectations that parents have for their children are natural and inborn tendencies. As human beings, that is our composition; that is the way we are made and wired to care for our young ones, the up-and-coming generation.

Parents/carers get old, frail, and weak and can no longer help as much as they would like. In some instances, the reversal of roles becomes the case. The parent/carer now becomes more child-like because of natural old age or some debilitating conditions, and then the child becomes the carer (caregiver).

With all the goodwill and best intentions in the world, parents/carers cannot totally meet all their children's needs. Dependency on the Holy Spirit works somewhat like what we experience with our earthly parents on one level, but on another level, it is completely different. For one, we are human beings, and the Holy Spirit is Deity. We are limited in scope and abilities, whilst the Holy Spirit is unlimited. We get weak, ill, tired, and old, and our stay on earth is short and temporal. The Holy Spirit is an eternal being, so He reigns and rules forever.

There is no reversal of roles with the Holy Spirit; His strength is forever new, his power forever strong. His hands do not grow feeble, His eyes do not grow dim, and His ears do not grow heavy or impaired. He is God in us, He is the same yesterday, today, and forever; He is ageless and timeless. He does not have memory loss and He loves us with everlasting and unconditional love. He has been throughout all ages and is still the same. He looks after us from cradle to grave and will be with us for all eternity. He is infinite in knowledge, limitless in understanding, and inexhaustible in wisdom. He knows us intimately, He knows our every thought, He knows our every need at every stage of our lives, and He is willing and able to meet those needs if we let Him.

We need to trust Him and obey Him before we can begin to realise the benefits He has for us, and the changes He has come to make in our lives. The Holy Spirit's position in this regard is like that of our earthly parents; before they can help us or come to our aid, we need to allow them to do so by giving them our permission.

Just as our earthly parents expect us to fend for ourselves when we come of age, so does the Holy Spirit expect us to be more responsible for our actions as we grow and develop our walk in Him. The Holy Spirit does not take His hands off our case; he loves us with an everlasting love and when we go to Him for help, He is ever ready. He is the very present help in times of need and there is no job too small or too great for him to handle.

The Holy Spirit is very relevant in our day, our age, our culture, our values, our lifestyles, our belief system, and in all our activities because He is the oldest person on planet earth. There are no problems, issues, situations, or circumstances that are new to Him, so, nothing takes Him by surprise. He has everything figured out and under control and knows all the tricks in the book. He has seen many generations come and go and unlike our earthly parents, with limited experience in raising children, the Holy Spirit has seen and helped people to overcome impossible situations. There are no situations that befall us — or any situations peculiar to us — that many have not suffered. The Holy Spirit is well able, equipped, and experienced in dealing with such matters because he has been there before and has done it for countless people. He is the undisputed proven legend in overcoming any area of life's challenges. When we go to Him, He will always respond and deliver if we are willing to listen, trust and obey. He has all the answers to all our questions, cures for any ailment, and hope for hopeless situations. Whilst everything around us is crumbling, flaky, shaky, wobbly, unsteady, unstable, and insecure, He remains constant. He is the only consistent person on planet earth today. He has lived throughout all the ages and will live forevermore. There is nothing new under the sun; even fashion goes round in circles and so do our problems, needs, wants, and issues. No matter what the endeavour or venture might be, He has them covered and conquered under his belt; He has all the solutions.

We could say He is the font of all knowledge; this is not figurative or guesswork. He, really, is the font of all knowledge, wisdom, and understanding, and He knows what is best for us. Our life is already predestined, and when we present our lives and make our time available to the Holy Spirit, He will begin to unfold that pre-destined plan. So, there is no need to agitate, stress, be anxious, fret or worry over the plan.

As we grow from childhood to adulthood, we grow independent from our earthly parents but with the Holy Spirit, the reversal is the case. We grow and develop a dependent relationship with the Holy Spirit. As we begin to acknowledge the Holy Spirit in all that we do, He will make His relevance in our lives apparent and show us great and mighty things that we do not know, as we call on Him and draw closer to Him. The Holy Spirit is our ultimate helper, a trusted friend, and He will help us in ways that we cannot begin to imagine when we place our today, tomorrow, hopes, fears, worries, anxiety, trust, and cares on Him.

When we do not know, He knows. When we do not understand, He understands. When we are confused, He is not. When we are anxious and agitated, He is at peace. When we feel we are not in control, He is always in control. He is our one and only true trusted friend and guardian. When we do not love ourselves, He loves us. When we are lonely, He is our companion. He loves us more than anyone will ever love us.

TRUST AND OBEY

There are two basic requirements we need to know for us to walk with the Holy Spirit. The first one is ***to trust*** and the other one is ***to obey***. While there is a simplicity to saying this, working them out daily is not as easy as it may seem. The Holy Spirit Himself helps us to fulfil these requirements and it starts with believing and acknowledging Him as God living inside of us.

'***Listen, trust, obey, rest, wait and see***,' should be our motto and our approach to the Holy Spirit. ***Trust*** in the sense that He is trustworthy, going by His track record. When we ***listen*** to Him, we cannot go wrong. ***Obey*** His instructions because He knows what He is talking about and ***rest*** in His knowledge, experience, and expertise. ***Wait*** on His promises and He will put your mind at ease, then watch and ***see*** Him deliver the outcome.

2

PURPOSE OF THE HOLY SPIRIT

THE PROMISE OF THE HOLY SPIRIT

As Jesus was about to go to the cross of Calvary, before His death, burial, and resurrection, He said to His disciplines, "*...it is to your advantage that I go away; for if I do not go away, the helper will not come to you* [and stay with you forever]."

The 'Helper' that Jesus was referring to here was the Holy Spirit. Jesus, speaking in John 16:7, put it this way; it is profitable, good, expedient, and advantageous for us that He goes away because if he does not, then the Comforter, Counsellor, Helper, Teacher, Advocate, Intercessor, Friend, Standby, and source of strength will not come into the world to dwell inside of us. During Christ's earthly ministry, He was only physically able to be in one place at one time and the Bible gives accounts of how He was surrounded by crowds many times over. These accounts also show us the vulnerability of man; how we cannot help ourselves, and how we so desperately need the help of a Saviour and a loving Father.

Jesus, acknowledging our helplessness and hopelessness, promised that He would not leave us alone like orphans. He said that He would send us a Helper; 'another' Comforter in the person of the Holy Spirit. The word 'helper' is translated from the Greek word *paraclete*, which actually means 'someone who stands by another'. Jesus promised to send us a standby, just as He stood by His disciples and those who put their trust in Him, as their pillar, refuge, and strong tower.

The state of the world then, during Jesus' earthly ministry, could be described as dire and hopeless. Even with changes in the world, it can feel like the current world is similar, with doom and gloom all around us; we need the help of the Holy Spirit more, now than ever. Jesus was limited in where he could go and the places that he could be because He could not be everywhere at the same time, ministering to the needs of the people, during His days on earth. The good news is that, after the ascension of Jesus, the promised Holy Spirit, the '*paraclete*' came into the world to dwell in those who will believe.

The Ministry of the Holy Spirit on earth today is unlimited in range and power because He abides in us, and we carry His presence with us wherever we go. We all have needs and the Holy Spirit is here to help us meet our spiritual, physical, and emotional needs, and to have a close-knit fellowship with us.

MAKE HIM PRESIDENT AND NOT MERE RESIDENT

To enjoy the best of what the Holy Spirit has in store for us, we should not treat Him as a guest or stranger. To live a fulfilled and enriched life, we need to understand the Ministry of the Holy Spirit. We will be doing ourselves a disservice if we have a guest living in our house and this guest has a lot of skills to help us in areas that we are unaware of and we then choose to limit their stay to one room, and give them restricted access and strict instructions not to go into any other room. To further tighten the security, we may even fit the other doors in the house with alarm units that will trigger each time anyone attempts a forced entry. However, unknown to us, if given a bit of a free hand, this guest might prove to be very useful and able to help in many unimaginable ways.

I will share a story of when a friend came to stay with us, to illustrate this point further. My husband told me that his friend would be coming to stay with us for a while. I was a bit apprehensive about this as I had not heard about or even met this friend of his. My first instinct was to refuse. "No way, this will not happen, he will not come to stay with us," were my initial thoughts. I usually pray about issues like this before anyone comes to stay with us, however, I cannot remember praying about that particular issue or maybe I did, subconsciously. I was pregnant at the time and when my husband's friend came to stay with us, it turned out that he was very helpful to us in various ways. As his time with us came to an end, I found that I was sorry to see him leave and would gladly have had him extend his stay with us.

I am not advocating here that you open the floodgates of your house and allow just anyone to come and stay with you. You should prayerfully consider the proposal of anyone coming to live with you; if it is the will of God, let them in, no matter how you feel about it. There is always a reason why the Lord prompts us to show these acts of kindness. The reasons sometimes are not revealed to us beforehand, during, or even after the event. Pray about situations and let the Holy Spirit direct your actions.

The idea of '***Holy Spirit directed***' actions reminds me of my personal experience after salvation, when I began to yield consciously and intentionally to the Holy Spirit. I can describe the experience for me as similar to that of owning and using a microwave oven; after you have bought and had the experience of using one, you will begin to wonder how you coped without having one. In the same way, it is hard to imagine how I lived my life up until then, without the help, leading, direction, promptings, peace, and joy of the Holy Ghost. The depth of joy, peace, wholeness, and deep-down satisfaction of knowing that you have the Holy Spirit at the helm of affairs, directing your actions, is awesome. This joy can be experienced repeatedly by anyone who truly surrenders the running and leadings of their lives to the Holy Spirit.

Make Him president and not resident. If the Holy Spirit is treated as a guest in a house and told not to enter certain rooms, then we will not experience His Lordship over those areas in our lives. If He is kept in the guest room and not given permission to go into the living room, kitchen, garden, storeroom, or anywhere else in the house, then those areas will invariably suffer and will not benefit from the specialist help of the Holy Spirit. The Holy Spirit should not only be residing in our lives, but He should be given full permission to preside over all the areas, affairs, and issues of our lives. As He abides in us, we should allow Him to preside and yield the control of our lives to Him. As we do this, He will fill us with more and more of Himself. We will have everything to gain and nothing to lose if He becomes the president and not a mere resident in our lives.

We should allow the Holy Spirit to reign and have ownership over our lives. He is our only hope in this ever-changing world. I have heard people describe the Holy Spirit as a gentleman and I believe that this is an apt description. He will not meddle in our affairs uninvited and He will not go where He is not invited or topple our authority. Only when we allow Him to permeate our being, is He then really presiding over our lives.

No restrictions should be placed on what the Holy Spirit can do or where He can go in our lives. We should not operate a 'no-go area' policy with the Holy Spirit. No parts or aspects of our lives should be a no-go area for the Holy Spirit. Every area should be fully accessible by His indwelling presence. To enjoy an enriched life and to live life to the full, every detail of our lives should be submitted and come under the scrutiny of the Holy Spirit. He will only move in our lives to the degree that we yield to Him.

If we allow the Holy Spirit to saturate and permeate our entire beings, give Him pre-eminence in all that we do, succumb to His will and make Him president of our lives, then He will drench, captivate, and soak our beings with His presence. He will take our lives and Christian experience to a whole new level, one which we never dreamed possible.

POWER OF ATTORNEY

As the power of attorney was conferred on the disciples of Jesus, the same power of attorney has been commissioned and conferred upon those who make the Holy Spirit president of their lives. After His resurrection, Jesus appeared to the disciples and said, "*...peace be unto you: as My Father has sent Me, even so, I send you. And when He had said this, He breathed on them and said to them, receive the Holy Ghost...*" (John 20: 21-22)

He gave them the power to bind, to loose, to do the works of Christ, to live victoriously, and to show the power and share the love of God in this sinful world. We have the same power of attorney operating through the Holy Ghost in our lives today. Whatever we permit in our lives and on earth is permitted, and whatever we reject in our lives and on earth is rejected. We have a great work set ahead of us. We have the authority to cause many positive changes that will impact our lives and our world today, through the power of the Holy Spirit working in us and through us. ***Are you using the power of attorney conferred on you today***?

THE JOURNEY TO THE DESTINATION

Life is a journey; the purpose and role of the Holy Spirit in our lives is to help us run the race that is set before us. ***The Christian life is lived in the Spirit*** hence we cannot live a successful Christian life without the Holy Spirit.

Life can be described as going on a guided tour, with the tour guide showing us around and pointing out places of interest; telling us stories behind the interesting sights, why they are interesting, how they have become a must-see, and the do's and don'ts for tourists, etc. The Holy Spirit, likewise, helps and guides us through life, every inch of the way. As we see different scenarios, people, and places while on a journey, it is the same in life; we will have different experiences, some good and some bad. Success, as professed, is not a destination but a journey. In the same vein, we can say a Christian's successful journey in life is dependent on the Holy Spirit, but this journey does have a destination.

This is the reason the Holy Spirit was sent, to help us navigate life successfully if we decide to journey with Him. As believers, Christians, and children of God, we need to rely on the Holy Spirit to lead us through the journey of life, to the pre-planned destination.

Living by the dictates of the Holy Spirit is a habit-forming process; we form these habits by taking conscious, deliberate, and reasonable steps to change our old habits. We need to desire the change, and then commit ourselves to the change before it will happen. The way that we learn, grow, and develop in life is the same way that we need to learn, grow, and develop in our Christian walk. This can be summed up as a life of faith, trust, and obedience to the Holy Spirit.

Living in the Spirit is like building a house; it is a process of placing one brick at a time until the building blocks are formed. The Holy Spirit is our teacher; He is patient, He will teach and take us through the right path if we are pliable, patient, open-minded, tolerant, teachable, and obedient.

The Holy Spirit will lead us in many ways, as you will see echoed throughout this book. One thing we must remember is that the Christian walk is a two-way process; it is we, in compliance with the Holy Spirit. We cannot be travelling in two separate directions and expect to live a victorious Christian life. In Amos 3:3, the Bible says, *"Can two walk together, [except] they are [in agreement]?"*Our Christian walk is a partnership/working relationship.

As believers, we need to understand that ***the Christian walk is a process, and it does not happen overnight***. We also need to expect life's ups and downs because they will happen. One thing we need to realise is that when we are going through them, we are not alone; we have the Holy Spirit to ask for help, guidance, direction, and instructions on how to handle the issues we will encounter along the way.

Having the Holy Spirit in our lives does not mean that we have immunity from the hardship and hard times that people experience in this world. Christianity is not always a 'hunky-dory', smooth sailing, home-and-dry journey. If you have heard anything contrary, you have not been told the full story. The Bible clearly says that ***in this world, we will have trials and tribulations***. The Bible is clear on this subject; temptations and trialling moments will surely come our way and it happens to believers and unbelievers alike.

It is unfair, unscriptural, and misleading to tell or give the impression that the acceptance and presence of Jesus in our lives, means the absence of problems. This might explain some of the reasons why we have some people come to church and later leave when they experience obstacles. They make comments like, "the church thing did not work for me". Christianity is not a false pretence; we live in a world with various challenges. When we give our lives to the Lord, it is not 'done and dusted' and does not mean exclusivity from life challenges.

We are still in this world, and we will invariably experience moments of joy and sorrow, gain and pain, surplus and hardships, rough and smooth, hustle and bustle, and the ups and downs of life, just like anybody else. The only distinction with a Spirit-filled person is that we do not go through them alone because we have someone to help us carry the burden. As Christians, we are promised a safe landing but not necessarily smooth sailing all the time. We are not promised the absence of problems but the presence of the Holy Spirit. We grow and mature in our Christian walk as we face and tackle life's adversities, with the help of the Holy Spirit.

The Bible says that we will have trials and temptations in this world, but we should not worry because we have already overcome them. We have our anchor in the Holy Spirit; He will help us go through the storms of life if we ask Him because He is obligated to do so. The Bible, in 1 John 4:4 says, *"…greater is He that is in you, than he that is in the World."* In other words, no matter the situation and circumstances that we are going through, the Greater One living in us can help us quench all the fiery darts — any missiles, attacks, and challenges — that come our way. Believe me, if you go through trials and challenging times like I have, then you will feel the heat of the fire; you will feel like you are drowning, and you will feel like the very essence of life is being choked or drained out of you. You will feel stretched to the point of thinking that you are going to snap at any minute. If we rely wholeheartedly on the Holy Spirit in times like this, then we will come out of it gallantly. The Bible clearly promises us that ***we will not be faced with challenges beyond what we can bear***. You can be assured that God will not take you through challenges that you are unable to overcome. The Holy Spirit helps us through these moments when we invite Him in.

Isaiah 43:2 tells us that if we go through the fire, we will not burn and if we go through floods, we will not drown. It is a good thing to know that we are not alone when we are going through trying moments. Psalm 23:4 reinforces this point: "*Even though I walk through the valley of the shadow of death, I will fear no evil, for you* (the presence of God) *are with me.*" We have the presence of God in us through the person of the Holy Spirit.

We are commanded by scripture to work out our salvation, with fear and trembling. This means examining our Christian walk; are we walking in obedience or disobedience to the Word of God? Most of the trials we go through can make us better Christians. We find that we can come out of trials stronger than when we went in, building character and resilience in us. It also makes us trust more in the power and ability of the Holy Spirit to pull us through whatever situation we find ourselves in. ***With the power of the Holy Spirit, stumbling blocks that we experience through our journey in life can be turned into stepping-stones***.

GLORIFY JESUS

One of the chief purposes of the Holy Spirit is to glorify Jesus in our lives and in the lives of others. Our lives as believers and children of God are meant to show and demonstrate the power of God to the lost and dying world; to share the good news of the gospel and to point people to the Lord Jesus.

The Holy Spirit does not speak of Himself. Jesus, whilst on earth, said (paraphrased from John 5:19), "...whatever I see the Father do, I do. Whatever the Father, says, I speak. I have not sent myself." Jesus promised to send us the Holy Spirit in the latter part of John 16:13; "*...for he shall not speak of Himself; but whatsoever He shall hear [from me], that shall He speak...*" And in John 16:14:*"He shall glorify* (exalt) *me: [because] He shall receive[from me], and shall [show] it unto you."* John 16:15 likewise says, *"All things that the Father has are mine. Therefore I said that He will take [from Him] and declare* (show) *it to you."*

Jesus accomplished many things during His earthly ministry, and He said that we will do greater works than He did through the indwelling power of the Holy Spirit.

ANOINTING OF THE HOLY GHOST

One of the duties of the Holy Spirit is ***to equip us for service***; just as people in authority are set apart to carry out a special task, so we have been set apart to carry out our God-ordained purpose in life. We are divinely anointed by the Holy Spirit, at the time of salvation, to help us to carry out our tasks in life. This divine enablement is worked out over time, covering the span of our Christian lives. 1 John

2:20says: "*...you have an anointing from the Holy One, and you know all things*", while 1 John 2:27 says: "*...the anointing [which we have received] from him remains in you, and you do not need anyone to teach you...[because]his anointing teaches you about all things...*" We need the anointing, to fulfil the mandate and call of God upon our lives.

We need the power of the Holy Ghost to help us achieve extraordinary things for the kingdom of God and in our world today. The power of the Holy Ghost is called the anointing and we should depend on this anointing of the Holy Spirit to carry out our duties, tasks, calling, and assignments in life effectively. He wants us to have a dependent culture and relationship with Him. Dependences on anything else in this world are neither good nor healthy but I can tell you of the dependence and addiction that you need 24/7, and that is the dependence on the anointing and in-filling of the Holy Ghost. I have used the words 'Holy Spirit' and 'Holy Ghost' inter-changeably in this paragraph and indeed throughout this book. He is called the Holy Spirit or Holy Ghost for a reason; For one He is Holy and two He is the Spirit of God living on the inside of us. Some people say that they have seen ghosts; we do not see the Holy Spirit or Holy Ghost but as we surrender our will and lives to Him, He anoints us and leads us by His inward witness.

The Spirit of God that lives inside of us is Holy and having an addictive and vulnerable dependence on Him is safe; we can never be too close for comfort with the Holy Spirit. The closer we get, the better the comfort, help, and direction that we receive. When we are vulnerable to His leadings and promptings, we can be assured that He will not lead us astray. The anointing of the Holy Spirit is a life-changing and life-transforming power. It is the anointing that breaks the yoke and sets us free from what has ensnared and held us captive. The anointing of the Holy Ghost makes and will continue to make a difference in our lives.

Jesus was anointed for service and was dependent on the Holy Spirit throughout His Ministry on earth. In Isaiah 61:1, He said, *"The Spirit of the Lord is upon me, because [He] has anointed me to preach good tidings…"*

The anointing comes as a direct result of our surrender to the Lord; the anointing of the Spirit is received by faith, and at the same time, we receive the gift of salvation. When that happens, yokes are destroyed and burdens are removed in our lives, through the power of the anointing. A yoke can be described as anything that has held us bound or captive and burdens can be described as anything that weighs us down. In ourselves, we do not have the ability or power to set ourselves free from yokes and bondage. The Bible, in Isaiah 10:27, informs us that by the reason of the anointing, the power of the yoke is destroyed or broken. Nothing can withstand the power of the anointing in our lives, and we should not, for one moment, ever underestimate the power of the anointing of God upon our lives. It is this same anointing power that raised Jesus Christ from the dead! This is the resurrection anointing, the power of God Almighty on display. No one or anything can withstand the power or the anointing of the Holy Spirit and only we, ourselves, can decide to quench the flow in our lives.

INSPIRED MEN TO WRITE THE BIBLE

Another purpose of the Holy Spirit is His guidance and direction in helping us to understand and rightfully interpret the scriptures. He is, after all, the author of the Bible, which He inspired men to write (2 Peter 1:20-21). He is not only the originator of the Bible, but also interprets the scriptures for us and gives us personal revealed knowledge (John 16:14). It is a good starting point to ask the Holy Spirit for understanding, insight, and enlightenment when we read the Bible.

As the author of the Bible, He knows all the scriptures at His fingertips, and He can refer us to the right and relevant passage to meet a particular need. He makes the scriptures come alive to us as we read, meditate, and study the word. He knows the bits that will apply to every situation we might be facing or going through and He gives us personal revelations to meet our needs, situations, and circumstances.

Some principles used in the world originated from the Bible, so you can and should ask the Holy Spirit to direct you to the ones that apply to your life and to people within your sphere of influence. There are many revealed truths in the Bible; John 8:32 says that we will know the truth and the truth will set us free. It is the truth we know that will set us free, so ask the Holy Spirit to lead you to those truths. The truth has the liberating power to set us free from whatsoever predicaments that are presenting themselves in our lives.

CHRIST'S MINISTRY

The Holy Spirit had a defined purpose in the ministry of Christ. Jesus was conceived and born by the Holy Spirit, baptised and anointed for service by the Holy Spirit, and empowered by the Holy Spirit to do all that He did while on earth. Jesus was also crucified in the power of the Spirit (Hebrews 9:14) and at the resurrection, it was the power of the Holy Spirit that raised Christ from the dead. Romans 8:11 says, *"...the Spirit of Him [who rose Christ] from the dead dwells in you. He* (the Holy Spirit*) that raised up Christ up from the dead shall also quicken* (make alive*) your mortal* (human) *bodies by His Spirit that dwells in you."*

If we allow the Holy Spirit to dominate our lives, we can expect quickening and awakening of our mortal bodies; our bodies made alive to the things of the Spirit of God.

Jesus instructed His disciples and is now instructing us, His body, through the Holy Spirit. Jesus gave us the Holy Spirit as a gift to guide and help us through life. We will be dead to the deeds and the lust of the flesh and the world if we allow the Holy Spirit to quicken our mortal bodies from the inside out.

SETTING OUR AFFECTIONS

Another purpose and presence of the Holy Ghost in our lives is to help us to prioritise and put things in perspective. The Bible in Matthew 6:21 says, *"...where your treasure is, there your hearts will be also."* The question here is; where are our treasures? Are our treasures in the word of God? Do we place the things of God above every other thing in our lives?

In setting our affections, we ought to be mindful of how we spend our time and what we think about. Sports personnel are always trying to beat their personal bests and be recognised as the best in their chosen fields, students constantly pursue achieving success in their exam results, etc. Whatever we feed grows and whatever we do not feed dies eventually. If we feed our faith, our faith grows and if we feed our fears, our fear grows. Feed what you want to grow, being mindful that we can grow in both the positive and the negative areas as well.

We can apply this same principle to spiritual things. As we know, we are all products of our thoughts. What is it that is occupying our minds today, and what are the foremost desires of our hearts? The Bible says that we should set our affections on godly things. Therefore, we should place the love of God above all. If we really want the Holy Spirit to work through us, we will give Him top priority and place in our lives.

To locate where we put the things of God in our hearts, we will have to examine what we think about most of the time. If we are mindful of the things of God, it will feature and score top marks on our agenda and priorities for the day. Notice that I said 'for the day' because we plan things daily and they say our tomorrow is a result of our plan today. Whether we realise it or not, we prioritise daily what we see and count as important. If the things of the Spirit are not high or the most important on our daily priority list, reconsider your priorities and make them number one. If we really desire and want the things of God to take preeminence in our lives, we will have to consult the Holy Spirit.

He is the representative of the Godhead in our world today. Putting the things of God foremost in our lives can only be achieved with the help and assistance of the Spirit of God. This is not an impossible task to accomplish or too far-reaching to realise. With commitment, diligence, and persistence, we will attain the goal by making a genuine effort to reschedule our daily plan to accommodate the number one priority.

We cannot serve God and mammon (riches); the Bible makes a sharp comparison between the two. In Luke 16:13, it says that no servant can serve two masters; you will either like one, while hating the other or hold on to one, while despising the other. We cannot serve God and put the cares of this world, and all its lusts, as top priorities. What men esteem so highly is an abomination to God. Let us take our cue from Joshua when he charged the children of Israel in Joshua 24:15 to 'choose this day whom you will serve'. He presented the options to them; would they rather serve the gods their fathers served on the other side of the river or the god served in the land where they dwell? Joshua ended the verse with this bold declaration and confession: "*...as for me and my household we will serve the Lord.*"

We should critically examine who is occupying our thoughts in life and who is sitting on the throne of our hearts. Choose to make this confident declaration that Joshua made, for the Lord to occupy our moments, our thoughts, and our daily lives.

God does not give us conflicting priorities; the Bible is very clear on this issue.1 Corinthians 14:33 says that God is not the author of confusion. He is a God of peace and does things in an orderly manner. When we submit to the leading of the Holy Spirit, it is done on a step-by-step, precept-by-precept basis. Many people that live this way can attest to the fact that it is by far the best and highest type of life to live. This type of life is called ***the life of***

faith, trust, and obedience in the Lord, through the person of the Holy Spirit.

WIN-WIN SITUATION

Another Ministry of the Holy Spirit in our lives is to help us live by faith. The Bible says the just (justified) shall live by faith. Who are the justified? The justified are people who allow God and His teachings in the Bible to be the final authority in their lives. This kind of living requires absolute trust in the abilities and leading of the Holy Spirit.

Living by faith, simply put, is living by the dictates and directives of the Holy Spirit. There is an adage that says, 'Do not put all your eggs in one basket.' With the Holy Spirit, we can stake all our eggs in one basket. With the Holy Spirit, we can say it is a win-win situation, all the time. The outcome might not always be what we expected or bargained for all the time but one thing that I can say for sure is that it is always a good outcome. It might be over and above our expectations or at other times fall short of our expectations but in both instances, we should be pleased because there is always a reason. What we need to be mindful of is that whatever the outcome, we are on the winning side and within the will and plan of God for our lives rather than our own will and plans. ***The Holy Spirit is not obligated to carry out our plans; the only time that happens is when our plans align with His plans and purposes for our lives***.

The reasons why some of our plans do not materialise can sometimes be revealed to us, or we might have to wait until when we get to the other side of eternity to find out. One thing is certain; when we ask the Holy Spirit for leading and direction, **He will NOT lead us astray.** Whatever the outcome, favourable or not, we can be certain that it is in our best interests and in the hands of the Master. The Bible says everything works out together for good, to those who trust Him. Another certain thing that you will notice when you yield to the help of the Holy Spirit for decision-making is the peace we feel deep down in our being. We have an awesome sense of peace when we leave things in the capable hands of the All-Knowing Master.

To illustrate this point, I will relay an experience that I had some time ago. A few years back, my husband and I planned to take the kids to Nigeria for their summer holiday. Three of our children had not visited Nigeria before then, and their knowledge of the country was restricted to what people had told them and what they saw on television, watched in movies, or read in books. So, we thought it would be a good idea for them to visit their homeland and have their own first-hand experience and memories.

We started to pray earnestly for the journey, months in advance. We prayed for a safe journey and for the Lord to keep them safe and healthy throughout the duration of the trip. We also asked the Lord if it was His will for them to go on holiday to Nigeria. We did not hear any audible voice that said 'go' or 'do not go' and we did not have any dreams for or against the trip. All we had was the peace of the Holy Spirit. We were guided and led by that peace we had on the inside; we knew without a shadow of a doubt that the Lord's hand was upon the journey, so we purchased the tickets and prepared for the holiday.

The plan was for all four of the children to travel ahead with my mother, and I would join them for the last two weeks of their stay and then travel back to the UK with them. While planning the trip, my husband shared that he did not think it was a good idea for our youngest son to go with my mother and our other children. He suggested, instead, that my son travel with me when I was ready to go, while his three siblings could travel with my mother. So that was the plan. Our first three children went first with my mother, and then I went afterward with our youngest son; my husband did not go on the trip with us.

Everything went smoothly and according to plan, with only a few hiccups here and there. When I arrived, the kids were happy to see me, and everything went well for the first week. In the second week, the Lord delivered us from what would have been a fatal accident. What I can say is that it was nothing short of a miracle that the accident did not happen; I am sure that angels were dispatched to avert the fatal collision. Our driver was not very careful when he turned onto an express road/speed lane. As we turned into the road, we saw a bus filled with passengers approaching us at full speed. I had already screamed with my hands up in the air and my eyes closed because I could not see how we could have avoided the accident but, suddenly, our car came to a halt by the side of the road and the bus went past us without a scratch. A narrow escape that could have only happened by divine intervention.

While that experience was put behind us, we could not stop thanking God for His divine protection. I still recall the incident and will raise my hand in the air and say, "Thank you, Jesus."

While on this trip, our youngest son, who was a three-year-old at the time and the one whom I had travelled with, fell ill with malaria. He was admitted to the hospital for one day and was discharged with some medication. Due to the illness, he lost his appetite and did not eat much, and consequently lost weight. He was still poorly on the day that we were flying back and the doctor that we saw in Nigeria was so concerned about my son's drastic weight loss that he advised us to take him to the hospital as soon as we arrived in England.

During the flight back, my son mostly slept. However, about halfway into the flight, he suddenly woke up and threw up. I cleared the mess very calmly and off he went to sleep again. I tried to wake him up to give him some water at least but he would not have it. About an hour after the first bout, he vomited again; the guy that was sitting next to me became really concerned this time and asked one of the flight attendants to help me. This time, my son had vomited all over himself, and I had to change his clothes. The flight attendant that came took one look at him, and said, "This child is very ill, he does not look well at all. Let me see what I can do."

Before I knew it, she had informed the pilot and they made a public announcement on their PA system, enquiring whether there was a doctor or nurse on board, as there was a sick child that needed attention. It was like a dream, one that I did not want to believe was happening. I thought this was the sort of thing you would see in a movie; it was like a drama playing out before me.

Two medical practitioners came forward and one was asked to go back and wait as a standby while passengers were moved from their seats to create more room and privacy for us. The doctor felt for my son's pulse and took his temperature; he had a very high temperature. The doctor then administered Calpol (a paediatric pain killer) to bring down the temperature. Meanwhile, the flight staff had radioed the paramedics on the ground, and they were communicating with the doctor on board. When the doctor told them that my son was dehydrated, he was advised to try and administer a drip (intravenous fluid). So, the flight attendant got a drip line and drip to replace the body fluid he had lost. The doctor tried and tried but could not find a vein to administer the drip. During that process, my son suddenly woke up and asked for sweets and a drink of water, which were gladly given to him. Miraculously, after taking the drink and a sweet, he sat up and began to play and talk; it was as if nothing had happened. The doctors on the ground were informed of his progress and they said to keep an eye on him. The pilot told them to assure me that he would take the quickest route possible and that the paramedics would be waiting on the tarmac for the plane to land.

As soon as the plane landed, the paramedics rushed in to get my son out first but when they saw him, they could not believe that it was the same child they had been radioed about. He was sitting up, looking very radiant, happy, content, and surprisingly very well. When they saw his condition, they changed their minds and decided to allow all the other passengers out first and so, we were the last to disembark. Whilst the passengers were getting off-board, my son continued to play and chat normally. As the passengers were getting off, they would glance to see the boy that had caused so much commotion on the plane.

My other three children were escorted off the plane by the airline crew and their dad picked them up, while my son and I went in the ambulance to the nearest hospital. The paramedics did not even have to put their sirens on, they drove at a normal pace to the hospital. The hospital staff was informed about the reason for the visit, and they gave us a bed to check him over. They asked me to tell them what happened, and I relayed the entire story to the doctor. The doctor, a woman, said that she would have to do some tests to see if my son still had the malaria virus in his body. As the doctor went away, I noticed that his feet started to change colour; they were turning a bit greyish and when I felt his body, I noticed that it was getting very cold. So, I called the doctor, and when she came, they quickly whisked him into a special care unit ward. Before I knew it, my son had four medical staff attending to him, who wired him up to about three machines. I did not know what was going on, but I knew it was serious because they were not saying much to me, and they were moving very fast.

In the middle of this episode, my husband arrived at the hospital with the other kids. The hospital staff said the kids could not go into the room just yet and advised us to go to the cafeteria. They assured us that when the consultant showed up, they would come and get us. My brother was informed, and he came to the hospital as well and we were all in the canteen. After a while, I decided to go and find out what was happening, since no one came to fetch us. When I got there, I was told the consultant had come looking for us and left when he could not find us. Then they said my son was now stable and would have to be admitted to the ward because he needed to be on a drip all night.

My son slept right through the night and was looking radiant and well in the morning. At that time, the Consultant came to the ward to see us, with some student doctors.

My son was sitting up, drinking a bottle of coke; for some strange reason, all he wanted during that time was anything sweet. The consultant said that he was on holiday when he was informed about my son's condition, and he straight away ordered for my son to be taken to the children's intensive care unit and also informed the hospital staff that he was on his way to the hospital. He told us that he had never cut short his holiday to come to work before but when he heard about how critical and serious my son's condition was, he decided to come in. Surprisingly, when he came in, my son was still in the special care unit, and he was doing well, so he decided to leave him there and observe his progress and asked the hospital staff to inform me that he would see me in the morning.

The consultant said that one thing baffled him about the case; he had never seen a child so sick and yet in such a short time, get so well. He said it was a mystery and he intended to get to the bottom of it. I am sure by now it is clear to you that it is the power of the Holy Spirit and the hand of God, working on my son's mortal body.

I later came to understand the reason why the airline crew made so much fuss about my son on the flight. I was told that flying dehydrates ordinarily and for a young child to throw up twice on board an aircraft is not a good sign at all.

After a few days, we were discharged, and we came home. After about a day at home, I noticed that my son was not himself; he was not eating again and drinking very little. I then took him to our local hospital and by the time we got there, he needed medical attention urgently. He was admitted straight away and underwent a series of tests and treatments. To cut the long story short, he spent six weeks in the hospital to regain the body weight he had lost and to be medically fit and well enough to be discharged.

The reason I share this experience is to remind us that sometimes we pray, and the answer might not be what we expect. What helped and guided us throughout this whole ordeal was the peace we had when we had initially prayed about the holiday. Throughout the whole experience, we never doubted God because we knew we were within the perfect will of God for that occasion. God is faithful if we dare to trust Him. This experience demonstrates areas where the Holy Spirit can help strengthen our faith. It was supernatural faith in operation because to me, it was beyond the ordinary day-to-day faith.

The Holy Spirit has a definite purpose in our lives, and He will reveal Himself in many facets as we surrender whatever situation or circumstances we are going through, into His capable hands. He has many specific roles, duties, and responsibilities to accomplish in our lives and we can only realise the benefits of the Ministry of the Holy Spirit in our lives when we yield to Him. We receive to the proportion that we yield and avail ourselves to His provision and resources.

One of my husband's favourite sayings is, "The victory you win yourself is sweet." I must confess that it took me some time to understand what he meant but after much deliberation, I eventually got it. My interpretation is that when we surrender ourselves to the Holy Spirit, He helps us to accomplish what we think is impossible from the human standpoint. The experience we go through will be awesome because we will see the wonderful, supernatural demonstration of the power of God and what God can do with a life that is yielded to Him. Walking with the Holy Spirit is a partnership/working relationship.

When we walk in cooperation, complete surrender, and in compliance with the Spirit of God, the result is always good, especially when we have persevered and held on to His apron strings. We should not also forget or overlook growth, maturity, and character formation that can often come with painful and challenging experiences. I am sure you must have heard this saying: ***the Holy Spirit and you, working together in partnership, make a mightily explosive force***.

3

ATTRIBUTES OF THE HOLY SPIRIT

A GIFT TO THE CHURCH

The Holy Spirit is a gift to the body of Christ, whilst Christ is a gift to the world. When I say the body of Christ, I mean the church, Christians, or believers in Jesus Christ. For us to accept the gift of the Holy Spirit, we first must have received the gift of salvation. ***The gift of salvation is accepting Christ as our Lord and Saviour.*** This gift of salvation is an open invitation to the whole world, to accept Christ into their lives. John 3:16 says, *"For God so loved the world that He gave His only begotten Son* (Jesus Christ) *that* ***whosoever*** *believes in Him should not perish* (die in their sins) *but have everlasting life."* **Whosoever** denotes that it is an open invitation; it is free and you do not have to do anything but just believe that Christ died for our sins. After the acceptance of this gift of salvation, then we are ready to experience the Holy Spirit's gift to the body of Christ.

Christianity is dull and void of power without the Holy Spirit. The Holy Spirit is very much here on earth and dwells inside us; He has been sent by both the Father and the Son to take our Christian walk to a whole new level. The Holy Spirit has many roles and functions in our lives, as we have seen in chapter two. In this chapter, I have listed and explained some of the characteristics or attributes of the Holy Spirit and given examples of the kind of work He will perform in our lives if we give Him the free hand.

Do not limit the working of the Holy Spirit to the examples I have given as He can do far much more than I can ever write or explain. He deals with us on an individual basis, and He has customised solutions to all our needs, issues, problems, worries, and anxieties. He can help us with any menial, mid-range, or heavy-duty tasks.

COMFORTER

In the book of John 14:16 & 26; 15:26; 16:7, the Bible refers to the Holy Spirit as our Comforter. The word, 'Comforter' is translated from the Greek word, '*Parakletos*'. The English word, 'Comforter' does not really do full justice to the meaning of the original word. The full meaning of the Greek word, '*Parakletos*' can be translated in English to mean 'more than a Comforter'. The other meanings are an advocate, a helper, a friend, assistant, comrade, mate, buddy, one called to the side of another, a counsellor, and a standby'. ***The Holy Spirit is our Paraclete or helper on earth, as Jesus is our Paraclete or helper in heaven.***

The greatest comforter now resides inside of us and nobody will know how you feel more than the Holy Spirit. So, let

Him comfort you in times of need, sorrow, loss, painful periods, and other low moments. People will not always be there to comfort us, but the Holy Spirit will be there to comfort us always. The Bible, in John 14:16, called the Holy Spirit 'another Comforter'. He will comfort us like no one else can if we invite Him in, He will drench us with His presence, and people will not be able to understand how we can be so unruffled and at peace during difficult times. He is our *Paraclete*.

This reminds me of how I received comfort from the Holy Spirit during some trying moments in my life. I had about four or five miscarriages, one after the other, within the space of four years. What I noticed was that after each miscarriage, I would feel this sense of peace deep down inside of me; even if I wanted to grieve, I could not. It felt like the capacity to grieve at those times was taken away from me. Instead, I was filled with overwhelming peace and joy. At the time, we were trying for a second child. When friends, having heard of the miscarriage, came to sympathise, on seeing how composed and unruffled I was, they were often shocked. On one or two occasions, some of them passed comments like, "Nobody would believe that you have just experienced a loss, you look as if nothing has happened to you." They were right in their assessment, as that was exactly how I felt. During one of the miscarriage episodes, one of the nurses commented about my blood pressure, saying it was amazing that my blood pressure was normal, considering the number of miscarriages I had experienced. At the time, I must have been walking in serious obedience with the Holy Spirit and had surrendered all my cares, anxieties, and worries into His capable hands. I remember I used to say something along these lines to myself, "I do not understand what is going on, but you know and understand."

When you surrender all, you alone will be able to testify to the fact that you have yielded the circumstances and situation to the hands of the Comforter. He will come alongside you and help you to carry whatever the burden might be. Are you going through any circumstances that require the intervention of the Comforter today? Please, yield it all to Him now and stop carrying the burden alone. Isaiah 43:2 says if we go through the fire, it will not burn us and if we go through the waters (trouble), we will not drown. Psalm 23: 4 says even if we walk through the valley of the shadow of death (depression, addiction, lack, need, problems, afflictions, sorrow, pain, mourning, illness, failure, agony, danger, anger, hurt, unhappiness, suffering, heaviness, hardship, misery, gloominess, sickness, illness, disease, misfortune, trials, test, loneliness, temptation, etc.), we will fear no evil because the LORD is with us. He is our rod and staff, and He comforts us, no matter the issue, situation, or circumstances.

Shepherds carry rods and staff to protect and defend their sheep from attack and danger. The Holy Spirit directs, protects, and leads us with His indwelling presence. We can take comfort in the rod (protection) and staff (leading) of the shepherd because they are there to protect us and see us through the trying periods and moments. We will have supernatural confidence and assurance when we allow the Holy Spirit to lead events in our lives. We should allow the Holy Spirit to shepherd us through the storms of life and provide the needed comfort; the supernatural comfort that only He can give in times of need.

HELPER

We sometimes look for help in other places. We should covet an attitude of consulting the Holy Spirit inside of us for help; after all, we have the helper, the greater one, living on the inside of us and we should utilise this. We should let the Holy Spirit be our umpire and direct us in all our help campaigns. He is the ever-present helper in times and moments of need. The word 'helper' in Greek is also interpreted as a standby, confidante, or one who assists.

When my children tell me that they have lost anything, I will always ask them if they have asked the Holy Spirit to help them find the items because He knows everything. An example of this was when one of my sons misplaced his school tie. I only ever buy my children one school tie each and will replace it when the tie is worn out, lost, or damaged. On this occasion, my son came to me one morning and said that he could not find his tie. Some of you that are reading this may be aware of how children get when they cannot find something that they want or really need. After endless searching, I asked him if he had prayed about it, to which he replied that he had not. I then suggested to him that he prays about the matter.

He grumpily began to search all the rooms, going upstairs and downstairs. After a while, he shouted with a sigh of relief and with a big grin on his face, announced, "Mummy, mummy, I found it!" When I asked him where he found it, his reply was, "You will not believe it, mummy. I found it in the laundry basket downstairs." We have two laundry baskets, one upstairs and the other downstairs and there is no way he would have known it was there. He said that after he prayed and asked the Holy Spirit for help, he went downstairs, looked in the laundry basket, and found it. The tie was not on top of the laundry basket, considering that he wore it to school the day before; it was buried halfway down the basket.

I like the way the Holy Spirit drops thoughts in our minds and makes us own them. In His dealings with us, most of the time He drops the thoughts in our hearts, and we think that they are our own. The Holy Spirit helps us with what we count as significant or insignificant matters or issues if we dare place our trust in Him and listen to Him. Had my son not listened to the prompting of the Holy Spirit and, instead, chose to reason his way out of his problem, he would have gone to school grumpy that day and would have been told off because his school had a very strict uniform policy. It pays to ask the Holy Spirit for help in times of need and to listen to His promptings.

The Holy Spirit helps us in different ways, all we need to do is just ask and let Him lead us. I can tell you that, after that experience, whenever we are looking for any item of clothing, clean or dirty, I will automatically look in the laundry basket.

This same son of mine who had the school tie episode, when he was ten years old, said to me one day, "Mummy, can we overuse the Holy Spirit?" I asked him why he was asking, and he said that he felt like he is overusing Him. I shared that I sometimes felt that way too. I remember saying to my mother once, "It's like I am using the Holy Spirit like one who may take maid services for granted." The truth of the matter is: ***we can never overuse the Holy Spirit***. That is one of His purposes in our life. Jesus told us that he would send us another helper. He is the helper, and He is here to help us when we let Him.

I have read various books in which people said the Holy Spirit has helped them cure sleeplessness, overcome shyness or the fear of public speaking, get over bereavement, and addictions of various kinds — embarrassing things that we cannot mutter to anyone, help us with our thinking, learning; the list goes on. The Holy Spirit knows us and has the answers to any issues, problems, ailments, situations, or circumstances we are facing. Help is at hand with the Holy Spirit.

COUNSELLOR

I particularly like this one: the Holy Spirit is our official counsellor. When we need advice and direction in our life, we should seek the Counsellor. He counsels and shows us the right way out and leads us on the way to what He has predestined for us. We are familiar with debt counsellors, marriage, financial, and career counsellors, or counsellors in other areas. We should seek the ultimate counsellor for all our counselling needs.

I am not advising or suggesting here for one moment that we should not use the services of or approach professional counsellors. We have, by way of educational qualification and experience, trained and skilful counsellors. Go to them and utilise their expertise if you require their services. The service of the person I am referring to here is the service of the Ultimate Counsellor. He is the Chief Counsellor, the Counsellor of counsellors. When we turn our worries, anxieties, counselling needs, and cares unto Him, He will order our steps. He might give us the solutions directly or direct us to use the help, knowledge, and expertise of professional counsellors. He might advise us through friends, family members, Ministers of the gospel, church leaders, acquaintances, coaches, or mentors. The key point I am making here is to ask, consult the Holy Spirit ***first***, and let Him direct us.

There are many counselling experiences narrated in the scriptures. I would like to refer to one of Moses' counselling experiences in Exodus 18. Moses was counselled by Jethro, his father-in-law, after he relayed the victory of the Red Sea and what the Lord did for them, and how He delivered them from Pharaoh and the Egyptian armies. The aggregate number of the Children of Israel that left Egypt, as told in Exodus 12:37, was about six hundred thousand men. With women and children, the number would be in the range of 2.4 million. After observing Moses for a while, Jethro called Moses and told him that he cannot carry all the work of leadership on his shoulders alone. He advised him to appoint men to support him with daily administration, planning, organisation, and governance, so that he will not single-handedly carry the burden of being the chief, servant, and worker. The advice that Jethro gave Moses saved his life because he would have probably died a premature death from shouldering all those responsibilities alone.

There is always a shoulder to cry on. ***The Holy Spirit's shoulders span the world***; lean on Him and let Him advise you in times of need. The advice we require might be simple, complex, straightforward, or common sense. It does not really matter what the magnitude or size is. What really matters is; who is our backbone, who is our counsellor, and who is the person that is with us when we are going through these periods, bouts, and episodes. Have you noticed that when you are going through a situation, are in a muddle, confused, or under pressure, you cannot see the obvious, even if it is standing on the road and blocking your view. You cannot see the woods for the trees, i.e., you are so overwhelmed by the details (the trees) of a situation that you cannot see the whole picture (the woods). At moments like this, we need to go to the Holy Spirit to de-clutter our minds and receive direction, clarity of thought, and refreshment for our spirit, soul, and body. Consequently, we will find that a lot of needless weight will be lifted off our shoulders.

ADVOCATE

An advocate acts on our behalf, and the Holy Spirit acts as our advocate. There are many instances in life that will require the help of an advocate. Sometimes, decisions about important matters are made in our absence. It might be a decision about a promotion, a new job opportunity, a court case, a business deal, a proposal, etc.; the list is endless. The Holy Spirit, if we ask Him, will plead our cases for us. Remember that ***He is one called to the side of another***.

The Bible, in Proverbs 16:7, records that if our ways please the Lord, He will make our enemies be at peace with us. Even those who do not like us will favour us when our ways please the Lord. The Holy Spirit sometimes lays our cases in the heart of godly people to advocate for us. In the story of Peter's imprisonment in Acts 12:1-11, the Bible recalls that the Word of God grew mightily and the people in the corridors of power did not like the rate at which the Word was spreading. Therefore, they decided to use some of the disciples as scapegoats. They had already murdered James and then they laid their hands on Peter and threw him in prison. He was chained in a maximum-security prison and the intention was to leave Peter in there until after the feast of the Passover (Easter), before they would pass their judgement. It was customary for the Jews not to do anything during this feast, let alone soil their hands with murder.

Whilst Peter was in prison, the rest of the disciples were praying, advocating on his behalf. On the eve of the day that King Herod would have Peter brought before him, the angel of the Lord went to the prison, woke Peter up, and the chains fell off him. Peter was instructed to put on his sandals and clothes, and they preceded to the first and second maximum security gates that led to the city. As they approached the gates, they opened of their own accord.

It was not until Peter got to the house where the apostles were praying for him that he realised it was not a vision but a miraculous deliverance. The moral of the story is that when we allow the Holy Spirit to lead us, in more ways than one, the outcomes will nine times out of ten seem like a dream.

If you leave the issue, the bother, or whatever you are believing God for, in the hands of the Holy Spirit, He will deliver you, plead your cases and work on your behalf, in the hearts of people, just as he raised up people to pray for Peter and miraculously delivered him from a death sentence. He will rescue us, and show us mercy, kindness, favour, and the way out. The Holy Spirit might even use you to plead for other people's cases, as He uses others to plead on your behalf. He sometimes works in the heart of men at a sovereign level, on our behalf.

INTERCESSOR

Romans 8:26 says that the Holy Spirit also helps our infirmities and our weakness because we do not know how and what to pray about as we ought. The Holy Spirit Himself makes intercession for us, with groaning which cannot be articulated in human speech. Mind the emphasis used in the verse, the Bible did not say we do not know how to pray, it says ***we do not know how to pray, as we ought***. The prominent word is 'ought'. Due to our human frailties, limitations, imperfections, and self-agenda, we do not and cannot pray the perfect will of God for others and ourselves. When we yield to the Holy Spirit during prayer times, He takes our prayer life to another level. He takes over, making intercession (praying on our behalf) for us with groaning (unutterable, indescribable gushing and cry of the heart) that we cannot articulate, express ourselves, and at the same time ensure that we are praying the perfect will of God for the issues, situation, or circumstances.

Many times, we find ourselves in the neck of problems and we do not know how to pray. We are just confused, thinking, 'How do I get out of this one?' The Holy Spirit is a specialist in this area; He will help us to pray for the solution and the will of God, if we turn to Him.

Prayer is the lifeline of a Christian. Everything we do, achieve, and accomplish in our Christian life has a bearing on prayer. Back in the day, before digital technology and instant pictures, photographers used to develop negatives of pictures in the darkroom. Prayer acts as the darkroom, where picture negatives are processed and developed. When we lose our prayer line, we lose our connection line with heaven. To be effective in our Christian walk, we cannot ignore or rule out the power of prayer. Prayer is simply communicating with God and should be offered daily. It is a good habit to start the day with prayer and continue conversing with God throughout the course of the day. Can you imagine calling someone your friend and you do not talk to them or get to know them? I tell you, that friendship will not be very intimate or strong. But with the help of the Holy Spirit, if we ask for it, we can have and maintain a successful prayer life.

Also, in intercession, the Holy Spirit can help us to pray for others. I am sure that some of you would have experienced this happening to you many times over. Sometimes, whilst minding your business, a thought, a picture, or the name of someone just pops into your head. If you are like me, you will probably just want to disregard it and carry on minding your own business. However, I have learned from experience that it is a way that the Holy Spirit prompts us to pray for that person or group of people. You do not have to know what is going on in their lives or what they are going through. You might not be privy to that information. On such occasions, I have often prayed until the burden is lifted off my chest. Sometimes it takes a few minutes, and at other times, it might take longer.

Sometimes you just get burdened to pray for a particular situation; it might be for yourself, a person, community, or country. Again, I have learned to respond to these types of promptings with obedience. We might not have the full information of what we are praying for at the time, or we might never have the full information. All that is required of us is to respond in childlike obedience, and to just pray when we receive these promptings. As we are being led by the Holy Spirit, from time to time we will get this sudden urge to intercede or pray for others and ourselves. Yield to the Holy Spirit during these moments and let Him pray through you.

STRENGTH

The Holy Spirit strengthens us. I am sure this must have happened to you just as it does to many others. When it feels like we have come to the end of the road, we will say things like this to ourselves, 'I cannot take this anymore, I do not know how much longer I can bear this for, I cannot carry on anymore, this is too much for me,' etc. The Holy Spirit comes alongside us, at these times when we are at our lowest ebb, to give us strength.

On most mornings, I pray the Ephesians 3:16 -21 and Colossians 1:9-11 prayers. The verses talk about the Holy Spirit strengthening our inner man, which we need to be strengthened to live victoriously. The Bible says the joy of the Lord is our strength and that we should be mindful not to allow the cares of the world to choke and steal our joy. When we lose our joy, it has a knock-on effect on our strength as well but with the help of the Holy Spirit, we can preserve our joy and strength. 2 Corinthians 12:9 says that His strength is made perfect in our weakness. The kind of strength that we require will depend on our present needs. These might include;

1. The strength of character to stand for what's right when others are compromising in the face of opposing views.
2. The strength to resist bullying.
3. The strength to overcome peer pressure.
4. The strength to resist stress.
5. The strength to carry on.
6. Mental strength.
7. Emotional strength.
8. Spiritual strength.
9. Physical strength.

Many people in the scriptures displayed these kinds of strength; Joseph in Potiphar's house, Daniel and the three Hebrew Children in Babylon, David in his many dealings, and Sampson with raw strength, just to mention a few. The Apostles and other Biblical characters in the New Testament also displayed inner strength.

Sometimes, the shutters come down and we cannot bear the thought of seeing another day when we have come to the end of our tether, crossroads, or our wit's end. At these times, we will need the rejuvenating dose of the Holy Spirit's supernatural strength. This world we are living in can be hostile, competitive, challenging, and stressful at the best of times and we need the help and strength of the Holy Spirit to get through each day. His strength is made available for us if we want to tap into His endless and ever-flowing supply.

When we are physically, mentally, emotionally, and spiritually weak, He is strong, He is forever strong, and He is God Almighty in us. He is forever mighty, all-powerful, all-purposeful, and all-meaningful. He is the same yesterday, today, and forever constant; His principles and ways never change. The Holy Spirit will give us a daily dose of strength if we ask, so make a daily habit of asking Him for renewed strength every morning of every day.

STANDBY

The promised Holy Spirit is just standing by us. He is a friend that sticks closer than a brother. Indeed, the Holy Spirit is nearer to us than anyone else.

There is a saying that goes, '*If you do not ask, you will not get.*' The same is true about the Holy Spirit; if we do not ask, we will not receive. He is there, standing by us, to help us in times of need. Therefore, we should ask, so that our joy may be full and not partial.

As bodyguards stand by the people they are guarding, to protect them from danger and unsavoury characters, so does the Holy Spirit act as our protector and shields us from problems, dangerous situations, and events. He will not leave us alone; He will stand by us in times of need.

I once read a story about a girl who was walking down an alley at night. It was dark and she said to herself, "If I take the long way home it will prolong my journey," and so she decided to take a shortcut through an alleyway. As she was walking down the alley, she saw two menacing-looking boys. Fear-stricken, she began to recite Psalm 23 while she walked past them and continued all the way, until she got home safely. The next day she heard on the news that a girl was killed walking down the same alleyway the night before and there was a public appeal for witnesses. So, she came forward and reported that around that same time, she had walked down the alley and she could identify the two boys that she saw. The boys were caught, and when they were asked why they killed one girl and spared the other one, they said that the girl they spared was not walking alone. According to them, two huge men were holding the girl on either side as she walked through the alley, so they were panic-stricken and could not attack her. This is one of many examples of what our Standby can do for us.

When the Spirit of the Lord is upon us, He sends His angels to protect us. We carry the presence of God, in the person of the Holy Spirit, everywhere we go. The Bible says, "*...He will never leave you* (abandon, give upon you) *nor forsake you...*" (Deuteronomy 31:8).

The Spirit of God is with us always; He is the ever-present help in times of need. He is obligated to stand by us and not abandon us, desert us, or turn His back on us when we call on Him.

REVEALS THE FUTURE

The Bible says that the Holy Spirit will reveal to us things to come. The Holy Ghost in Luke 2:26 revealed to Simeon that he would not see death until he had witnessed the birth and dedication of our Lord Jesus Christ. Have you ever wondered about the plans and purpose of God for your life? If you have ever wondered, and want to know, your task will be to ask. Then the Holy Spirit will begin to reveal His plans for your life, as you walk in obedience to His leading, prompting, and direction. Learning to walk with the Spirit of God is a progressive revelation and a walk of faith.

This reminds me of a personal story. I was reading the first chapter of the book of Jeremiah, on how God had called and commissioned Jeremiah for special work. I was pregnant with our second child at the time, and, as I read, verse five stood out and I paused for a moment to meditate on it. The verse reads, *"Before I formed you in the belly I knew you; and before you came out of the womb, I sanctified you, and I ordained you to be a prophet unto the nations."* It was the first part of the prophesy that grabbed my attention; I said that if God knew, called, and commissioned Jeremiah before he was born, then surely God must know the name of the baby I was carrying in my womb at the time. Therefore, I began a quest of praying and asking the Holy Spirit to reveal the name of the child to me.

Well, I can tell you that the name did not come immediately. I was about two months into the pregnancy when I read Jeremiah's commissioning account and the name did not come until two weeks before delivery. After about four or five months of asking for a revelation of the child's name and no name was coming forth, I began to relent and said, 'You know what, when I have the baby, we will look at the baby's face and give a name that suits the face.'

As is typical of God most times, the name was revealed when I least expected it. I had two more weeks to go and had yet another scan. I forgot to add that because I had a series of miscarriages before this pregnancy, I had more than the usual antenatal care at the hospital. As a result, I was offered many scans to ensure that everything was fine. None of the scans revealed the child's gender, even though I asked at every appointment. On this momentous appointment, I chose not to ask but as the ultra scan staff were doing the scan, they said to me for the very first time, "Oh, we can see the gender now. Would you like to know?" After months of asking to no avail, I said yes, although not very enthusiastically.

I went for that scan on a Tuesday and on the Sunday before, at church, the Minister had preached about the story of David, Nabal, and Abigail. The name Abigail resonated with my spirit straightaway. I tried to discount the thought, saying to myself that it was my idea, and it was not a so long-awaited answer to prayer. I must say up until then if I was given a list of names, I would not have chosen the name Abigail. In my attempts to discount the name, I even told a friend of mine during an outing on that Sunday, that when she has a baby girl, she should call the baby Abigail. She looked at me and said, "Between you and me, who is pregnant? That is your child's name if you do not know."

Going back to the scan at the hospital; they told me that I was going to have a baby girl. Immediately, the name from the Sunday sermon came back to me and for the first time I thought to myself, 'You know what? Even though Abigail would not have been my first choice of name, I am going to make sure that it is among one of her names.' A few days later, I gave birth. The midwife, as a matter of routine, asked, "Have you got a name for the baby?" and without hesitation, I said, "Abigail."

The midwife came to me the next morning and said, "I am about to send the baby's name to the registry, but before I do, I thought I'd check one thing with you." She went on to say that my husband did not seem convinced when I said to call the baby Abigail, as he looked a bit puzzled. She went on, "So, I thought it is best to just check if it is okay to send the name or if I could just write 'Baby Babudoh' for now and then, when you go to the registry, you can give them her names."

I thanked her for checking the name with me and added that I would like Abigail to be part of the names on her birth certificate.

My mother came to stay with us for a while after the birth of the baby. As you would imagine, she asked the obvious question, "Have you got an English name for the baby?" Without hesitation, I said, "Abigail." My mother was equally puzzled by the name; I could imagine what was going through her mind. Both my husband and mother were clearly not in agreement with my choice of name, so for the first two weeks, they called her Baby, and I was the only one calling her Abigail.

One morning, as I was coming down the stairs with the baby in my arms, I noticed that my mother and my husband were unusually quiet and looking somewhat perplexed. My husband said to me, "You will not believe what happened," and went on to explain that we had received a letter from his father congratulating us on the birth of the baby. His father's letter arrived about two weeks after the birth of the baby. In the postscript of his letter, he wrote that my mother-in-law said to call the baby Abigail. My husband said, "I just cannot believe it," my mother just looked stunned, and they both gazed at me in sheer amazement. As soon as I heard the news, I said to myself that I was going to ask my mother-in-law how she decided on that name for her newest grandchild because I knew how I got my own inspiration.

Well, the opportunity came when she came to visit us and I asked her how she got the name. She told me that she went to a church cell group where they were discussing David, Nabal, and Abigail. Inspired, she said to herself, 'I will name my next granddaughter Abigail,' and my new baby was indeed her next granddaughter. My mother-in-law had already written me a letter earlier that year, before I conceived, saying that she is standing in the gap with me and believing that God would give me a baby boy. ***There are no coincidences with God; there are God-incidences.*** The Holy Spirit foreknew the name and when I took that bold step of faith to ask, He revealed it, maybe not at the time I wanted the name but nevertheless, at the right time, even with confirmation that was over and above my request.

The Holy Spirit searches the deep things of God; He knows everything and will reveal things to us if we ask Him. I must add that He reveals according to His will and plans for our lives. If He chooses not to reveal, He has a better plan and expects us to follow Him by faith, trust, and obedience.

THE SPIRIT OF TRUTH

God is a Spirit and they that worship Him MUST worship Him in Spirit and in truth. (John 4:24)

Have you believed a lie? Has someone told you a lie about yourself? Or have you believed your own lies? Apart from people telling us lies about ourselves, we sometimes lie to ourselves as well. If we have believed a lie, no matter how it came – either through other people or ourselves, we can be set free from those lies by the Spirit of God.

The Spirit of truth will help us to discern the lie from the truth. The Bible, in John 16:13, says that the Holy Spirit will guide us into all truth. Do not let the lie that people have told you, or the lie that you have told yourself, to hold you back from fulfilling God's best in your life. Be what you are created for, victorious over all the lies of the enemy. The Bible says Satan is a liar and the father of all lies (John 8:44). He wants you to believe what is not true, so you can be enslaved in your thinking, not making any real progress, and living a defeated life.

The world is a marketplace and there are many voices competing for our attention. What voice are you listening to? Are you listening to the voice of deceit or lies? Are you listening to those voices that say, 'I am not good enough', 'I am lazy', 'I cannot succeed', 'I am a failure', 'it is too difficult', 'people like me do not make headway in life', 'it is too late', 'I am too old', 'too young', or 'I am too weak'? Are you giving ears to ideas full of self-pity, self-doubt, feelings of inadequacy, lack of confidence, lack of motivation, low self-esteem, and feelings of being incapacitated, amongst others?

The Holy Spirit will lead, direct, and guide us if we dare trust Him and commit all our inadequacies into His hands. Let the Holy Spirit be the umpire, let Him help us to discern the thoughts, abilities, and intents of our hearts. The latter part of John 16:13 tells us that He will show us things to come. The Holy Spirit can show us what is to come when we approach Him and follow His leading and directions. Have you ever imagined what the future might have in store for you? Ephesians 3:20 put it this way: "*Now to Him* (Holy Spirit) *who by* (in consequence of) *is able to [carry out His purpose and]do superabundantly* (far over and above) *all we dare ask or think* (infinitely beyond our greatest prayers, desires, thoughts hopes or dreams), *according to His power that is at work within us...*"

The Holy Spirit is the right person to approach for your future. The opposite of truth is a lie; if we do not have the Spirit of truth guarding and leading us, we will be operating in lies and falsehood. The world will attempt to ensnare and enslave us, and we need to break out from its grip and ask the Holy Spirit to take ownership of our lives. In that way, we can really experience true freedom from the lies we have been led to believe.

There is a story about a man who led masses of people in a city to believe a lie, in chapter eight of the book of Acts. This man, called Simon, practically bewitched the people of Samaria with his magical arts, claiming that he was an extraordinary man with great powers. All the people, from the smallest to the greatest and amongst the high and low, gave him their attention and regarded him as a man with divine powers. For a very long time, he amazed, bewildered, and dazzled the people of Samaria with his skills in magical arts. Does this sound familiar? We still have people like Simon today, deceiving people with magical arts, and they think it's true.

Little did Simon know that his reign was about to come to an end when, one day, a man of God called Philip (one of Jesus' disciples) came to Samaria. Philip preached the gospel (the good news) about Jesus Christ and the kingdom of God. The people – both men and women, great and small, high and low – believed and were baptised, and even Simon himself believed and was baptised. Simon followed Philip and was utterly amazed at the great signs and miracles he saw take place.

Now when the apostles in Jerusalem heard that Samaria had accepted and welcomed the word of God, they sent Peter and John there. When they arrived in Samaria, they prayed that the people might receive the Holy Spirit, for they had not yet been baptised by the Holy Ghost, but had only been baptised in the name of the Lord Jesus. And when the disciples laid their hands on the people, they received the Holy Ghost. When Simon saw this, he brought money and offered it to the apostles saying, *"Give me this power as well… so that everyone on whom I lay my hands may receive the Holy Spirit."*

Peter said to him, *"May your [money] perish with you, because you thought you could buy the gift of [the Holy Spirit] with money! You have no part or share in [the work that we do] because your heart is not right before God. Repent, therefore, of your wickedness, and pray to the Lord. Perhaps He will forgive you for [having such a thought in] your heart. For I see that you are poisoned by bitterness and captive to [sin]."*

When Simon heard this rebuke, he said to Peter, "Pray to the Lord for me so that nothing you have said will come upon me."

Peter rebuked Simon in this way, so that he could repent and be freed from the wickedness of wanting to buy the gift of the Spirit of God with money. We have the gift of the Holy Spirit with us, and we should not go anywhere near fortune-tellers, deceivers, magicians, false prophets, people with fake powers, or liars who specialise in making merchandise of people in the name of solving our problems. You should not let anyone subject you to sit under false teachers, sit under false doctrine where they preach error, or go to false teachers who specialise in telling people the things that they want to hear, which clearly goes against the grain of the gospel. We should watch and pray that we do not fall into the hands of these kinds of people and make up our minds that we are going to believe and pattern our lives after what we hear or what we read from the word of God. We should also cultivate a habit of asking the Holy Spirit to give us illumination and light as we read the word. He is the author of the Bible, and so He can explain what He has inspired men to write when we ask Him.

The Holy Spirit does not speak of Himself; He is in perfect harmony with the rest of the Godhead. John 16:14 says that He will honour and glorify Jesus by receiving from Him and revealing them to us. And in John 16:15, Jesus said: *"All things that the Father has [belongs to me]. Therefore, I said that [the Holy Spirit] will take of Mine and [show] it to you."* This will happen if we ask and really want to know the unsearchable riches of God for our lives. God has innumerable things to show us, and the Holy Spirit will take these things and show us, so that Jesus will be glorified because all things are His.

1 John 2:21 says, *"I have not written to you because you do not know the truth, but because you know it, and that [there is no lie in] the truth."* Verse 24 goes: *"...If [you abide in the truth], you also will abide in the Son and in the Father."* And verse 26 continues: *"...I have written to [confirm the truth you already know and to warn you against] those who [would seduce] you."*

So, if we abide in the truth, we will not be subject to the lies and bondage of the enemy and no man will deceive or seduce us. The Word of God is true, and the Holy Spirit will help you to appropriate the truth to your life.

GUIDANCE AND DIRECTION

The Holy Spirit has been given to guide and direct us. John 16:13 says, "*But when He, the Spirit of truth comes, He will guide you into all the truth...* Follow the leading of the Holy Spirit; He is our leader and will guide and lead us into what has been already prepared for us. Take note of the tense used (has been), which shows that God knows the end from the beginning; our direction in life has already been planned and mapped out. We do not know it but God knows the plan, and that is why it is good to go to Him for direction because He knows. Believe me when I say doing that will save us from a lot of unnecessary headaches. The average person worries about what tomorrow will bring. Now, suppose you know someone that has been acclaimed, proven, and tested, and has a track record of 100% accuracy all the time, at predicting what tomorrow will bring, I am sure you will go to the person, without hesitation, for predictions. Well, we have the person that knows tomorrow living inside of us. We do not want to be like the Children of Israel, who through disobedience and lack of faith wandered in the desert for forty years (a 4-day journey became one of forty years).

The Holy Spirit reveals to us just what we need to know when we need to know it, a step at a time. We can find ourselves acting in a hesitant way, always rushing, or wanting things instantly. Just like the Children of Israel, God revealed to them what they needed to know when they needed to know it, but they had a few ideas of their own. There is nothing wrong with having your own ideas, but the problem begins when your ideas do not line up with God's ideas and ideals for your life and you want it badly and, sometimes, immediately. As a matter of fact, you may even want it yesterday. When we find ourselves running ahead of God's agenda, it is likely to lead us into all kinds of problems, temptations, frustrations, and fatigue. ***If we go at God's pace, we cannot go wrong***, and we have to be prepared to accept that the Holy Spirit will not reveal the entire vision at once. There is always a starting point, a middle part, and an end to all stories. When we have accomplished one task, then the rest will begin to unfold on a step-by-step, line-by-line, and precept-by-precept basis.

The Lord knows our tomorrow better than we know our yesterday. There is one thing that is worth remembering all the time and that is: we and God are walking in two different directions. God is walking from tomorrow into today and we are walking from today into tomorrow. Have you ever been lost or felt that you do not know where you are going? Do you need guidance and direction in life? Ask the Holy Spirit.

AIDE MÉMOIRE

The Bible says that the Holy Spirit will bring all things to our remembrance. We all need to remember things at various stages of our lives. The Holy Spirit will help us to remember what to say when we are ministering our faith to others, applying scriptures from the Bible, or for other endeavours that will be of benefit to others and us. Have you ever been in a position where you needed to remember something at a particular point in time? When next you find yourself in such a situation again, pause, say a quick prayer under your breath, and ask the Holy Spirit to help jog your memory.

One of the workings of the Holy Spirit is to avail Himself to believers who expect and look to Him to bring things to their minds when it is needed. When we are in tune with the indwelling presence of the Holy Spirit, sometimes we do not even have to ask as what we need to remember at that point just comes into our mind. The Holy Spirit moves as He wills; the latter part of John 14:26 says that the Holy Spirit will teach us all things and bring all things to our remembrance for personal and spiritual life.

AIDS OUR LOVE WALK

The Holy Spirit aids our love walk. Romans 5:5 puts it this way: "*...the love of God is shed abroad* (poured out) *in our hearts by the Holy Ghost which is given unto us.*" The Bible says we should not owe anyone anything but love, and the love being referred to is the agape kind, the God kind of love. This love hangs on the two commandments that Jesus gave to us in the New Testament; to love God with all our soul, might, heart, and all our being, and to love our neighbour as ourselves.

If we notice that certain things are not going the way they ought to in our lives, we should check our love walk. Are we at peace with our neighbours, or are we harbouring and not letting go of any misunderstanding, walking in unforgiveness, strife, or jealousy? Are we unfriendly, do we have many enemies, are we cheating, lying, or stealing from our neighbours? Do we have temper, anger, hatred, and rage that we cannot control, that is robbing us of our joy? Would we like to stop these habits and begin to love our neighbours as we ought? Do we love God the way we should? Are we reverencing God in all that we do? Do we give Him first place in our lives? When we invite the Holy Spirit into these areas of our lives, He will shed, and pour out His love in those areas, which helps us to mend broken relationships and initiate corrective measures in our love walk. The Bible says that love does not keep records of wrongs and love covers a multitude of sins. If we love someone, we will be quick to forgive them and would not want them upset.

The ultimate sacrifice of love was when Christ was crucified on the cross at Calvary for our sins. God's love has been and is still being demonstrated in our lives today. In John 3:16, the Bible says, "For God so loved the world that He gave His only begotten son that whoever believes in Him will not perish but have everlasting life." Love is an attribute of the Holy Spirit. God Himself says He is love, in 1 John 4:8 & 16. Without the help of the Holy Spirit, we will fail in our love walk. Love activates the blessing of God in our lives and helps us to live enriched, peaceful, purposeful, fulfilled, and fruitful lives.

SPIRITUAL COMPASS

The Holy Spirit is our spiritual antenna and radar, He knows our human spirit and what is in our hearts, and He knows what is in the heart of God for us. He helps us to navigate our way through the maze and jungle of life, leads us through the right pathways, and brings us to the place that has been predestined for us. 1 Corinthians 2:10 put it this way: "*...The Spirit searches all things, even the deep things of God.*" The Holy Spirit helps us to conduct a deep-down search of what God has placed on our hearts and helps us to fulfil them. The last thing we need is to be lost when the person that can show us the way lives on the inside of us.

Romans 8:27 has something to say about this same subject; it says in the New American Standard Bible: "…*and He* (the Holy Spirit) *who searches the hearts knows what the mind* (intent and purposes) *of the Spirit is, because He intercedes* (pleads and prays) *for [us] according to the will of God."* The Holy Spirit will help us to filter and weed out what is not in God's divine plan for our lives. Therefore, we need to be tuned to His station/frequency to pick up the signal of what He is saying to us.

I once heard a lady's testimony; she prayed and asked God to use her as a missionary but not to send her to America or Japan, because she believes that they are the two most capitalist countries in the world. As events would unfold in her life, she went to live in Japan for several years and then she married an American. She added that she loves her husband dearly and she is now working with her husband to help underprivileged people. God knows what is best for us, even when our heads are not in agreement with our hearts. The Holy Spirit works out His perfect plans for our lives when we let Him. He is our spiritual compass.

GREATEST TEACHER

The Holy Spirit teaches us many things in various ways. He is the supreme, ultimate teacher, who quickens our intellect and understanding. He enlightens our minds, reveals hidden things to us, and helps us to recall forgotten things, and He teaches us all things that we need to live effective, fruitful, and fulfilled lives. We can only learn from a teacher when we listen, because when we are distracted, we do not learn or retain much. Our attention and obedience are required to learn from the Holy Spirit.

He will teach us all things — pertaining to things that we need for life — and to live a life that is pleasing to God. As students, professionals, and businesspeople, we all need teaching, to develop and improve our quality of life. Whatever our calling in life might be, we need teaching. The Bible in 1 Corinthians 2:13 says that The Holy Ghost will teach us all things and that our wisdom should not only rest in the wisdom of men but in the wisdom of God. We live in this world, so we will invariably need the knowledge the world gives but we also need the wisdom of God to apply them rightly in our everyday lives.

If you are a person in a position of authority, you need the help of the Holy Spirit to teach you how to use the power rightly. If you hold official positions and can influence the law and legislation, you can pray and ask the supreme teacher for divine wisdom. The Bible in Proverbs 29:2 says: *"When the righteous are in authority* (in a position of power and rulership) *the people rejoice; But when a wicked man* (people who do not know God*) rules, the people [mourn, grief and lament]."*Every one of us has our own sphere of influence; we can pray and ask the Holy Ghost to teach us, so that we can positively impact our generations, communities, families, friends, children, colleagues, etc., with His divine wisdom.

We need the Holy Spirit to teach us to operate in the wisdom of God and not the wisdom that the world gives, to live decent, peaceable, and morally acceptable lives. As believers (Children of God), the word of God is our final authority. The Holy Spirit is our teacher, and He will help us to live the God-given and God-acceptable kind of life if we ask Him.

4

ENDOWMENTS OF THE SPIRIT

We are all born with in-built gifts, talents, skills, and abilities. These natural gifts are freely given to us. The endowments we will be looking at here are supernatural endowments. The Holy Spirit endows and equips people with special skills that they have not specifically learned, to benefit and enhance their lives. These gifts, I believe, mainly come by way of ideas for witty inventions, concepts, insight, supernatural wisdom, and knowhow.

ENDOWMENTS OF SKILLS

I once heard a story about a woman who invented a baby's feeding bottle that controls colic, which is a condition that is painful and uncomfortable for babies. In the early stages of a baby's life, before they learn to sit up, they are always lying down and wind becomes trapped in their intestines. That is why it is a good idea to burp babies, especially if they are bottle-fed, so that they can expel the wind. At the time, this woman was nursing a baby with colic. She had an idea of how to design a feeding bottle that would control the amount of wind absorbed during bottle-feeding. So, she put her ideas to work and became the first person to manufacture anti-colic feeding bottles, which turned out to be a huge success. There are many variations of anti-colic bottles produced today, by different manufacturers.

I heard another story about how Isaac Newton gained one of his greatest mathematical formulas whilst on his knees, praying. Albert Einstein, another great scientist, developed his inventions through special gifts of endowments. God has placed minerals and natural resources in the earth and solar system for us to discover and use for the benefit and enrichment of our lives. The Bible did say that knowledge will increase, and we are seeing the increase of knowledge all around us today, with many discoveries, inventions, and modifications being made. The Holy Spirit helps with this gift of special abilities and knowhow. It will be a worthy endeavour to ask the Holy Spirit to help you to locate your special gifting and abilities.

Another inspiring story in this area of special gifting is that of another young person. A fourteen-year-old girl started to post wise sayings on her website, and before long she had a considerable number of young people visiting her platform. One day, out of the blue, she received a phone call from an advertising company, saying that they would like to advertise on her website. So, she'd had an idea, and instead of sitting and brooding over it, she put it out, blessing children and young people of her age with the wise sayings. Her ideas and talent paid off financially, yet she was only a teenager at the time.

Bill Gates, described as one of the world's greatest philanthropists, is another example of a person with witty ideas. He made computers so user-friendly that even young children could use them. When interviewed and asked why he set up Microsoft, he said he wanted to make routine work easy for people, by lightening their workload and helping to computerise routine work. His inventions made it easy for people to store, retrieve and use information readily, without the laborious task of trawling through filing cabinets or wherever the information is kept. Computers, as we know them now, are being used for various activities that range from pleasure to fun and other intricate to complex things.

I am sure that there are many more examples of people that you know of, have heard of, or have read about. The woman that invented the anti-colic bottle, I think, is a Christian. For the other four examples, I am unsure if they are Christians or not and if it is by natural abilities that they have come up with these ingenious and fantastic ideas. But how much more do you think we can achieve with the influence and help of the Holy Spirit? When we have these witty, inventive ideas, they are not really for our own use and consumption only; they are generally given to us to benefit mankind, the environment, and the world at large.

BEZALEEL AND AHOLIAB

The Bible, in Exodus 31, described how the Holy Spirit endowed two people with special abilities. There are many stories of how the Holy Spirit specially endowed many other people in the Bible. By way of an example, I would like to relay the account of these two ordinary people that were like you and me. In the days of the Old Testament, we know the Holy Spirit would come on people, enable them, and then leave (what can be described as ***touch-inspire-and-go ministry***). After Pentecost in, the New Testament, the Holy Spirit does not have a *touch-inspire-and-go ministry* with believers because He has taken residence in us. He lives within us and we carry Him wherever we go, both in our sleeping or waking moments.

Bezaleel and his business partner, Aholiab, were commissioned, endowed, and filled with wisdom, understanding, knowledge, skills, abilities, and intelligence in all kinds of craftsmanship, to assist Moses in building and furnishing the tabernacle. Both men were commissioned by the Holy Spirit to work creatively with their hands and between the two of them, they carried out skilful work such as cutting out shapes, patterns, and designs, and creating artwork with gold, silver, and bronze. They were supernaturally gifted and talented in arts and crafts, stone cutting, wood carving, building and construction work, furniture building and design, textile making and design, and diverse manner of workmanship, pertaining to the call and course the Holy Spirit placed on their minds.

They built the tabernacle for the congregation, and built the ark of the testimony, the mercy seat, the altar of incense, the burnt offering altar, and all the furniture required to furnish them. They constructed tables, desks, benches and chairs, pews, pulpit, altars, candlesticks, candle stands, and a building for the congregation. These were in addition to crafting the clothes and service garments for the priest and his sons. These men were gifted in different ways even though they did not attend any school in carpentry, construction, handwork, needlework, tapestry, or design technology. They were divinely gifted under the tutorship of the Holy Spirit.

In general, Bezaleel oversaw metal, wood, stone, and apothecary, while Aholiab oversaw textile work. Both of these gifted men were specially endowed to help Moses to carry out his assignment and, by divine endowments and appointments, were specialists in their trades. Likewise, we all have special tasks and endowments. It is our duty to seek the help of the Holy Spirit to discover and carry out our assignments, tasks, and purposes in life. In John 16:23-26, Jesus said we should not be afraid to ask Him for anything, but He said to ask, so that our joy will be full. Our duty is to ask, and the Holy Spirit will do the delivery, according to His will and purpose for us to live life to the full or fullest.

The Holy Spirit does not only want to help us in spiritual things alone, but has also been sent to help us in every area of our lives. We are after all tripartite beings (spirit, soul, and body), and when we submit these members of ourselves under His hospice, leadership, rule, and control, He will help and bless us materially, physically, emotionally, and spiritually. He will lead us to discover and live out our full potential and make our lives focused, wholesome, purposeful, and impactful. John 16:24 says: *"Until now you have not asked for anything in My name. Ask [in faith] and you will receive, so that your joy [will be full]."*

Take note that asking is not limited to spiritual things alone but extends to all other needs, so that we can function as holistic beings. If you know your purpose and calling in life, do not forget to enlist the continuous, never-ending, never-failing guidance, help, and direction of the Holy Spirit, so that you remain on course and do not go off the right path.

Noah operated in this special endowment in building the Ark. There is a saying that goes along these lines: amateurs built the Ark, but professionals built the Titanic. Solomon did not attend a world-renowned school of leadership and management, yet under the schooling of the Holy Spirit, he was endowed with wisdom that enabled him to serve as one of the wisest Kings of Israel. As history stands, King Solomon is recorded as the wisest and richest person that ever lived. This is not an excuse for us not to acquire knowledge, because knowledge is good, knowledge is power. We should enrol in educational courses that will broaden our knowledge and minds. However, the knowledge I am referencing here is a supernatural endowment, and part of the supernatural abilities needed to boost our natural abilities.

The Bible, in Psalm 119:99, recorded that David knew more than his teachers. The book of Daniel, chapter one, records that Daniel and his friends were so supernaturally gifted in knowledge, understanding, skills in all learning, and wisdom, that they were ten times more astute than the Babylonians. There are many more examples of these occurrences and gifting in the Bible and in our world today.

When ideas come into our minds, we should not discount all of them by saying that they might not amount to anything because some might, and some might not. With the support, advice, and guidance from people you trust, these ideas might not just be wild dreams, they might be God-given ideas that could help mankind in a way that advances and enriches our lives.

We have dream-shapers, people who are strategically placed to help us shape our dreams to make them a reality, and we have dream-breakers, those who sabotage our dreams. So, be selective regarding whom you share your dreams with. In the story of Exodus 31, God gave Moses the vision and specially endowed and commissioned Bezaleel and Aholiab to help carry out and fulfil the mission as He commanded. These gifts of endowments are usually given to benefit mankind; they are God-given and Holy Spirit-directed.

ENABLER

Do you aspire to be somebody extraordinary in life? Ask the Holy Spirit and He will give you the power and enablement. I have always wanted to be a good communicator. When I hear people who speak with impact, clarity, and eloquence, I say in my heart, 'Lord, I would like to sound like them someday.' Do not be a spectator and do not let life just pass you by, while belittling yourselves by saying, "I am not cut out for this," that is a lie. Ask the Holy Spirit to enable you to reach your dreams and fulfil your God-given life goals, potential, and purpose.

Do you have an ambition? Do you have a dream, vision, or desire that you want to accomplish? Once it is aligned with the will of God for your life, then it will come to fruition. The reason we think we cannot do what God places in our hearts is that the vision is too large for us to comprehend. God is not a small God; He is a big God and so when He gives us an assignment, it seems larger than life to us. We say to ourselves, "How on earth can this dream, vision, or goal be accomplished?"

I once heard Joyce Meyer say, "God has not called us to do what we cannot do. God has called us to do what we are afraid to do." That is where faith, trust, and obedience come in. The vision, nine times out of ten, is always bigger than our imagination can conceive or comprehend. Take a step of faith and ask the Holy Spirit and, together, you can accomplish the dream, taking one step at a time.

The Holy Spirit will help us to accomplish our dreams and take us to better, mightier, and greater heights than we dare to imagine. Read the stories of Abraham, Joseph, Moses, Joshua, Gideon, Ruth, Esther, David, Solomon, Daniel, and countless others in the Bible, and see what God did in the lives of ordinary people like you and me. I once heard the story of Martin Luther King Jr., the American Civil Rights Leader, during the tense days of the Montgomery boycott and after receiving threats and opposition from those who did not believe in his course. He prayed, and he said, 'I am taking a stand for what I believe is right but Lord, I am afraid, weak, faltering, losing my courage, and the people are coming to me for leadership. I need strength to enable me to carry on.' He later wrote that when he made that prayer, he experienced the Divine presence of God, and the fear began to subside, the uncertainty vanished, and he was ready to soldier on. David, in the Bible (the book of Psalms), prayed this kind of prayer many times. My prayer for you today is that the Holy Spirit will enable you to run the race that is set before you and finish your course with joy.

QUICK SUMMARY

Below is a quick summary of the attributes and functionalities of the Holy Spirit:

1. We ask God for His presence; He sent the Holy Spirit to dwell and abide in us forever.

2. We ask for an instructor; He sent us the Teacher that will teach all things.
3. We ask for help; He sent us the Helper to help at our beck and call.
4. We ask for an adviser; He gave us the Counsellor.
5. We ask for justice; He sent us the Advocate.
6. We ask for a friend; He gave us the Permanent Standby, the Friend that sticks by us 24/7.
7. We ask for strength; He gave us His unwavering strength on tap.
8. We ask for direction; He sent us the Guardian.
9. We ask for truth; He sent us the Spirit of truth and discernment.
10. We ask for good memory; He sent us the memory bank that will bring everything to our remembrance.
11. We ask for comfort; He gave us the Comforter.
12. We ask for energy; He energises us, giving us a constant supply of energy.
13. We ask for wisdom; He gave us the Spirit of wisdom.
14. We ask for understanding; He gave us the Spirit of understanding.
15. We ask for an eye-opener; He gave us the Spirit of revelation.
16. We ask for power; He gave us the Spirit of power and boldness.
17. We ask to be commissioned; He gave us the Commissioner.
18. We ask for wholesome thinking; He gave us the Spirit of a sound mind.
19. We ask for safe keep from fears and phobias; He gave us the Spirit of boldness.

20. We ask for companionship; He gave us His presence.
21. We ask for self-worth (self-esteem); He gave us the right of adoption and sent the Spirit of His Son into our hearts to nurture us.
22. We ask for a Father; He sent us His Spirit, whereby we can call Him Abba (Daddy, Papa), Father, assuring us that He is our Father.
23. We ask for love; He gave us the Spirit of love.
24. We ask for knowhow, skills, and abilities; He gave us the Spirit of Knowledge.
25. We ask for confidence; He gave us the Confidant, Mentor, and Coach.
26. We ask for personal identity; He gave us a personal companion, seals us, and baptises us with the Holy Ghost.
27. We ask for prayers; He gave us the Intercessor, who prays on our behalf non-stop.
28. We as for joy; He gave us the Source of joy.
29. We ask for supplies; He gave us the Supplier.
30. We ask for sanctification; He gave us the Sanctifier.
31. We ask for peace; He gave us His peace that surpasses understanding.

And the list goes on and on. We cannot exhaust God's resources because His ways are past finding out and inexhaustible, and He is forever yearning to do good things for us because He is good.

Ephesians 3:20 says God can do exceedingly and abundantly above all we can ever think or imagine. The Holy Spirit can do more for us than we will ever know. Ours is to do the believing, trusting, and acting out our faith in the light of His supreme power, and He will do the rest.

Talk about a helper and a friend that sticks closer than a brother, then you are talking about The Holy Spirit, who can do so much through us, as we tap into the rich, overwhelming, and all-encompassing resources He has made available for us.

Invite Him into every area of your life and the areas where you have shut the doors.

5

FILLING AND BAPTISM OF THE HOLY SPIRIT, AND SPEAKING IN TONGUES

The Holy Spirit, as we know, is a gift to believers and was promised to manifest at Pentecost. I would like to draw our attention to two more scriptures that point us to the promise of the Holy Spirit. In Luke 24:49, Jesus said, "*...I send the promise of My Father upon you; but [wait] in the city of Jerusalem until you are endued* (clothed) *with power from [heaven].*" In Acts 2:33, Peter testified and referred to the promise in Luke 24:49, when he said, "*...[Jesus]being exalted* (lifted high) *to the right of God, and having received from the Father the promise of the Holy Spirit, He poured out this which you now see and hear.*"

BORN OF THE HOLY SPIRIT AND BEING FILLED WITH THE HOLY SPIRIT

There is a difference between being born of the Spirit, being filled with the Holy Spirit, baptism of the Holy Ghost or Holy Spirit, and water baptism. I will keep my explanation very simple and clear, so it is not muddled. This important aspect of the Holy Spirit can be misunderstood if it is not dissected properly.

BORN OF THE HOLY SPIRIT (SALVATION EXPERIENCE)

When a person believes in their heart and confesses with their mouth that Jesus is Lord and that God raised Him from the dead, they receive the gift of salvation, new birth, or eternal life. At this point, the person's spirit (human Spirit) is reborn, regenerated, or born again by the Spirit of God, and they are made a new creature (species) in Christ. Old things and old ways of life will change and from then on, everything becomes new as they embrace this walk of regeneration and transformation. This event is described as 'born of the Spirit of God' and is also known as 'the salvation experience'. The term, 'born-again' is also used to describe this experience. Other terms you would hear people use to describe their salvation, their relationship, and affiliation with Jesus are, 'I gave my life to the Lord', 'I am a believer', 'I am a Christian', 'I am a Child of God', 'I have accepted Christ as my Lord and Saviour', 'I am saved', 'I have eternal life', etc.

I have heard people describe what they physically noticed after their salvation experience, and it is something that other people might take for granted. What these people say is that the grass they have been seeing every day is suddenly greener, the sky is clearer, the day is brighter, etc. It is good to know that salvation can change people's emotional state, perception, and environmental outlook. For me, I felt joy unspeakable, un-comprehend-able, and unquenchable bubbling on the inside of me. I also felt a renewed hope and a sense of calmness and peace within myself. Having said all that, some people do not experience any physical or outward manifestations at all.

The Holy Spirit is instrumental in our salvation and plays a pivotal role. He enables us and gives us the unction to confess Jesus as Lord, to accept the gift of salvation, and at the same time, He recreates our human spirit and dwells within our spirit. Our human spirit, which was once estranged and dead to the things of God, becomes regenerated, infused, and ignited with the power of the Holy Ghost. We receive the anointing and illumination of the Holy Spirit, and our human spirit is quickened, made alive, and aware of the things of God. The Holy Spirit baptizes us, anoints us, and places us into the body of Christ the moment that we receive the new birth. All this might sound like a lot, but it all happens at the same time. So, we do not need a checklist to say 'has this happened' or 'has that happened'? That is why salvation is called a package; all the work happens simultaneously at the new birth of every believer in Jesus Christ.

We refer to salvation as an experience, because when it occurs, people can talk about it. Anyone that has gone through this encounter should be able to relate a personal story of what their life was like before salvation, what lead them to salvation, why they felt it was necessary when they received their salvation, where they received their salvation, how it happened, and who lead them to salvation. They should also be able to measure the remarkable changes and visible difference that has taken place in their Christian and personal life since they made the commitment. On the contrary, I have met Christians who cannot remember when they were saved and that does not mean that they are not saved.

I have heard people give vivid accounts of their salvation experiences, just as they would for their weddings or any other memorable life events. They can remember what, why, who, when, how, and where it took place. I was born a Roman Catholic and I remember my first Holy Communion Ceremony; I was about eight years old at the time. I remember the classes that I attended in preparation for the ceremony, remember passing the test, and remember the dress I wore for the ceremony. Our salvation experience might not be as formal as a wedding day, or any other memorable occasion in our life, but the point remains that it is a conscious experience, and we can relate and attest to the fact that it's one of the most joyous and memorable moments of our lives and an experience that is not easily forgotten.

FILLED WITH THE HOLY SPIRIT

Immediately after salvation, the indwelling presence of the Spirit of God within us is activated. The second experience after salvation (being born of the Spirit) is known as being filled with the Holy Spirit, receiving the Holy Spirit, or being baptised with the Holy Spirit. When this happens, the believer is filled with power for service. We can describe this event as when the Holy Spirit comes upon our spirit and fills us with Himself. This initial in-filling of the Holy Spirit happens at the same time that we receive our salvation.

There is a difference between the initial in-filling of the Holy Spirit and the ongoing in-filling of the Holy Spirit. For the Apostles, we can say the initial filling of the Holy Spirit happened on the day of Pentecost while, for us, the initial in-filling happens on the day we give our lives to the

Lord. After our salvation experience, we will now commence on episodes of in-fillings, as the Apostles did in their day. The initial in-filling is automatically given the moment we accept Christ as our Lord and Saviour, and the subsequent in-filling is something we seek daily.

The Apostles, in the book of Acts, were continually being filled with the Holy Ghost as they made their lives available for Him to use. They experienced many episodes of filling, one after another. We too can experience many episodes of filling of the Holy Spirit, if we choose to; it is a matter of choice, by making ourselves available for the Master's use and asking. When we ask, the Bible guarantees that we will be filled. The scriptures command us to be filled with the Spirit of God and not with worldly lust and desires that will perish and pass away (Ephesians 5:18). Being filled with the Holy Spirit sets us on the right path and helps us to stay focused on our individual endeavours. Without the in-filling and fillings of the Holy Spirit daily, we might step out of line and out of the will of God for our lives. So, we need daily doses of the in-filling of the Holy Spirit.

To stay full of the Holy Spirit, one would have to receive an initial in-filling and thereafter, we are commanded to continue to be full of the Spirit. This subsequent in-filling of the Spirit is available to every believer who desires more of God. Jesus, in Acts 1:4-5, commanded us to be filled and to desire the in-filling of the Holy Spirit.

To be full of the Spirit does not mean that we should be acting weird, or looking solemn, pious, or holier-than-thou. What it simply means is that we acknowledge the Holy Spirit by prioritising Him in our daily agenda and asking Him for His help, direction, and leading. When we perform these basic steps, presumably on a regular basis, then we can be assured that we are being filled with the Holy Spirit. Ephesians 5:19 summaries it this way: it says it involves speaking to yourselves in psalms and hymns and spiritual songs, and singing and making melody in your heart to the Lord, coupled with reading the Bible, praying, and meditating on the word. When we are conscious of the presence of God in this way, we are acknowledging Him and prioritising Him and He will begin to direct our daily activities. As we implement these processes, we are being filled and re-filled with His presence and power.

Think about it this way, you have a full glass of water; if you drink the water, the glass is emptied, and if you need more water, you will need to refill the glass. God wants to do new things in our lives and fill us anew with Himself. And when we read the word, pray, meditate on the word, listen to His promptings, trust His instructions, guidance and obey them, we are presenting and putting ourselves in a position to be filled daily, with the Holy Spirit.

With this daily act of worshipping, reverencing, serving, yielding, presenting, meditating, and dedicating ourselves before the Lord, to be used for His purpose, we are gradually being transformed and conforming ourselves to the image of who He wants us to be. The Lord, in return, will pour and fill us with the Holy Spirit. The book of Acts 1:8 says, *"…you shall receive power* (ability to do my work) *when the Holy Spirit has come upon you…"* Just as the Holy Spirit powerfully changed the Apostles and filled them with His power when they yielded themselves over to Him, so He will do the same for us today, as we yield in obedience to His Commandments.

BAPTISM OF THE HOLY SPIRIT

At the time of our new birth and salvation experience, Our Lord Jesus Christ, Himself, baptizes us with the Holy Spirit, and this is called the Baptism of the Holy Spirit. These experiences happen all at the same time, so that we cannot pinpoint or differentiate when one took place. Salvation, as I said before, is a package, and it goes well beyond the day we give our lives to the Lord.

John the Baptist, in relation to the baptism of the Holy Spirit, in Matthew 3:11 said, "... *[The One] who is coming after me... will baptize you with Holy [Ghost] and fire.*" And in the book of Acts 1:5, before he ascended into heaven, Jesus promised his disciples: "*...you shall be baptized with the Holy Spirit...*" The baptism of the Holy Spirit that John spoke about, and the baptism of the Holy Spirit that Jesus promised, is received during our salvation experience. These two passages refer to the same experience, which we now call the Baptism of the Holy Spirit. The scriptures said you will receive power after the Holy Ghost has come upon you, and 'Power' here refers to the baptism with the Holy Ghost and fire. This Baptism gives us the enablement and the impartation of power, which equips us for service. As the Apostles were equipped for service after the Baptism of the Holy Spirit, so are we today. The phrase "baptism of the Holy Spirit" means to be immersed, dipped, and soaked in the power of God, and filled with the Spirit of God.

Jesus promised to send us the Holy Spirit after His death, burial, and resurrection. He said, "When I go, I will send the Holy Spirit and He will fill you with power to do my work." The promised gift of the Holy Spirit was inaugurated at Pentecost and is given to every believer by Jesus

Christ, at the time of our salvation. Salvation, being filled with the Spirit, baptism of the Holy Spirit, regeneration, and being sealed with the Holy Spirit, all happen together and at the same time. These events are intricate; one comes after the other successively without us noticing the sequence, as they practically take place simultaneously.

WATER BAPTISM

Water baptism is different from the baptism of the Holy Spirit. Water baptism is a visible act of identifying with the death, burial and resurrection of our Lord Jesus Christ. Water baptism is a public affirmation of our belief and not a prerequisite for eternal life, although it is good to do this, and it can take place any time after our salvation experience. Water Baptism, as the name suggests, involves water. People that are being baptised in this way are physically baptised with water or immersed in water. Water Baptism is another memorable experience in that people remember the why, what, when, where, who and how, especially when it is done when they are old enough to remember. Water baptisms are occasions to which people can invite their families, friends, and loved ones to witness if they choose to.

COMPARISON

By way of comparison, salvation is the baptism into the body of Christ, orchestrated by the Holy Ghost. The initial in-filling of the Holy Spirit happens at the same time as our salvation experience. The baptism in the Holy Spirit occurs when Jesus fills us with the Holy Spirit and endows us with power for service. First, the Holy Spirit sets the scene for us to receive our salvation and baptises us into the body of

Christ. Secondly, we are filled with the Spirit after we have already received salvation. Thirdly, Jesus Christ, Himself, baptises us with the Holy Spirit, thereby empowering us for His service on earth. Water Baptism is a separate event that happens later than the other three.

The Holy Spirit helps us to acknowledge and accept Jesus as the Lord and saviour of our lives. 1 Corinthians 12:3 says that no one can say that Jesus is the Lord except by the Holy Ghost. Baptism of the Holy Spirit is an experience that happens once, and then there are many subsequent episodes of in-filling throughout our lives. We are filled on the day that we are baptised with the Holy Spirit, in the same way that the apostles were filled. By way of daily maintenance, we need to be re-filled and re-fired. So, in effect, the baptism of the Holy Spirit is a one-time occurrence but there are many in-fillings. Baptism of the Holy Spirit can be described as when you open the door to let the Holy Spirit into your house and the in-filling is described as when you allow Him to dwell in your house and – I would like to add – with unrestricted access.

BENEFITS OF BEING FILLED WITH THE HOLY SPIRIT

As a believer, you may say, "I have already been born of the Spirit and placed in the body of Christ. Why do I need the additional experience of being filled with the Holy Spirit?" Here are some of the benefits of being continuously filled with the Holy Spirit. This list is by no means exhaustive.

1. To be filled with the Spirit is a commandment and this commandment is helpful and beneficial for our spiritual and personal growth.

2. Being filled with the Spirit gives us insight, clarity, and illumination into understanding the word of God better. As we study the scriptures, we will receive more light and revelation.
3. The Bible becomes a living word (the words become alive and active) as we begin to apply its instructions to everyday living circumstances and situations.
4. Our Christian life and indeed our lives, in general, will no longer be dead, filled with drudgery, and boring. We will begin to see life, or indeed each day, as an exciting adventure.
5. As we begin to explore life from a brand-new perspective, we discover more of God and begin to develop a deeper yearning to know more of what God has in store for us.
6. Our outlook on life takes a whole new dimension as we begin to have more understanding, wisdom, and knowledge, as well as a sense of new significance, identity, fulfilment, and real purpose.
7. We all need power, and being filled with the Holy Spirit is a source of spiritual God-filled power.
8. We will experience a new boldness and power to be effective witnesses for the gospel.
9. Timidity is reduced or removed when we are filled with the Spirit.
10. Cowards are turned into heroes when filled with the Spirit.
11. People with little education, or even uneducated people, receive understanding, powerful insight, and wisdom that outstands when filled with the Spirit.

12. You will notice that you will begin to enjoy the presence of the Lord more and you will long for more of His presence.
13. You will not want to take the things of God for levity; they will now be of uttermost priority, and you will begin to find them more interesting.
14. Your experience of prayer, meditation, praise, and worshipping will take on a new meaning.
15. You will enjoy, basking daily in the Holy Spirit, as you become mindful of His indwelling presence, filling, leading, and direction.

HOW CAN I BE FILLED WITH THE HOLY SPIRIT?

To be filled with the Holy Spirit you should:

1. Be sure that you are born again or you can say the salvation prayer at the end of this book on pages 281 and 282.
2. Simply ask and receive the Holy Spirit by faith (Luke 11:9-13).
3. Begin to read, study, and meditate on the words you read in the Bible.
4. Begin to yield to the Holy Spirit's promptings.
5. If you are already a believer, you can enjoy the continued in-filling of the Holy Spirit by being mindful of the things of the Spirit and by trusting and obeying His commandments.

God is not separate from His Word, so as you read the Word and act on it, you will notice that your conduct, your character, and your way of life will begin to change to what God expects of us as believers. This will be the ultimate evidence that your life is being influenced and filled with the Holy Spirit. Others will also notice and see these changes in you.

If you want a new dose of the filling of the Holy Spirit, you might want to say the prayer below and ask the Father in the name of Jesus, to fill you anew with the Holy Spirit:

> *Heavenly Father, I ask that you fill me anew with the Holy Spirit so that I may receive the fullness of Your Spirit. Lord Jesus, I want to have the power to be a witness for You. As you breathed on the disciples of old and said receive the Holy Ghost, I receive now. I want to be able to praise You from my innermost being, speak Your word boldly and be an effective tool for your Kingdom. You said if I ask, I should believe and I will receive. You said that You will give the Holy Spirit to those that ask. Father, I thank You for filling me anew with the Holy Spirit now. In Jesus' name, I pray. Amen*

SPEAKING IN TONGUES

As we receive our salvation by faith, we can also receive speaking in other tongues by faith. Some people say they spoke in other tongues on the day they got saved. For me, it happened much later. For other people, it does not happen at all. Speaking in tongues is not an indication that we are more spiritual. I would like to emphasise that receiving the Holy Spirit is normal to everyone who is born again, but some don't speak or "choose" not to speak in tongues, and that does not make them less spiritual than those who speak in tongues.

Like every other subject in the scriptures, speaking in other tongues has its place and it is useful for our spiritual growth, especially in our prayer life. I would not like to minimise or underplay the importance of speaking in other tongues because it is extremely useful and beneficial in my life.

Most children that attended Sunday school have been brought up with this song, 'read your Bible, pray every day, if you want to grow.' One of the growth areas ascribed to in this song is prayer. I can attest to the fact that the Holy Spirit has helped me in my prayer life, to pray in other tongues and in my own understanding. We can pray in our known tongue, which is extremely effective, and we can also pray in other tongues that we have not learned, and it is equally as effective, if not more so.

Sometimes, we find ourselves wanting words when we pray; we cannot articulate as we ought or want. This is because we are limited in our known tongue, limited by what we can say, how we say it, what we do not say, and what we cannot say. Praying in tongues helps to bridge the gap in these scenarios and enables us to pray beyond our understanding and praying abilities. Praying in other tongues also enables us to pray the will of God more effectively into our lives. This reminds me of an experience I went through some time ago while driving. During this episode, I became very impatient and easily irritated. Anytime a sluggish driver was in front of me, or the traffic light changed to red just before it passed me, I became filled with anger and felt so enraged. This kind of behaviour gets people in trouble, big time. They have even coined a phrase for this kind of behaviour; it is called "road rage".

Most drivers will agree with me that some of the challenges we experience on the road (like putting up with bad drivers and having traffic lights changing as you approach them) are irritating, inevitable, and can be frustrating for motorists. I am normally what you would describe as a calm, laid-back person. During that time, I allowed the situation I was going through to get the better of me. I did not ever lash out at anyone, but I had plenty of opportunities to do so. One day I found myself again in these moods. As I was about to get angry again, muttering words under my breath and working myself up, I had a notion in my spirit suggesting that when this happens again, I should not get angry but pray under my breath in tongues instead. I thought this was weird, but I decided to put it into practice.

To my sheer amazement and utter surprise, it did not stop at praying in other tongues. Sometimes, I will find myself singing in other tongues and known tongues. I really began to enjoy the experience every single time. Unbelievably, I even began to enjoy being stuck in traffic as well because it gave me more opportunities to express myself to God in prayer and in tongues. You might say this sounds weird- I know, I was of the same opinion in the beginning. Looking back now, I can say the experience acted as a check and balance to what could have been a bad habit for me, and well out of my character.

The other thing I noticed was that I stopped minding if a sluggish driver was driving in front of me or if the traffic light changed to red as I got there. I just continued doing what Ephesians 5:19 told us to do, by speaking to ourselves in psalms and hymns and spiritual songs, singing and making melody in our hearts to the Lord. No doubt, I was being filled and refilled with the Holy Ghost during those times. With the help of the Holy Spirit, my adrenalin was diverted into doing something worthwhile. The experience had a soothing, calming, and refreshing effect on me, to the extent that the problem I was going through then just began to seem so insignificant. It was later I realised that all this had happened because of deciding to obey the promptings of the Holy Spirit; to pray in tongues. You see, I had the choice to respond negatively (which I did for a long time) or positively. By way of comparison, I preferred my newly discovered way of coping with the situation, which was far better for my health and wellbeing.

A few months after this episode, I went to visit my sister-in-law and as usual, we talked about everything and anything. Somehow, our conversation drifted into road rage, and I relayed to her how the Lord had taught me to deal with potential road rage situations. She told me that what I described could only be what God can do, and that I could see the hallmark of God all over it. She really made me see the whole scenario in a different light. The valuable lesson I learned from the experience was that instead of getting upset, whining, and moaning, I can decide to use the time wisely. I can tell you that from that day, and up to this day, I still pray in tongues when I am stuck in traffic. The Bible teaches us to redeem (buy back, use) the times wisely, for the days are evil. Speaking in tongues goes beyond the experience I have just relayed.

1 Corinthians 14, Acts 2:4, Mark 16:17, and other passages in the New Testament, give us more insight into the subject of speaking in tongues. This example of my personal experience is just an instance of how the Holy Spirit helped me to get out of the predicament that was presenting itself in my life at that time. The Holy Spirit deals with us on a personal level. In this instance, He chose to use the ways explained above to bring the solution to my problems. I must say that I am one person that now really enjoys speaking in tongues on the go.

Another example I would like to recount, happened during a canvassing job a few years ago. During one of my canvassing jobs, as I was praying in tongues, the Lord gave me a profound insight. Each time this memory comes to my mind, it just fills me with a deep sense of appreciation, awe, and assurance that God really cares for us and has our best interests at heart. To continue, this canvassing job involved going to households, cold calling, and sometimes delivering official papers. I would always pray in tongues as I did this job, as it could be very boring sometimes. I would pray for the salvation of the souls of the people in the households, and sometimes I would pray for the entire neighbourhood and locality, pray for myself, family, friends, and whatsoever comes to my mind.

I remember that on one of those occasions, I was praying in tongues and as I was praying, I heard in my spirit, "Some of your finest battles are won whilst praying in tongues, on this job." Each time I remember this episode, it leaves me in awe and adoration of how God longs to fellowship and fill us with His presence at any given moment and opportunity, no matter the circumstances, situation, or place. God is indeed a good God.

God delights in blessing and giving gifts to His children. Speaking and praying in tongues is one of the gifts of the Holy Spirit and it is not a mindless exercise or a spooky experience. When we examine praying in tongues with the natural human mind, it may appear silly because it is a spiritual exercise. When we pray in other tongues, we bypass our minds and intellect, and pray to God directly from our spirit. Our natural minds are unfruitful when we pray in the Spirit because we do not understand the language ourselves sometimes, but in the Spirit, we are speaking mysteries and praying for the will of God.

Praying in tongues can be described as a battery that helps to charge our spirit and at the same time helps to stir and build up our faith. Have you ever had an experience of someone buying you a gift unexpectedly and it is just what you needed at that point in time or it was what you had always wanted? You might find yourself making comments like; 'I did not tell anyone about this need, so how did they know? I did not ask, and I did not even pray about it.' You might probably be lost for words in expressing your appreciation for the timeliness of the gift and the genuine met need. I will liken praying in tongues to these experiences.

The gift might be a direct or indirect result of obedience or might just be God in his infinite mercy, performing His acts of grace, kindness, and blessings. God sometimes likes to surprise us and loves to bring smiles to our faces. Praying in the Spirit (known and unknown tongues) is a gift that will meet all our spiritual needs, hunger, and thirst; it helps us to stay focused and builds us up spiritually. Such a gift should be received with thanks and gratitude, embraced, appreciated, desired, and nurtured. For all we know, there might be an element of pleasant surprise in store for us, as we diligently exercise this gift.

As we pray with our understanding or pray in tongues and carry out other spiritual commandments in the Holy Scriptures, we are positioning ourselves to be filled and being refilled daily with the Holy Spirit.

6

COMMANDMENTS TO BELIEVERS

We sometimes fall into our default position, which is not to do anything and expect things to happen. We should force and apply ourselves to get out of this. As they say, nothing good comes easy, so we should be prepared to work on our flaws and weakness, to achieve our best. Living up to the commandments of God requires the same amount of commitment, courage, and compliance.

Our inquisitive natural mind wants to know and understand everything before it believes, and that is not necessarily the case with the things of the spirit, because they are discerned spiritually. The human mind cannot fully understand the things of the Spirit without the Holy Spirit. Now you can begin to see the reason why we tend to quit before we even start or why we find it difficult to obey the commandments. That is why faith, trust, and obedience are essential ingredients in our Christian walk.

We are commanded to be led by the Spirit, to live, walk, pray, and be filled with the Spirit. We are also commanded to worship God in Spirit and in truth, and to carry out a host of other functions and commandments in the Spirit. Our services to God can only be rendered effectively with the aid of the Holy Spirit. The Holy Spirit guides us through these commandments because we cannot do them with our own human power, wisdom, determination, or abilities.

LED BY THE SPIRIT

We are commanded to be led by the Spirit; being led by the Spirit is a testament that we are indeed the children of God. Romans 8:14 says: *"For as many as are [being] led by the Spirit of God, these are the [children] of God."* Verse 15 of the same chapter says that we have not received the spirit of bondage again to fear but we have received the Spirit of adoption, whereby we can call God our heavenly Father. Bondage, in this verse, means the nature of the enemy, which is slavery to relapse again into fear and terror. Adoption means freedom and given the right of sonship to break every form of bondage. Adopted children share the same rights and privileges as one born into the family. Verse 16 says that the Holy Spirit bears witness with our spirit that we are the children of God. Galatians 5:18, in the same vein, says that if we are led by the Spirit, then we are not under bondage.

Being led by the Holy Spirit is like being on a journey. Life is a journey and by no means static, so as we progress through the journey of life, we have many varied experiences. Being led by the Spirit is essential because we need someone that has walked the road before to help us navigate our paths through the wilderness, tunnel, and maze of life. The Bible refers to God as the ancient of days and the only person who knows the end from the beginning.

We walk in opposite directions from God; as mentioned earlier, we are walking from today into tomorrow whilst God is walking from tomorrow into today. So, we need someone who knows the way to shadow us through the maze of life. When we allow the Holy Spirit to lead us through life's hurdles, we cannot go astray, and we will be certain that we will arrive at the appointed destination.

How do we know we are led by the Spirit?

How do we know that we are being led by the Spirit? We are being led by the Spirit if we consult the Holy Spirit in all that we do and listen to the inward witness. There is often a formidable peace that comes with the decisions that we make when being led by the Spirit of God. The Bible says that God is not the author of confusion. When we allow the Holy Spirit to lead us, we will not be confused when making choices, even when we do not fully understand the reasons behind our decisions. This is one of the requirements that come with being led by the Spirit; you put decision-making in the hands of the person who knows best. The decision might seem grim, going by our five senses, but we need to trust the unshakable peace inside of us even though it might not seem logical to our minds.

This reminds me of the story of Peter and his partners in Luke 5:1-11. Peter and his fellow fishermen partners went fishing as usual. On this occasion, they had fished all night and did not catch any fish. By the time Jesus came on the scene, they were washing their nets and getting ready to go home.

Whilst they were washing their nets, Jesus, being followed by a crowd, saw two ships, and decided to get on one of them since the fishermen were not there. He got into Peter's ship and, from there, taught the crowd. After the teaching, Jesus said to Peter, "Launch out into the deep, and let down your nets for a catch." Peter, being a professional fisherman, on behalf of the other fishermen, decided to give Jesus a lecture on fishing. He said (paraphrased), "Master, the reason fishermen fish in the evening is because the fishes swim to the surface and it is easier to catch many fishes. Moreover, it is hard for them to see the net at night, so they fall into the trap. Just before you came, we were washing our nets getting ready to call it a day. Now you are asking us to throw our nets into the deep for a haul. During the day, the fishes swim in the deep; besides, they see the net and they will not swim into the trap and our net might be too small to reach them in the deep."

After delivering his logical, rational, and reasoned lecture, Peter half-heartedly concluded his speech by saying, *"[It is a fruitless venture] nevertheless at your word, I will let down the net."* We know the rest of the story; they let down the net, they caught so many fish that the net broke, Peter had to call his partners to help him to pull out the net, and they had two ships filled with fish, to the extent that the ships began to sink.

We might not see Jesus physically in our ships today, but we have the promptings of the Holy Spirit. He knows the solution to our problems, answers to our questions, and results to our prayers, and He knows how to bring us out of any situation and lead us. The instructions of Jesus did not make logical sense to Peter, but he trusted and obeyed and the rest, as they say, is history. We should not let our limited minds hinder us from enjoying God's best for our lives.

The key to being led by the Spirit is to listen, trust and obey, and this should be exercised daily. The Spirit will lead us on a minute-by-minute basis. Sometimes, the Holy Spirit just prompts us to check our obedience radar; it might not be for something significant. You can call it a practice run, drill, or exercise but it is always worth it in the end when we obey.

LIVE IN THE SPIRIT

To live in the Spirit means living in the supernatural abundance, and overflow of God. We call the place where we live a place of abode, our home, or our dwelling place. Psalm 91:1 says, *"... [the person that] dwells in the secret place of the Most High shall abide under the shadow of the Almighty."* So, in effect, if we dwell (live) in the secret place of the Almighty, the Bible says that we will be under His constant supervision, leading, protection, provision, covering, and guidance.

Living in the Spirit means taking our place of abode in the Holy Spirit; in Him, we live, move, and have our being. When we pattern our lives to live in close communion with the Holy Spirit, then and only then will He begin to direct us and unfold His plans for our lives according to His will. Galatians 5:25 says, *"If we live in the Spirit let us also walk in the Spirit."* When we live in the Spirit and walk in the spirit, our lives will manifest the fruit of the Spirit but when we live and walk in the flesh, our lives will manifest fleshly lust. Galatians 5:16 tells us that if we live in the Spirit we will not gratify, fulfil, or satisfy the desires and lust of the flesh.

In our own ability and strength, we cannot live in the Spirit. The Christian life is lived in the Spirit and not anywhere else. The Holy Spirit will help us to live in the Spirit if we make up our minds to live that way. The Bible says the just (justified) shall live by faith. The justified means people who allow the teachings of the scriptures and the promptings of the Holy Spirit to act as an umpire for their lives. This kind of living requires absolute trust and obedience in the leading of the Holy Spirit. Living in the Spirit is a walk of faith, and faith in this instance, means putting absolute trust in the person that is leading the way.

How do we live in the Spirit?

Living in the spirit is a choice. We first need to make up our minds that we want to live in the Spirit and then we ask the Holy Spirit to come and make His abode or dwell in us, and to give us the ability to live the kind of life that is pleasing to Him. If we live in the Spirit, the Spirit is invariably leading us. In Revelation 3:20, Jesus said: "*…I stand at the door and knock. If anyone hears My voice and opens the door, I will come in to him and [eat] with him, and he with Me.*" Another passage in the Bible (Psalm 16:11) says that in the presence of the Lord, there is fullness of joy and at His right-hand, pleasures forevermore.

We can only enjoy this kind of life and pleasures when we allow His presence and ways to reign in our lives, and when we resign from being the landlord of our lives and hand over the keys to the Holy Spirit. This is easier said than done but it is achievable with practice and commitment to live in the Spirit.

WALK IN THE SPIRIT

Galatians 5:16 commands us to walk in the Spirit. Walking in the Spirit also comprises walking in the supernatural abundance and overflow of God. We will not fulfil the lust/work of the flesh if we walk in the Spirit. What are the works of the flesh? Galatians 5:19-20 says the works of the flesh manifest themselves in our lives as adultery, fornication, uncleanness, impurity, indecency, immorality, idolatry, witchcraft, hatred, enmities, jealousy, fits of rage, strife, selfishness, dissensions, factions, seditions, heresies, envying, drunkenness, orgies, and the like. The Bible warns that those who live like this will not inherit the kingdom of God. Because our flesh and the Spirit of God are travelling in two opposite directions, we need the Holy Spirit to help us travel in the right direction. Romans 8:1 says that there is no condemnation to those who walk, not after the flesh, but after the Spirit. This suggests that there is condemnation for those who allow their flesh/human nature to lead, direct, guide and dictate to them.

We are commanded to walk in the Spirit and refusing to do that is tantamount to disobedience. We will bear the consequence of our actions if we choose to live otherwise. The Bible says those who live according to the dictates of the flesh will not inherit the kingdom of God unless they confess their sins and by the power of the Holy Spirit, put away the deeds of the flesh.

How do we walk in the Spirit?

We need to make up our minds to receive freely what Christ has done for us. We need to ask the Holy Spirit to help us walk in the Spirit. The Bible says when we ask, we should believe that we have received. It is as simple as that: ***ask and believe***. The answer to what we have asked will begin to unfold itself in our life if we have asked with a sincere heart. Walking in the Spirit is an act of faith, simple obedience, and trust in the Lord. Insincerity, ask the Holy Spirit to grab you by the hand and walk with you.

Do not expect bad habits to disappear overnight. It took days, weeks, months and even years to perfect some bad habits. So, just as it took a while to form the habits, it might take some time to break them. Sometimes, the Lord in his infinite mercy can decide to supernaturally break some bad habits immediately, whilst some other habits might take some time to break. However, it is certain that with the passage of time, the outcome of the deliverance from bad habits will become more apparent.

When you begin to walk in the Spirit, you will notice that your conscience will begin to prick you if you are tempted to fall into the old sin again, unlike before when it was seared. When you fall into old sin or any sin, repent, get up and continue walking. Do not look back, wallow in self-pity or say, 'poor me'. The Bible says, in 1 John 1:9: *"If we confess our sins, [God] is faithful and just to forgive us our sins…"* Sometimes when we sin or miss it, our hearts keep condemning us even after we have repented of the sin/s. The Bible, in 1 John 3:20, says, *"…if our heart condemns us, God is greater than our heart…"* So, do not let that condemnation affect or stop your faith walk. God is bigger and greater than our hearts and conscience.

Christ's death on the cross is sufficient for the payment of our sins, misgivings, and mishaps. Confess the sin/s and believe you have been forgiven according to the word of God; if you feel any condemnation in your heart, bring it under the blood of Jesus that was shed on the cross, for the remission of our sins and keep walking in the Spirit.

As conveyed earlier, walking with the Holy Spirit is a partnership walk; it's not a lonely walk. To walk with the Holy Spirit requires our cooperation, commitment, and obedience. The test of walking in the Spirit is measured by our lives yielding the fruit of the Spirit, which Galatians 5:22 lists as love, joy, peace, patience, kindness, goodness, faithfulness, gentleness, and self-control. When our lives begin to yield these fruits, then we know that we are walking in the Spirit.

PRAY IN THE SPIRIT

Prayer can be described as our lifeline. Prayer is one of our sources of communication with God. Prayer is simply talking to God. We must not let anything sever this line of communication. Prayer may sound simple but, at the best of times, can be one of the hardest things to do. We have a real enemy out there who does not want us to pray. When it comes to prayer time, our minds begin to wonder, things crop up in our minds and it is hard to keep the mind under control. So, we need the help of the Holy Spirit to sustain a healthy, powerful, and successful prayer life. Our flesh does not want to pray, as it is not designed to pray; we pray most times from our spirit.

Have you ever wondered why it is that during prayer time and time to study the word, we want to do anything else other than pray? All the menial things that we have been putting aside or saying we will do when we have some spare time, suddenly become urgent, top priority, and particularly important. Have you ever stopped to think that if there is nothing good and beneficial about praying, perhaps our minds and flesh will not be fighting it so much?

The good news is that we do not have to fight this battle alone; the Holy Spirit can help us in this struggle when we yield to Him every time we want to pray by asking Him to help us pray. The Bible commands us to pray without ceasing; that is praying any time, any place, and anywhere. It is good practice to have a dedicated time for prayer, alongside praying on the go. Many victories are won during prayer and we also receive directions, renewal, rejuvenation, instructions, a new sense of hope, refreshment, joy, satisfaction, etc. Accomplishing anything for God and in our lives, will have to be done on our knees. Several things are accomplished during prayer, that's why the enemy fights tooth and nail to stop us from having a successful prayer life.

Romans 8:26 explains how the Holy Spirit helps us to pray. The Holy Spirit knows what we ought to be praying about, how we should pray, and what is best for us. When we are in tune with His frequency, our prayers have a bearing, target, focus, and are on course with God's will for our lives. Before we start to pray, it would be good practice to acknowledge the Holy Spirit. Present our request to Him and ask Him to direct our prayers, as He knows our past, future, and present needs. The Bible says we should not put our confidence in the flesh (Philippians 3:3).

God knows our tomorrow more than we know our yesterday, so we will not be praying amiss when we cultivate this type of prayer life. We will always be in the know when the

Holy Spirit is praying the will of God for our lives, through us. Believe me, this is a good place to be. It is good for us to know that someone who knows better is directing our prayers rather than directing our prayers ourselves with limited knowledge.

How do we pray in the Spirit?

Praying in the Spirit is a supernatural ability supplied by the Holy Spirit. We put this ability into practice whenever we yield to the Holy Spirit when we pray. All we need to say is, "Holy Spirit, you said you will help me to pray, I now yield myself to you, please pray through me." Then, open your heart and begin to pray. We pray well beyond our understanding when we pray in the Spirit, which is Holy Ghost-led and Holy Ghost-energised prayer. Some prayers might not necessarily be for us, it can be for friends, family members, loved ones, neighbourhoods, locality or region, people you do not know, or those that just randomly pop into your mind. It might also involve praying for the world at large. As we walk in the Spirit, we are also led to pray in the Spirit; to pray for different events, issues, situations, scenarios, circumstances, and God's will, plan and purpose for our lives and the lives of others.

When babies are born, they learn the art of talking by mimicking and imitating until they finally form and gain the art of talking and communicating. When we give our lives to the Lord at our second birth, we learn the act of praying properly and our teacher is none other than the Holy Spirit Himself. He will teach us to pray for God's plan and purpose. When the Holy Spirit leads our prayers, we cannot pray amiss. Prayer is, plain and simple, talking to

God. A prayerful Christian is a powerful Christian. We receive power, boost, clarity, strength, and the ability to have an effective prayer life, as we yield to the Holy Ghost to pray through us daily.

As well as asking the Holy Spirit to help us to pray; an acronym that I find useful when praying is ***P.R.A.Y***. The P is for ***praise*** (praise God), R is for ***repent*** (repentance of sins), A is for ***ask*** (your request) and Y is for ***yield*** (yield to the Holy Spirit and He will help you P.R.A.Y. effectively).

FILLED WITH THE SPIRIT

We are also commanded to be filled with the Spirit. Ephesians 5:18 says that we should not get drunk with wine, which leads to indecency, shameful, senseless, and immoral acts but instead to be filled with the Holy Spirit. It is an awesome privilege for every believer to be filled with the Holy Spirit. This kind of filling is good for our general well-being and welfare, and it is recommended that we crave the filling of the Holy Spirit daily.

As intoxication affects our bodily functions, physically, mentally, emotionally, and spiritually, so does the Holy Spirit permeate our entire body, spirit, and soul with His life-transforming power, which helps us to successfully accomplish our purpose and helps us to lead fulfilling and satisfying lives. Considering the ill effects of alcohol intoxication, or any other form of addiction we see all around us, we must indeed count it a privilege to be filled with a different kind of wine, which does not devalue, but instead *adds* value to our lives.

When we are filled with the Holy Spirit, we are equipped with the power to live holy lives. We will find that we struggle to do the simplest of tasks when we are not filled. It takes being filled with the Holy Spirit to witness. Filling of the Holy Spirit takes the shyness from us and gives us boldness. Filling of the Holy Spirit puts the joy and zeal back into our Christian walk. Without the filling of the Holy Spirit, we will not have compassion for the lost and dying world. Without the filling of the Holy Spirit, we will find it hard to live purpose-filled lives or give the things of the Kingdom of God, first place in our lives.

The filling of the Holy Spirit empowers us to carry out our secular work and provides the wisdom that we need. Being filled with the Holy Spirit makes us better people. To be filled with the Holy Spirit is not open for negotiations; it is a commandment and a necessity to live effective lives.

How do we get filled with the Spirit?

This can be summed up in a few words: ***willingness, belief, trust, listening and obeying***. We need to *act* as if God's word is true. We know God's word is true, so when we act it out, we can only see the victories and rewards. The Bible says faith without works is dead. In effect, what the verse of scripture is saying is that faith without corresponding action is dead. If you believe the word of God, then act it out. This might sound ironic but as we are acting out the word of God, we are being filled with the Holy Spirit. As we read and act on the word of God, the word is working in us and conforming us to the image of God. We can describe this process as being filled with the Spirit. We will notice that children do a lot of role-playing, if we observe them very well; they are forever acting out one thing, one person, or another. That is what the Lord expects us to do – to act out the Word, like children.

Actors are paid to act for a living and some of them throw themselves into the part so well that we begin to mistake the role for real-life scenarios and occurrences. For some, you can conclude that they were born for that role but then you see that same actor go on to act in other roles just as well. Just as children and actors role-play, we can take our rightful stand, enlist the Holy Spirit's help, and begin to model Jesus and role-play His words in our lives. As we begin to do this, the real thing begins to happen; we are no longer acting, we are being led and being filled with the Holy Spirit.

We have the Almighty power of God backing us up, the host of heaven as our fans cheering us, and the Holy Spirit helping us to make and live out this choice. It starts with a Will, and the Will is, "I want to be filled with the Holy Spirit daily" and then begin to act it out. The Holy Spirit does the rest; He fills us with Himself. If we want to fill something, we make room for it and if we do not make the room, the filling will not take place.

We should be imitators and actors of the word. Paul made a profound statement in this regard, when he said in 1 Corinthians 11:1: *"Follow my example* (copy, mimic me), *as I follow the example of Christ* (the Anointed One)." The statement means to walk, speak, and act in the manner of another person. Paul made another similar statement in Ephesians 5:1 when he said we should be imitators of God as dear children. This means to imitate God's nature, words, ways, graces, and Spirit as children imitate their parents. When we do all these things, then we will and are being filled with the Holy Spirit.

Being filled with the Holy Spirit means that when the Holy Spirit teaches, we listen; when He prompts us and give us an inner witness, we believe; when He gives guidance, we trust and follow; and when He says to pray and give instructions, we obey. I am not for one moment suggesting that this is easy because, as we know, we have the tide of the world, the materialism, the lust, and the deception of riches, against us. However, with the help of the Holy Spirit and a willing and obedient heart, we can overcome and be filled with the Holy Spirit daily.

By giving ourselves to be filled daily, we are learning, gaining experience, growing, and maturing in the things of God. The Bible says that God has given us the Holy Spirit and if we ask Him to, He will fill us with His Spirit. What we need to do is just believe with a childlike attitude. The Bible says until we become like children, we will not see the Kingdom of God. ***Childlike faith works in the Kingdom of God***. We need to trust the word because the Bible says His words are trustworthy and they will not return to Him void, without fulfilling their intended purpose.

The Lord deals with us differently, He gives us specific instructions according to His Will and we are to listen and obey His instructions. When we follow this simple plan, we are being submissive. As we surrender our Will the Holy Spirit will direct us, fill us with power, His Will, and Himself.

7

THE SPIRIT AND THE FLESH

SPIRIT AND FLESH STRUGGLE

One thing we need to realise is that we are in a battle every day of our lives, from when we are awake to when we go to bed. Even in our dreams, we sometimes find ourselves in this struggle, as what goes on in our minds during the day finds its way into our dreams. As Christians, we are called to be the light in this world, which is no easy task. But by the power of the Holy Ghost working in us, we can overcome these influences and conflicts.

Apostle Paul in the book of Romans 7:15-23 said (paraphrased), "What I do not want to do, I find myself doing," and this is not peculiar to Paul alone. If we are in this world, living in a body made up of flesh and blood, then we will experience this inner conflict. We have two natures inside of us. The nature of the world (called flesh), which is the nature we are born with, and the nature of God (called

Spiritual nature), which is received after we have given our lives to the Lord.

John 3:6 says: *"That which is born of the flesh is flesh, and that which is born of the Spirit is spirit."* This means that before we were born again by the Spirit of God, we had the spirit of the world in us, with its fleshly feelings and lust. Our flesh, mind, and spirit, before the new birth, were under the control of sin. We are prone to sin; we were born into sin, and we are like accidents waiting to happen. The attraction to sin is like a magnetic force, over which we have no power. To an extent, we still feel like that after the new birth, but the difference is, we now have a new search engine in our hearts, highlighting the sins that had been there for a time but we had not realised. This is why it feels like we Christians have more challenges than when we were not yet believers in Christ.

In fact, Christians do have more challenges and more to contend with; for one, we have the power of the enemy at work, with the lust of the world and other forces of the world against us. These forces make the Christian life even harder. The flesh wants to dominate us, and wants us to live defeated Christian lives. Because of this, we experience tug, pull, and stretch times. We ought to wake up to the fact that we live in a war zone, in a battle over good and evil conduct. If we are in this sinful world, we will from time-to-time experience this raging battle of the will. With our lives under the auspices of the Holy Spirit, we have a good chance of survival and of winning the tug of war and will.

We can try to live right with our own strength, and carry out good deeds, but it will often not last long, because the human nature we are born with, cannot sustain that kind of behaviour for too long. Eventually, the old flesh will rise because it is not in its nature to live right, be kind or carry out good deeds all the time. In fact, it is foreign to the flesh to behave like that all the time. Before we gave the reins of our lives over to the Lord Jesus, our five senses, the things of this world, what we exposed ourselves to and the nature of the devil, governed us. As we know, nothing good comes from the enemy. Even if we try to live right and carry out some acts of good deeds, it is only temporary; it is only a matter of time before we fall flat on our faces. To do good all the time in the power of the flesh is hard and virtually impossible; we need the power of the Holy Spirit to help us sustain this kind of life because it is not in-born or within the realm of our natural human nature to do good and live right all the time.

We have two natures ruling and reigning on the inside of us and each one tries to get superiority over the other, even after we have given our lives to the Lord. You see, we have one nature at our natural birth, which is the nature of the world –that is fallen and defective. At the new birth, we inherit another nature, which is the nature of God, the perfect nature, where the Holy Spirit comes to dwell in us, with His infinite power and abilities.

You might ask this question; why is it that we are susceptible to the fallen nature, the nature of the world, even after we have given our lives to the Lord Jesus? The answer is simple: as you have seen, we did not trade in one nature for another at the new birth, but we inherit the nature of God at the new birth. Therefore, we have the two of them living inside of us. We do not change our names at the new birth, nor do we have a new spirit body that makes us invisible. We are still on this earth, looking the same on the outside, but something has changed on the inside of us that would soon begin to work its way out.

This brings me to the question of feeding. What we feed ourselves will determine what we manifest. If we feed our spirit, mind, body, and soul with the wrong food, we will manifest and deliver the wrong outcome. Our flesh is still very much actively demanding its fleshy food. When we feed our flesh with its worldly lust, then we lose the battles of our wills to the flesh. On the other hand, if we are mindful of the things of the Spirit and we concentrate and spend most of our time feeding our spirit with the right kinds of food, then our spirit will be stronger, and we will be led by the Spirit of God. The 'just' (those that allow the Spirit of God to lead them), as we know the Bible says, will live by faith. Our goal as spirit-filled children of God is to live a life that is pleasing to God.

Hebrews 11:6 says, "*...without faith, it is impossible to please God.*" To be successful over these conflicts and struggles inside of us, we should make it a constant, daily regime and a conscious effort to follow the leadings of the Holy Spirit. As we cannot overcome these struggles with our own power and strength, the power of the Holy Spirit is there and available for us.

We will still feel tempted to do the things of the flesh, as Apostle Paul said, (paraphrased from Romans 7: 15-23), "I find myself doing the things I do not want to do." If Paul, who wrote two-thirds of the New Testament, struggled with this, then we can begin to imagine the magnitude of temptation that you and I face today. To live by faith is not the easiest of things in this world. We know how hard it is to live by faith and to be in form all the time; but by the power of the Holy Spirit, we can live a life that increasingly brings glory to God.

What we feed eventually gets stronger; if we feed our flesh at the expense of our spirit, then the flesh will be stronger, exert itself on us, and win the battle. But if we feed ourselves with the things of the Spirit, then the opposite is the case. The rulership of our lives should be handed over to the Lord, and this needs to be done on an ongoing basis, with the power of the Holy Spirit guiding us. It is then and only then, that we will begin to experience some victories in the areas of our struggles.

This area of what we feed our flesh and spirit reminds me of a story I once heard. The story went along these lines: there was a certain man that had two dogs that he engaged in dog fighting as a means of livelihood. He would bring the dogs to town on a certain day and get people to bet on them. Before the fights, he would sometimes tell them the dog that was going to win, and every time, his prediction would happen. The punters would ask him, "How do you do it, how come your predictions are always right?" In the end, he finally told them the secret; he said, "I starve the dog I want to lose and feed the dog I want to win."

The moral of the story is that whatever we feed will eventually get stronger, grow, dominate, win, and have more control and power. My advice to you is that: you know which one to feed. The flesh does not profit us in any way, shape, or form but the Spirit gives us life and life in all its fullness, richness, and abundance in all ramifications.

It goes to show, if you want to win the fight against the flesh, you have to feed on the things that empower the Spirit's working in you. This is how to win the struggle between the flesh and the spirit.

8

OBEDIENCE AND DISOBEDIENCE TO THE HOLY SPIRIT

The question is whether to be obedient or disobedient. My advice is to be obedient as the Holy Spirit wants open, frank, and honest communication with us. We cannot have Him living inside us and detach ourselves from Him. He is gentle, yet authoritative; He is a firm and steady voice. God is not the author of confusion, so when we give the Holy Spirit a free hand to lead and rule in all the affairs of our lives, we know that we are on the right track. He gives us a clear head, steers us on the right course and there is peace with the decisions we make under the influence of the Holy Spirit.

He does not force His way; He speaks to us, and our spirit bears witness, even during those times when we feel uneasy in our minds or are debating whether to obey or not. Many a time, the Holy Spirit has instructed me inwardly to do something that I just conveniently ignored. I have had several instances where I had the conviction in my spirit but because my human mind could not comprehend the reason, I chose not to obey the inward suggestions and decided to ignore them. We will find that each time we decide not to yield to the Holy Spirit, we feel a bit uneasy.

Our minds are so conditioned to our five senses and in the moments when we cannot comprehend why we should do something, it is easy, natural, and convenient to ignore any promptings. This is especially so if there is no compelling reason to obey it and if there are no burning or pressing issues at the time. The promptings might seem insignificant when they come, but when we obey, we will always reap the reward and when we do not obey, we pay for the consequences. We should not forget that the Holy Spirit is all-knowing; just because we do not know or understand, does not mean that we should shun the promptings of the Holy Spirit.

We are wired, created, and designed to be in control. Hence, we feel insecure when it seems as if we have lost this natural ability and that is why things need to make sense before we choose to believe. If we cannot fathom the reason for doing something, we dismiss and talk or reason our way out of it. I suspect that you have done this on several occasions. If we are attentive and obedient, then we will reap the rewards of obedience. I believe that you can think of many times in your life when you have chosen to obey or ignore the promptings of the Holy Spirit.

CASE OF DISOBEDIENCE

I have my own fair share of disobedience, and here is one. A few years back, a friend who had just had a baby called me and asked me to drop something off for her. So, I put what she asked me to drop off, in the passenger seat of my car and embarked on my journey to her house. I cannot remember what I was thinking about while driving to her house but I guess that as usual, my mind was preoccupied and crowded with the cares of life. As I was parking my car in front of her block of flats, the Holy Spirit impressed on my mind to open the boot of the car. As I could not see any logical reason to look in the boot even though the impression was firm and constant, I decided to ignore the promptings. As I was locking the car, the impression came again to check the boot of my car. I struggled with the thought and said in my heart, 'this is not necessary', ignoring the voice again. I went to the entrance door, entered her door number on the panel and I was buzzed in. I pulled the entrance door open, walked to the lift, pressed the lift button, and waited for it to come down. Then I got in the lift and pressed her floor number.

Throughout the time I was in her flat, I thought nothing of the promptings. But when I returned to my car after my visit, I needed to put something in the boot and when I opened the boot, I saw a present that I had bought for the baby several weeks ago. I had put the present in the boot of my car with the plan that whenever I was next in her area, I would drop it off. If I had yielded to the promptings, I would have saved myself a second trip upstairs.

CASE OF POTENTIAL DISOBEDIENCE

I would like to share another example, this time from the Bible, to further buttress this point of obedience vs. disobedience. It is the story of a Noble captain with leprosy, his maid, and the prophet, found in 2 Kings 5:1-19.

Naaman was the captain of the Syrian army, who had fought and conquered many opponents in his time. On one of his conquests, he brought a captive from Israel, a little maid, to wait on his wife. This little maid noticed that her master had leprosy and one day, she said to her mistress that there was a man of God called Prophet Elisha in Israel who could cure leprosy.

The advice of the little maid filtered to the King of Syria. The King of Syria immediately wrote a letter to the King of Israel, saying one of his captains had leprosy and that he had heard about the Prophet Elisha, who could help to cure him. When Prophet Elisha heard about the man's plight, he invited Naaman to come and see him in Israel. After Naaman's arrival at Elisha's house, the prophet sent out a message to him, saying, 'Go and dip yourself in the River Jordan seven times and you will be cleansed.' Naaman was outraged, saying Elisha did not even have the courtesy to come to see him face-to-face, so that they could have a man-to-man chat about his condition. Instead, the prophet had instructed him to go and wash in the river Jordan. He was so angry and left Elisha's home in a rage, asking if there were no better rivers in Syria, where he had come from, and why must he go to a particular river? He queried why just any old river would not be sufficient.

When the maid heard her master's reaction, she was sad. One of Naaman's servants went to their master and said, "If the prophet had asked you to do something more strenuous and spectacular, would you not have done it?" They begged their master to reconsider his decision to go back to Syria and instead do as the prophet had instructed. Naaman, moved by their concern and plea decided to obey; he went to the river Jordan, dipped himself in it seven times. When he came out of the water on the seventh occasion, his skin was like that of a baby, and he was completely cured of leprosy.

Sometimes, we are looking for the spectacular, when the solution we seek is in the small, still voice. One of the morals of the story above is that we do not necessarily have to understand, but all we need is a little bit of faith, trust, belief, and obedience.

For us to obey, sometimes, we might need to seek counsel from a third party. The third party in this story was the little maid (who can be likened to the Holy Spirit in this instance). There is nothing wrong in running our thoughts past people sometimes, but we should be very careful that we seek wise counsel, so that our obedience can be complete.

As there are rewards for obedience, so are there consequences for disobedience. This is the right place to mention two things you should know. No subject about the Holy Spirit will be complete without mentioning the concepts of 'not grieving the Holy Spirit' and 'the question of the unpardonable sin'.

GRIEVE NOT THE HOLY SPIRIT

As human beings, we are free moral agents; we can decide to shut down or allow the move and the flow of the Holy Spirit in our lives. Some of us from the old school may remember a song that says, 'I am young, free and single, I just want to mingle with you…' which was first released by Sunfire in 1982. We can be young, free, and should want to mingle with the Holy Spirit. We will be limiting the activities and power of the Holy Spirit and doing ourselves a disservice when we just want to do things our own way and not mingle with the Holy Spirit. We should be open to His leading and look forward to how He can help us get over life's ups and downs. The more we yield or open our hearts, the more He leads, speaks, and directs us. We should not quench the flow of the Holy Spirit in our lives, nor grieve Him.

Imagine that you are a beneficiary of a huge sum of money and living like a pauper. When your benefactor finds out, they will try to intervene by helping you to see what you have, and to try to guide and advise you. If all they get in return is shunning and "no thanks," how do you think they will feel? We indirectly do this to the Holy Spirit sometimes, without realising it.

Ephesians 4:30 says: *"And grieve not the Holy Spirit of God, whereby ye are sealed unto the day of redemption."* To seal something means to put protective tape around it, to make it secure, or to put a stamp of ownership on something. If we allow the Holy Spirit to operate in our lives, we will be sealed with His presence, and the seal proves that we belong to the heavenly family. Some young people — and even adults — looking for identity get into all sorts of groups, gangs, and associations, so that they can be accepted. These kinds of groups only promise false hope and false identity. I am sure you will agree that the best position to be in life is where we are sealed, secured, firmly rooted, looked-after, hidden, loved, directed, cared for, concealed, and owned, by the Spirit of God. We should be mindful not to do anything to grieve the Holy Spirit. As the Holy Spirit has sealed us with Himself, our goal should be to bring Him joy and not grieve Him.

We can grieve the Holy Spirit through our actions, thoughts, words, and deeds. These are some of the ways we grieve the Spirit of God in us:

1. By entertaining unwholesome and impure thoughts.
2. By being selfish, unkind, and by not esteeming the things of the Spirit.
3. Being unholy; displaying a bad temper and behaviour.
4. Uttering careless words, not trusting, and disregarding His promptings.
5. By ignoring Him and doing our own things.
6. By not revering Him; by pride and disobedience.
7. Allowing unbelief and doing things that we are not supposed to do, as believers of the gospel and children of God.

It would be unwise to grieve a person that well and truly cares for us, who has put a seal of protection, security, health, wealth, deliverance, wellbeing, welfare, love, and care around us, and who helps us to run and accomplish the race that lies ahead of us.

We do not want to make grieving the Holy Spirit a habit. If we catch ourselves grieving the Holy Spirit, the wise thing to do would be to repent and ask Him to help us to obey and not disregard His promptings, and to fill us with His ways, so that we can be good disciples and children that will bring Him honour and not shame.

UNPARDONABLE SIN

We cannot talk about the Holy Spirit without mentioning the unpardonable sin. The Bible records, in Mark 3: 28-29, that you can sin against God (the Father) and sin against Jesus but if you sin against the Holy Spirit, it is unpardonable. To commit this sin, you would have had to commune with the Holy Spirit and know Him. There is no fear of unbelievers committing this sin because they do not know Him. If you have committed the unpardonable sin, you will know. Put it this way, it is the sin that Satan and his cohort committed and were kicked out of heaven.

Having communed with the Holy Spirit and then wilfully, maliciously, slanderously and deliberately blaspheming Him by saying He is an unclean Spirit and ascribing the work of the Holy Spirit to Satan, is what the Bible calls the unpardonable sin. If you are wondering if you have committed the unpardonable sin, the chances are that you have not. People that have committed this sin will know because it is a wilful act. If we blaspheme God the Father or God the Son, the sin can be forgiven, but if we blaspheme the Holy Spirit, there is no forgiveness.

THE HOLY SPIRIT AND OUR SPIRIT

Obedience is a vital ingredient in following the leading and promptings of the Holy Spirit. As human beings, we have our own will; to develop a close partnership or working relationship with the Holy Spirit, we will have to unlearn, re-learn, and learn new things. This learning process will require some elements of training and re-training our minds, spirit, soul, and body.

As humans, we are made up of spirit, soul, and body. The human composition comprises our intellect, will, mind, conscience and other invisible faculties that make us free moral agents and rational beings. With our spirit, we are in contact with the spiritual realm and within our souls, we have our minds, will, emotions, intellect, and desires. We are in contact with the world with our bodies and our body is nourished by the physical food we eat.

We are also fundamentally spiritual beings; we have a soul and live in a body, and we respond to God with our human spirit when it is being fed with the word of God. Our soul tugs between our spirit and body. If we are more mindful of the things of the body (the flesh), the world, and its lust, our soul feeds off this and we will be operating in the fleshly realm most times and not mindful of the things of the spirit. If, on the other hand, our spirit is being fed with the word of God, our souls will be mindful of the things pertaining to the Kingdom of God, which will invariably cause us to live a victorious life, the one that we are born to live.

The Holy Spirit and our human spirit are distinct. We communicate with the Holy Spirit through our human spirit. The Holy Spirit speaks to our spirit, and not to our heads or minds. That is why it is impossible to understand the things of the spirit with our heads, intellect, human knowledge, or minds. The things of the Spirit are spiritually discerned. The Holy Spirit will constantly commune with those that acknowledge Him and have given Him the pass-code into their hearts.

THE HOLY SPIRIT AND OUR CONSCIENCE

We all have a conscience; it is the joint knowledge of God and man in us. We are born with this trait. It is the faculty, power, or principles that decide the lawfulness of our actions and affections, and approve or condemn them. It can also be described as a state of awareness or a sense that our actions or intentions are either morally right or wrong, along with a feeling of obligation to do the right thing.

By the very act of creation, regardless of our religious belief, our age, or status in life, we are all capable and possess the ability to decide right from wrong, if there are no health issues impinging on these natural abilities. As believers, with our faculties, we can decide to allow or disallow the workings of the Holy Spirit in our lives. The Holy Spirit is not the same as our conscience.

The Holy Spirit is an individual, He is a person. He is God personified inside of us and He is greater than our conscience. Our conscience can neither carryout nor replace the work of the Holy Spirit in us. The conscience functions like any other inbuilt sense in us, it is the moral faculty in us that guides and judges our actions. So, it should not be confused or seen as a substitute for the Holy Spirit.

The Holy Spirit is constant; while our conscience along with our other faculties, are relative (change with circumstances). The state of our conscience will depend on what we have been exposed to i.e. our set of beliefs, our value systems, our environment, circumstances, etc. Some people can be doing something that is seemingly wrong and yet their conscience does not condemn them because it's deemed right, it's what they are used to, or it's what they choose to believe.

The Holy Spirit changes the state of our conscience, gives us moral codes to live by, and causes us to comply with the things of the Spirit, if permitted. As Christians, we have the Bible as our final authority and if we are raised knowing right from wrong according to the word of God in the Bible, our conscience will prick us if we go against the grain of the scriptures. If we have done something wrong, sinned, or done what we are not supposed to do, our conscience will rightfully convict us.

Once we have confessed our sins, we pray and ask for forgiveness, and we are forgiven, our conscience should adjust and act accordingly. Sometimes, we may find that this is not the case; our conscience still condemns us even after we have repented. I would like you to know and remember that the Holy Spirit is greater than our conscience, even when we have these experiences. I learned this lesson the hard way, as a new convert. When I know I have stepped out of line, I would pray for forgiveness and in my heart of hearts, I know that I have done the right thing by repenting and asking for forgiveness and I know that I have been forgiven but my conscience would carry on pricking me. I got my deliverance from this one day, when I was reading 1 John 3:20, which says, *"If our [conscience] condemns us, God is greater than our [conscience]."* I beg you, please, do not carry the guilt in your conscience forever and a day; when you confess the sin sincerely, you are forgiven, and the message will get to your conscience later. With the passage of time, your conscience will catch up and adjust accordingly.

The point I am making here is that we should not subject or compare the Holy Spirit to our conscience. There are good, bad, or seared consciences, and how people see good, bad, right, or wrong is subjective (by perception) and is dependent on their exposure, environment, and experiences in life.

WHAT ABOUT INTUITIONS, INSTINCTS, HUNCHES, INKLINGS AND THE HOLY SPIRIT?

The Holy Spirit is not a feeling and cannot be described as such. When we are being directed by the Holy Spirit, we have a knowing and such knowing can sometimes manifest as a hunch, an intuition, an instinct, an inkling, an impression, know-how, gut-feeling or what people refer to as the sixth sense (a knowing without any logical explanation).

Our five in-born senses are the sense of sight, smell, taste, hear and feel; the sixth sense is referred to as the sense of knowing, which is what I have briefly touched on in the paragraph above. The Holy Spirit is not in the same league as our senses; He is, by far, much more superior than our feelings. He is God embodied in us and can sometimes give us these feelings of knowhow and answers to questions that we have not thought or imagined. He also nudges us on when we are on the right track or gives us warning signals when we are on the wrong track.

The distinction that I would like to make clear is that we must never confuse or replace the Holy Spirit with a feeling. He is our compass in life, leading and steering us in the **right** direction. Notice the emphasis on the word *right*, as we can sometimes experience negative feelings that are not right, and they tend to lead us on the way to destruction if they are not guarded.

We can have good or bad feelings, wrong or right feelings, and positive or negative feelings. Feeling is one of our five human senses, and a Deity cannot be in the same category as our feelings. We cannot rely on our feelings solely when it comes to following the Holy Spirit. We are commanded in the scriptures to allow the Holy Spirit have utter pre-eminence in our lives.

HOLY SPIRIT, SOMETIMES CALLED HOLY GHOST

Some people might often wonder why the Holy Spirit is sometimes referred to as the Holy Ghost in the scriptures; I certainly did, (especially if you are a reader of the King James Version of the Bible, like I am). To my understanding, I think this is because He leads us by the inward witness. Some people say that they see ghosts, but this Ghost is Holy and cannot be seen with the naked eye, but we can sure see His mighty acts and deeds in the lives of those people that put their trust in Him and let Him lead them.

You can call Him Holy Spirit or Holy Ghost; it does not really matter. All we need to know is that we are being guided by His invisible presence and we do not have to see Him before we believe. We do not want to be like doubting Thomas. Remember that the Bible says: ***blessed are those who do not see, but believe***.

9

GIFTS OF THE SPIRIT

I once worked as a sales rep for a company. Before we went out to the field each day, we would have training sessions that mainly consisted of role-playing i.e. we would practice selling the products to ourselves. We used to go door knocking, cold calling, stopping people in the streets, shopping centres, etc. One of the useful lessons I learned from that experience was that if you do not ask, you will not get.

This reminds me of an account in the Bible about ask, seek, and knock. In Luke 11, Jesus was responding to His disciples when they asked Him to teach them how to pray. Jesus went on to tell them that if they ask, they will receive, if they seek, they will find and if they knock, the door will be opened to them. In verse 11 of that chapter, Jesus asks them that: if a son asks his father for bread, will his father give him a stone? If he asks for fish, will he be given a serpent? If he asks for an egg, will he be given a scorpion? Jesus concluded by saying that if we who are sinners (not perfect) can give good gifts to our children, how much more shall our heavenly Father not give the Holy Spirit to those that ask? The Holy Spirit reference here is not that of the new birth, which we receive as part of the salvation package, but is in relation to asking for other benefits and gifts of the Spirit.

This gift can be wrapped up in what we need for physical, spiritual, and emotional wellbeing and welfare. They can be gifts of healing, raiment, food, prosperity, protection, happiness, deliverance, health, wealth, and whatever would make life comfortable for us. You can add any need you might have to the list.

The Bible passage here equates receiving the Holy Spirit to receiving a good gift from our earthy parents. When we receive the Holy Spirit, it is the best gift anyone can ever ask for or receive. The same way that Jesus was sent to the world to die for our sins, is the same way the Holy Spirit has been given to us as a gift to help us live through life, fulfilling our God-given call, potential, purpose, and assignments in life.

The Holy Spirit is the whole embodiment of heaven, so, we have the whole resources of heaven at our beck and call. No wonder the Bible says that we are the temple of God. With the Holy Spirit dwelling inside of us, we carry the good gift inside us, to everyone, everywhere, and anywhere we go, to manifest the purpose and kingdom of God on earth. God gave us more than what we can ever begin to imagine, understand, or fully utilise when we receive the Holy Spirit.

GIFT MANIFESTATION

The gifts of the Holy Spirit are manifested or shown in different ways. The Holy Spirit manifests or demonstrates the promises of God's word through us. We can say He is the conduit/pipe; a pipe is a channel through which things flow. The gift (endowments) of the Spirit flows from the Holy Spirit through us, to enrich our lives and enable us to make a difference in the lives of others. We can also describe the Holy Spirit as the postman that assists in delivering and distributing the gifts and promises of God, according to His Will. We cannot live a happy, fruitful, fulfilled, and contented life without the help of the Holy Spirit. He is the carrier and the courier that dispatches what God has promised and done for us in Christ Jesus. He makes the blessings of God evident in our lives and enables us to share this in the lives of others.

The purpose and manifestations of these gifts given by the Holy Spirit are to give spiritual illumination, to benefit us, and to be used for the common good of humanity.

ORDERLY AGENDA

God is big on order; 1 Corinthians 12:4-7 shows this agenda very clearly. This is how it explains the functions and working of the Godhead when it comes to the manifestation of the gifts (endowments) and indeed any other agenda spearheaded by the Godhead. This shows the perfect order of the triune God.

Firstly, in verse four, it is emphasised that we have different varieties of spiritual gifts (endowments) and these gifts are made manifest (brought to light and to our attention) by the embodiment of the Holy Spirit in us, as being the preferred chosen executor and deliverer of the gifts.

Secondly, verse five says there are different ways to serve in our ministerial offices or callings, in relation to the gifts and any other duties we have been assigned to fulfil. One thing that is worth stressing here is that we are all placed here on planet earth to serve one another and be our brothers' keepers. Jesus was our perfect example; during His time on earth, He displayed the attitude of a servant King. He came to the world to serve us and point us in the right direction. Who will be the best person to help us to serve in our ministerial offices, other than the Lord Jesus Christ Himself who qualifies in all realms as our exemplary Leader? The execution of the service mentioned here is administered by the Lord, Himself.

Lastly, verse six says God the Father works and moves within us in different ways. He is the Chief Commander; He holds the helm of affairs and has a diversity of operations under His belt. He has called us to execute specific missions in life, and He oversees all of them. He is directly in charge of all the operations, and they are all under his perfect control.

Therefore, we have God the Father as the head of the operations (Managing Director, MD), God the Son as the Administrator (Project Manager), and God the Holy Spirit as the Executor (Executive Officer, EO). You might be wondering and saying to yourself, 'How does all of this concern me?' Verse seven of the same chapter puts it in context; it says the Holy Spirit makes the gifts visible. Here is where we come into the picture. The gifts are manifested through us and so, we have a crucial part to play in this whole agenda. We are not left out of the equation. As we can see, the Holy Spirit does not act alone; He acts on behalf of the Father and the Son in perfect harmony. They have distinct offices and functions, yet are inseparable and totally unified.

To enjoy the benefits of these gifts, we should agree with the Holy Spirit. Verse eleven of that chapter says that the Holy Spirit divides the gifts to everyman, as often as He will. The principal idea of the gift is to profit everyone (in this context that is the church, which is the body of Christ), and to glorify Jesus. Our duty is to carry the gifts far and wide, under the leadership and directives of the Holy Spirit.

I would now like to look at the gifts of the Spirit. I have classified the gifts under three headings below: Revelation, Vocal, and Working gifts. The gifts operate at the **will** and command of the Holy Spirit. In effect, we ask Him for the manifestation of the gifts when we require them, and He decides when to manifest them. Sometimes, we do not have to ask because if the Holy Spirit knows that we need them, He still manifests them all the same. These gifts of the Spirit are listed and explained in 1st Corinthians 12:8-10. There are other gifts of the Spirit mentioned in the Bible, other than the ones explained below.

REVELATION GIFTS

1. Word of wisdom — this refers to supernatural revelation or insight into the divine will and purpose of God, which gives us timely words to solve any problem that may arise. Have you ever found yourself in a situation where you needed a word to save the moment? Through words of wisdom, this is possible. It is not usually a pre-meditated event; the timely word for the season just drops in our spirit and we speak it out of our mouths as if it is our own. This kind of wisdom is different from the wisdom we use daily.

This gift is operational in any situation; I have had instances where I have operated in this gift in face-to-face conversations, when people call me on the telephone requesting advice, at work meetings when we need ideas, to make decisions, or find solutions, at family meetings, witnessing about the Lord, social engagements, settling disputes, decision making, giving counsel, problem-solving, etc. I will always say a quick prayer under my breath, asking the Holy Spirit to give me wisdom for the issues at hand. Try it, believe me, it works. You will notice that the gifts are not solely for yourself; they manifest to help, encourage, build up and support others, and glorify Jesus.

King Solomon, as narrated in 1 Kings 3:16-28, operated in this kind of wisdom, when he presided over the case of the two women, with one living and one dead baby. To get the full gist of the story, read the account in the book of Kings. There are many examples of this kind of wisdom demonstrated in the scriptures, I encourage you to find and study them.

2. The Word of Knowledge – this is a supernatural knowledge or insight of the divine mind, will or plan, and the plans of others with divine intervention. When this gift is in manifestation, we have supernatural insight into matters that we have not studied or known. We can say it is the Holy Spirit leading us beyond our knowledge. This gift is particularly evident when we are deep in thought, struggling with something, or just seeking a way out, and suddenly, a supernatural knowing comes into our spirit, giving us clarity, direction, light, answers, solutions, etc. Sometimes, you might find that you know the answer to what you want but somehow cannot seem to access the information because there is a mental block, or your mind just goes blank. The Word of knowledge comes in handy during those moments.

These kinds of knowledge can be described as light bulb moments when the knowing just pops into your mind and you know without a shadow of a doubt that this is the answer you have been expecting. A friend once told me that she had been experiencing frequent headaches and did not know the cause. So, she decided to take the situation to God in prayer. She said that one day, she just heard in her mind to stop drinking coffee. True to the word, she stopped drinking coffee and the headaches stopped. I am not advocating that people stop buying or drinking coffee. In her own case, drinking coffee was not good for her body.

Essentially, the gifts of the Spirit are given to profit others, and sometimes manifest to bless ourselves as well. Word of knowledge can be used to benefit others and ourselves. The gift is usually operational when the need arises. I have only just given a personal experience in relation to this gift. As with all gifts, they work at any level, corporate, congregational, personal, family, or friends, in any circumstances, situation, or scenario. Words of wisdom and Words of knowledge usually help us to make good and wise decisions without precedence.

3. Discernment of spirits – this is a supernatural insight to discern and distinguish between the utterance of truth and falsehood. It also gives divine insight into the realm of spirits, to detect plans and read the minds of men. In this time and age that we are living in, we need to be able to discern between good and bad, because the days are evil. This gift of discernment will give us supernatural insight and help us to discern the intent and plans of evil people who want to lead our children or us astray, or land us in trouble and muddy water. If the enemy presented himself the way he really is, as the devil, we would not fall for his tricks and strategies to distract, distort, and destroy. The enemy is the master of disguise and falsehood, and he comes in many guises to deceive; his number one weapon is deception and lies. With this gift of discernment of spirits operating in us, we will not naively fall prey to his devices.

The Bible also warns us of false teachers and false doctrine. With the spirit of discernment working in us, we will be able to discern the true teachers and true doctrines and not be swayed by every wave of doctrine. 1 John 2:20 says we have an unction from the Holy One and we know all things.

I would like to add here that, as Christians, the God we worship is the God of the Bible, who is the God and the Father of our Lord Jesus Christ. If we go anywhere and another God is presented, we should be able to discern.

This gift is not called discerning of devils, as some people think is only for discerning evils. It is about us relying on God the Holy Spirit on the inside of us, to help us supernaturally discern and distinguish between good and bad, and the utterance of truth and falsehood. With this gift, we can discern between holy, decent, pure, and immoral activities, so we will not be caught up and entangled in the lies and deception of the enemy.

VOCAL GIFTS

1. Prophecy – this is a supernatural utterance not conceived by human thoughts or reasoning; it should not be confused with fortune telling. Prophecy is given to edify, build-up, and encourage.

Prophecies can be given collectively in a church service, public meetings, and gatherings, or privately to individuals. I have heard many prophetic utterances given in church, over the radio, on the internet, on television, whilst reading, via emails, text messages, and listening to CDs and DVDs; I have claimed some of them because they apply or relate to my circumstances and with what the Lord has been telling me. I have also had one-on-one prophetic utterances.

Prophecy often acts as confirmation. If anyone gives you a prophecy that does not encourage you but instead it fills you with confusion, fear, and doubt, then I would advise you to bin that prophecy because it is not from God. When God gives prophecies, there is a confirmation and witness in your spirit, and you can relate to it. Sometimes, you might get a prophecy about your future that might seem unclear; my advice would be to put it on the cooler/back burner, as it were, and refer to it at some time in the future.

God will not bypass you and tell your business to somebody else; God does not work that way. Most prophecies come as a confirmation of what God has already told you. God is not the author of confusion. We should guard what we hear and receive with all diligence because there are many falsehoods out there. Let the Holy Spirit lead and garrison your heart.

2. Diverse kinds of tongues – this refers to supernatural utterance in other languages that are not known to the speaker. This gift involves praying out what God wants to do, in tongues. Sometimes you might just be minding your business and a situation, and the name of someone or a picture of them pops into your mind. Nine times out of ten, it is the Holy Spirit wanting you to pray concerning a situation. This gift is best exercised by praying in tongues because the situation might not be revealed to you, nor are you given the full information, and all you need to go by is the stirring-up, quickening, and uneasiness you feel in your spirit. There have been many occasions when I have felt stirred up in such a way and I have responded by praying earnestly. There have been other times, I must confess, when I have just ignored the urge or struggled to mutter a word or two. The reason why we struggle sometimes is that we do not fully understand the urge. Working with the Spirit requires an element of faith, trust, and obedience. If we do not know, believe me, He knows. If we walk in obedience, we will always reap the benefit. If we nurture and exercise this gift, it will grow, and we will not only be a blessing to ourselves but to the world at large.

Diverse kinds of tongues, as the name suggests, involve praying and speaking in a whole variety of tongues, known or unknown to us. The Apostles in Acts 2 spoke in diverse kinds of tongues, to the extent that people thought they were drunk. The order of the day was saved when various people of Jewish descent, who had come to finally settle in Jerusalem, said that they could hear the disciples speaking in their own languages. I once heard a story of a missionary who was church planting in a certain area. She had toiled for about ten years and the programme did not take off as anticipated. So she decided to go back to her home country (country of origin) to become an itinerant minister. She visited a church when she got back and during the church service, someone began to speak in tongues. After the utterance, the pastor of the church asked if anyone had an interpretation of the tongue. The missionary stood up and said that there was no need for an interpretation. She said the message was for her, as the tongue was the dialect of the place she was fleeing. The Lord had asked her to go back. She went back and within one year, she planted several churches.

3. Interpretation of tongues – this is the supernatural ability to interpret, in a native tongue, what was uttered in other languages not known by the one who is interpreting. This gift mainly operates in the church, public meetings, and gatherings.

Interpretation of tongues works in two ways; the person speaking the tongue is speaking in a language unknown to them and so is the person interpreting the tongue. I have been privy to working in an office adjacent to an interpreting service in the past. People come there speaking in different languages and I have no clue what they are saying. However, the good thing for them is that they have someone there who can understand what they are saying and is able to help them. Can you imagine what it would be like, if someone speaks in a tongue unknown to the congregation and some other person transcribes the language and take it to an interpreter for translation? Nobody would be edified, benefited, or blessed at the time the tongue was uttered, until after the interpretation has been received.

This gift is mainly operational in a congregational setting. Someone gives an utterance in tongues and somebody else interprets, and then the hearers are blessed. The interpretation might be a much-awaited answer to a prayer, it might be an assurance, or it might give general guidance and direction. It might even bring about conviction due to the proclamation of truth, leading people to repent, surrender, and worship God. I have been in meetings where this gift has been obviously in manifestation. When we pay attention and flow with the Spirit when this gift is in operation, we will be encouraged, built up, and receive solace and direction.

Interpretations of tongues also operate on a personal level. Sometimes, when you are praying in tongues during your quiet times, the Lord gives you interpretations of what you have just uttered in tongues. I do not know if you have experienced it, but I have, many times. Believe me, it is good when this happens, and you come out of the prayer closet feeling elated.

WORKING GIFTS

1. Special Faith – this is the supernatural ability to believe in God without human doubt, unbelief, and reasoning. The story I narrated earlier about my son, when we went on a visit to Nigeria, was the gift of special faith in operation. Ordinarily, in my own faith, I would have panicked but the gift of special faith took over my natural faith.

I am sure you can think of instances when you have operated in special faith. After such an experience, you will find yourself making comments like, "I just did not know where

I got the strength from" and "How did I overcome that situation?" During such instances, you have switched from your natural faith to the gift of special faith, without realising that you have.

As the name denotes, it is called special faith, because it is different from our natural faith and we do not operate in that kind of faith every day or willy-nilly. It comes when the need arises and it is required.

Sometimes, we operate in the gifts of the Spirit unknowingly because the gifts are given by the Holy Spirit as He wills or when they are needed. We can also ask for some of the gifts to be in manifestation in our lives, but our motive for asking must be right and according to the word of God.

2. Gifts of Healing – this is a supernatural power to heal all manner of sickness without human aid or medicine. I have had many instances where I have believed in God for supernatural healing. My journey of believing in supernatural healing started when I heard about Gloria Copeland, the wife of Kenneth Copeland from Kenneth Copeland Ministries. She said that since she read Isaiah 53:4-5, which says Jesus purchased our healings, and carried our disease, pain, and sorrow and so, by His stripes, we are healed, she has been standing on the healing scriptures not just for herself but for her entire family. She really challenged my faith and I have put it into practice since then and I can tell you that it really works. Try it for yourself. I also heard Joyce Meyer of Joyce Meyer Ministries say, "If you feel pain in your body, it is at that point you begin to use the word of God and quote the healing scriptures in the Bible." Do not wait until the pain gets worse before you begin to apply the word, because then you would need a bigger faith.

One thing I need to make clear is that the gift of healing is also subject to the Will of the Holy Spirit. The Holy Spirit helps us to exercise this kind of faith, in order to receive supernatural healing. I challenge you to do the same thing that Gloria Copeland did, which is to not just believe in God for healing for just yourself, but for your family and loved ones. There are many accounts of supernatural healings in the Bible; you can read the account of Jesus' earthly ministry, accounts of the apostle's ministries, and many instances of this gift in operation, in the Old Testament.

3. Working of Miracles – this is a supernatural power to intervene in the ordinary course of nature and to counteract natural laws, if necessary. Doctors will tell you they have seen miracles more than most people. This is because, sometimes, when they have washed their hands off some cases, done all they could, and left the patient to fate, then the most amazing miracles happen.

There were many instances of the working of miracles in Jesus' ministry, Elijah and Elisha's ministries, and that of the apostles, and the pages of the Bible give account after account of these types of miracles. The sorts of spectacular miracles that we read about in the Bible are still happening today.

The best miracle by a long stretch is that of salvation, which is when we are translated from the kingdom of darkness (this world) into the kingdom of light (God, heaven). I have heard and read accounts of people that used to drink, smoke, or are engaged in some form of habits and addictions of one sort or another, testifying that as soon as they gave their lives to the Lord, they were instantly delivered from the strongholds. From that moment on, they never desired, hungered, longed, or thirsted for the old habits anymore.

I have also read and heard accounts of the dead brought back to life, limbs growing where there were previously no limbs, blind eyes opening, the lame walking, the dumb speaking, the deaf hearing, tumours and growths that disappeared, aches and pounding pain vanishing, and diverse kinds of healings being manifested, as well as countless other workings of miracles. The ministry of someone that stands out in my mind is that of Kathryn Kuhlman. I read one of her books (I Believe in Miracles), and it clearly demonstrates the workings of this gift with documentary evidence.

In our individual lives as well, the Spirit of the Lord is working and breaking bad habits and addictions, healing diseases, keeping us safe, delivering us from adverse situations, and miraculously providing for all our needs. Working of miracles cannot be brought about by ourselves but can only be produced by the divine and supernatural power of the Holy Spirit.

The Bible calls the nine points that I have just described the gifts of the Spirit. A gift is something given to us. Are we using the gifts? Are they operational in our lives? As Christians filled with the Holy Ghost, the manifestations of the gifts should be evident in our lives. We should covet these gifts, and the Holy Spirit gives them as and when they are needed. Therefore, it is important for us to be in tune with the Holy Spirit always, so He will supply us with the resources, and the gifts we require, in our time of need. These gifts are received by faith and prayer and are distributed individually to everyone by the Holy Spirit, as He chooses.

WHAT IS THE BEST GIFT TO COVET?

The Bible, in 1 Corinthians 12:31, asks us to covet the best gifts. The best gift for us will be the gift needed at a particular point in time. So, if we need healing for ourselves or a loved one, we can covet the gift of healing. If we need words of wisdom, knowledge, discernment of Spirits, or working of miracles, we can covet them as and when they are required. We need to remember one thing; that our asking would have to be in line with God's Word. Also, remember that the Holy Ghost gives them as and when He wills.

10

CONCERNING THINGS OF THE SPIRIT

IGNORANCE IS NOT AN EXCUSE

The Bible clearly says in 1 Corinthians 12:1, concerning Spiritual gifts (special endowments of supernatural power), "*...I do not want you to be ignorant* (unaware or misinformed) *...*" I would like to add that we should not be ignorant of things pertaining to the Holy Spirit because we will pay the price for ignorance.

The Bible, in many places, talks about not wanting us to be ignorant of certain things, and it will be a worthwhile exercise to look up these instances. We are instructed not to be ignorant of the working of the Holy Spirit in our lives. Rather than doing things by our own strength and might, we should not forget that we have a Helper that can help when called upon.

I would like to relay a story to illustrate this point. I once booked a train ticket for the kids and myself to go on a trip. When we got on the train, we noticed that all the seats had numbers on them, and we were told not to sit on reserved seats. Cutting a long story short, I did not realise that our seats were booked and reserved for us when I purchased the tickets. So, while we were in another carriage, busy looking for free seats, our reserved seats were unoccupied somewhere else on the train. This is the price of ignorance.

Trial and error are good but if we have the attention of the person that knows, it will make common sense to ask. If the Holy Spirit is ignored in certain areas of our lives, He will not move, and we will not experience His best in those areas. The Bible warns that God's people are destroyed for lack of knowledge. If we do not know, the best thing to do would be to ask the Holy Spirit for direction, rather than to grope in darkness or swim in the sea of ignorance.

Ignorance can be displayed in many ways; it could be that we do not know about the existence of a thing or that we have never seen or heard about it. Whatever the case, we suffer the consequences of ignorance until we are liberated. A dear friend once told me a story about her mother. This friend left her illiterate mother in the village and went abroad in search of a better life, for greener pastures, and to fend for herself. From time to time, she would send her mother some money to change into the local currency and use for her upkeep. Her mother had not seen that type of money before, so she thought they were pictures. She would get someone to read the letter for her but hide the money under her mattress. One day, my friend went back home to visit her mother. Sure enough, her mother was glad to see her, and they had good times together catching up, and so on and so forth.

On the day that my friend was about to leave, her mother called her and said, "You have not talked about the pictures you have been sending me."

My friend said to her mother, "I cannot recollect sending any pictures."

The old lady then took my friend to her bed, lifted the mattress, and said, "Look, I have kept all the pictures here."

My friend counted all the money and there were at least a few thousand. It so happened at the time that my friend had some financial dilemma. So, she took the money, but she went to show her mother the place to change the money into the local currency in the future.

God has made His heavenly supplies and provision available for us through the person of the Holy Spirit. So, if we do not tap into the rich resources and inheritance, we will only have ourselves to blame. The ignorant, dear lady in the story I just recounted had instances when she suffered financial lack but had no idea that what she kept under her mattress could have brought the much-needed solution to her financial problems.

Just like the tale of the dear lady, we can suffer lack in many areas of our life and some of them are due to ignorance. I will tell you another story about an ignorant, faithful lady. This lady was such a hard worker and well-loved by her mistress. When her mistress died, because the lady had served her so well, she left something for the lady in her will. Before the mistress died, she called the lady and gave her a gift. This dear lady really treasured this gift so much that she decided to frame it. It so happened that a man of God, Charles Spurgeon, who was this lady's pastor, went to pay her a visit. He noticed the frame on the wall and asked who gave it to her.

With great fondness, the lady said, "My late mistress gave it to me."

Charles Spurgeon broke the glass of the frame and said to the lady, "This is not a picture, it is a cheque. Take it to the bank and withdraw the money, it is made out to you."

When the lady went to the bank to present the cheque, the bank manager invited her in and said that they had been waiting for her to come and cash the money. So, her situation changed as she became enlightened.

The Holy Spirit will enlighten areas that we are harbouring ignorance if we turn those areas loose to Him. He will also give us light in areas that we know nothing about if we are obedient to His promptings. Even if we think we know, there is always a better way of accomplishing the same thing and getting a better result. We have the person that knows everything we can ever think or imagine, living inside us. It will be an oversight and ignorance on our part not to consult Him. When we surrender our lives to Him, He has the power to transform us and make us better people, fathers, mothers, husbands, wives, and children and teach us a few tricks that will add spice to our lives and our relationships with other people. We can accomplish more within a few days with the Holy Spirit of God working in us, than we can accomplish in years, using our own natural abilities.

You might be right in saying, "I can achieve and accomplish things in my life without the gifts of the Spirit or without the help of the Holy Spirit." That can be true to a certain extent. But to experience ***all*** that the Lord wants for us, to live out our ***full*** potential, and triumph in ***all*** our endeavours, we need the help of supreme power, a power that is higher than our natural abilities. There is assurance and satisfaction in knowing that we are living within His will for our lives and that we are tapping into the abundant life He came to provide. That way, when life throws its ugly blows at us (which it will), we are able to cope better, and rest assured that we are within His perfect will.

I will throw in another story here to buttress my point. It is a story about two houses - one built on rock and the other, on sand. When the storms of life hit hard, the house on the rock, with a firm foundation in the Holy Spirit, was able to stand. However, the other house that relied on its own natural power, its natural abilities to solve problems, and its natural might, not knowing its depth was shallow, fell, and great was the ruin. The accounts of this story can be found in Matthew 7:24-27 and in Luke 6:47-49.

The things concerning the Spirit are not hidden from us, but they are hidden ***for us***. We should take the time to read them in the Bible and ask the Holy Spirit to expound them to us and help us to find our place and part in them, according to His will.

SUPERNATURAL LIVING

God wants us to live in the supernatural every day of our lives, to the extent that the ***supernatural will be the natural way of living for us***. This kind of life is possible through the power of the Holy Spirit in our lives. It is called the abundant life, ***Zoë***, or the God kind of life, which is living above the everyday problems, pressures, trial conditions, and temptations, to the extent that we are no longer moved or controlled by situations and circumstances but living by faith through the Holy Spirit. This kind of life is only possible under the hospice of the Holy Spirit.

BENEFITS OF THE HOLY SPIRIT

Here are some benefits of the Holy Spirit.

1. Fills us with Himself.
2. Gives us a new boldness and power to be effective witnesses of the gospel.
3. Empowers us for service, to serve God and our community, and to carry out God's intended purpose for our lives.
4. Endows us with gifts, talents, and abilities. Also enhances our natural gifts and talents.
5. Makes the scriptures come alive, interesting, and exciting.
6. The scriptures will not be like a chore, mechanical or drudgery, instead, it will take on a whole new meaning. It will become exciting, as we begin to receive more insight and revelations, and derive satisfaction from it.
7. Takes us to a deeper dimension in studying and meditating on the word.
8. Fine-tunes our spiritual antenna to the things of God, so that we can pick up Spiritual wavelengths quicker.
9. Help us to discern between good and evil. He is the Spirit of Truth.
10. Makes the presence of God real in our hearts and lives.

11. Takes worshiping and praising God to a new height.
12. Enables us to love God as we should and helps us to love our neighbours as ourselves.
13. Helps our weaknesses.
14. Enables us to speak in other tongues.
15. Energises our Christian walk, gives our faith a boost, and makes Christianity interesting.
16. Aids our prayer life.
17. Helps us to walk and live in the Spirit.
18. Leads, governs, and directs our daily activities.

These are some of the benefits and evidence that the Holy Ghost is operational in our lives. The list is by no means exhaustive.

MANIFESTATIONS OF SONS OF GOD

The Bible says that we will receive power after the Holy Ghost has come upon us. We may ask what power is being referred to here. Romans 8:19 says the whole of creation is earnestly awaiting the manifestation of the sons of God. Manifestation means to make something visible or evidential, to show or express something, to demonstrate or show a sign. In the court of law, the word evidence is commonly used to demonstrate what someone has seen or heard. In our generation, we are to make the truth of God's word visible to the lost, perverse, and dying world, by telling them about the prevailing truth of the gospel. We are called to make a difference and to make the power of God's word visible in our day.

2 Corinthians 12 lists some of these manifestations as simply demonstrating the gifts of the Spirit, which are healing, miracles, special faith, prophecies (being able to see beyond the present), speaking in tongues, interpretation of tongues, words of wisdom, knowledge, and discernment of various kinds. Manifestations of these gifts can be evidenced in our physical, mental, emotional, and spiritual lives, thereby enabling us to make and affect a difference in our generation. The demonstration of these gifts is one of the ways that God has chosen to make visible the truth of the gospel. On a personal level, the power of the Holy Spirit will begin to change our personality and character, as we allow Him to manifest Himself through us.

Galatians 5:22-23 also lists the fruit of the Spirit. This is another way that we can demonstrate and manifest the kingdom of God by our conduct and character. The fruit of the Spirit is covered in a later chapter.

The Apostle Paul and the other disciples manifested the Kingdom of God through their preaching and visible demonstration of signs and wonders, working of miracles, their lifestyles, values, conduct, and behaviour, and the other gifts of the Holy Spirit. Jesus evidenced this as well during His ministry on earth and countless others exhibited traits of the gifts of the Holy Spirit in the Bible. We are no exceptions; we are called to do the same today. We can only accomplish this mandate with the power of the Holy Spirit working through us. We are called to be the salt of the earth; if the salt loses its seasoning properties, it is good for nothing. We are also called to be shining light in the darkness; if light cannot illuminate the dark, then it is good for nothing.

We do not have to be rocket scientists to know that this world we are living in needs to be salvaged and ushered into the light of the gospel. All we can see around us is chaos, confusion, despair, and misery. The good news is that we have the solution, if we can dare step out and ask the Holy Spirit to help us manifest and use what has been deposited inside us. God does not want us to be ignorant concerning the things of the Spirit.

As believers, we are different; we are born of the Spirit of God, filled with the fullness of the Holy Spirit, and born to manifest kingdom principles on earth. This will not be achieved by the excellence of speech but in plain and simple English, by demonstration of the power of God. When we allow the Holy Spirit to lead and teach us, we will show forth these characteristics. Here is a challenge. Are you a believer? Are people that you know waiting for you to demonstrate and manifest the power of the Holy Spirit? It is time for us to take up the challenge, time to take up our rightful place, and time to stand and manifest the power of the Holy Spirit to the lost and dying world.

HIDDEN MYSTERY

1 Corinthians 2 says it is only through the Holy Spirit that we will see what God has in store for us. In this chapter, Apostle Paul said that he did not come to the people of his day with the excellence of speech but in demonstration of the Spirit and power, so that their faith should not stand and rest in the wisdom of men but in the power of God. In other words, he was saying that we should come to a place of utter dependence on the Holy Spirit, so that we will not be swayed by great orators using persuasive doctoring of

human wisdom. Our faith should rest in the power and might of the Holy Spirit and not in human wisdom.

The chapter goes on to say that we operate in the wisdom of God. The wisdom of God is a hidden mystery to the lost and dying world; they cannot understand and neither are they privy to the secret, which is only revealed through the Holy Spirit. The Holy Spirit enables us to have access and helps us to begin to understand and unravel this hidden wisdom of God. An example of this kind of wisdom was demonstrated when Christ was crucified. If the princes of this world knew that by crucifying Christ, they were crucifying one person whose death would result in many souls being saved, then they would not have done it.

At the time they thought they were shutting up and silencing one man forever but as a result, many children were born and are being born (including you and me) into the Kingdom of God, to show forth the demonstrations of His power and carry on from where Jesus and our predecessors left off.

Spiritual things are revealed and taught by the Holy Spirit. The same chapter in Corinthians went on to explain that eyes have not seen, nor ears heard, and neither has entered our hearts, all the things that God has prepared for those that love Him. However, the Bible says that God has revealed these things to us by the Holy Spirit. The Holy Spirit searches all things, even the deep things of God.

The things that God has prepared for us are concealed from our natural human spirit; it takes the Holy Spirit to reveal these things to us, as our natural minds are futile concerning things of the spirit. Have you heard or have you said, "I do not know what to do in this given situation," or

"I do not know what to do with my life," or even "I do not know my purpose in life?" The Bible says the Spirit searches all things, even the deep hidden things of God. Go on a quest with the Holy Spirit, and let Him do the searching for you. Once you are diligent, the hidden mystery, as it seems like now, will be unravelled in time.

SPIRITUAL AND NATURAL THINGS

Our natural human minds are not designed to know spiritual things and, in fact, things of the spirit are foreign and foolish to our natural mind because they are spiritually discerned (understood). This is why we need the Ministry of the Holy Spirit to do this work of revealing the hidden mysteries to us. Often, our mind is forever fighting to gain control, supremacy, and superiority over our spirit. This is a fight that happens to all of us, and that is why it is important to feed our minds with the right kind of food. Otherwise, we will do whatsoever our flesh (human nature) dictates to us, without a gauge.

Chapter two of the first book of Corinthians gives us the understanding that if we are led by the Spirit, we will not speak in the words that man's wisdom teaches but in that which the Holy Ghost teaches, in comparing spiritual things with spiritual. That is comparing like with like. Man's wisdom, or the wisdom derived from this world, cannot be measured or compared to the wisdom of God. Living under the influence of human nature, with no gauge, is a recipe for disaster. If we live in the fleshly realm all the time, we are just a disaster waiting to happen. People who live in the natural realm do not have a sense of spiritual values nor are they mindful of spiritual things. They just want to live by the lust and dictates of the flesh i.e. do whatsoever their minds tell them to do or whatsoever they feel like doing.

The spiritual person, on the other hand, lives under the control of the Holy Spirit and is mindful of the things pertaining to the Spirit of God. He has the mind of Christ, and discerns and esteems spiritual things above sensual things. Have you ever tried to explain things of the Spirit to someone that is not saved? It is hard for them to grasp the concept. When the Bible says, 'when you give you will receive, when you withhold from giving it will lead to penury, pray for those that use you, and love your enemies,' these ideologies are impossible for the person living in a natural realm to understand, much less use them as a standard of life. Even we as believers can only live out these principles by the power of the Holy Spirit operating in our lives. It is impossible for us to live the Biblical standards, the Christian charter, using our own power.

We are made up of spirit, soul, and body. Our human spirit is guided by our human composition, human reasoning, and natural faculties. The natural human spirit is limited and controlled by the five senses. When we allow the Holy Spirit to rule and guide us, the things of God are brought to our attention, knowledge, and reasoning. We are then not only being controlled and ruled by our five senses but by the supernatural power of the Holy Spirit. As a believer and children of God, through conversion and regeneration, the Bible said that we have not received the spirit of the world but the Spirit of God, and that we might know the things that are freely given to us by God. All the benefits that we derive from the Holy Spirit are given to us freely.

All we need to do is to ask and then begin to enjoy the greater knowledge, peace, understanding, victories, wisdom, love, joy, security, protection, and all the other benefits of the indwelling presence of God in us. To be triumphant over the things of the flesh (our inborn nature) and manifest the kingdom of God in our generation, we will have to surrender our thoughts, desires, ambitions, and affections, and yield the control of our minds, spirits, and souls to the Holy Spirit.

If we look around us today in the political, economic, and social arena, we will see that the government has no power or control over some of the things that are happening. They have passed, and are still passing, laws to compel people to behave and live in certain ways, but the legislation does not seem to have the desired effect, nor provide the solution to the lawlessness, chaos, social upheaval, or moral decadence in the world. It is impossible to legislate for the right living (righteousness). It is only with the help of the Holy Spirit, working through us, that we can make the difference the world desires to see. The world is indeed waiting for the manifestation of the children of God. We should take our lawful places as children of God and make a mark of difference in our generations. As children of God, we have the power at our disposal, and all we need to do is ask the Holy Ghost for wisdom, direction, strategies, and solutions.

The Bible, in Jeremiah 33:3 says, *"Call to me, and I will answer you, and show you great and mighty things which you do not know…"* The same book (in Jeremiah 29:11&13), records that the plans God has for us are good plans, not plans of woe, stress, and calamities but plans to prosper us to give us a hope, an expectation, and a future. The promise is that we will find Him when we seek Him and search for Him with our whole hearts. The prerequisite here is that we search for Him with our whole hearts. The question is, ***are we seeking and searching for Him with our whole hearts?***

I will leave one thought with you; the Bible says, concerning Spiritual things, we should not be ignorant, i.e. ignorant of our rights as believers, and events and world-changers. Ignorance simply means not knowing or being unaware. We have the Holy Spirit who is aware and all-knowing, so, ***are we tapping into His endless stream of knowledge?***

11

EMBLEMS OF THE HOLY SPIRIT

This chapter does not intend to cover all that the Bible has to say about the emblems of the Holy Spirit. I have only elaborated on a few of them in this segment.

The Holy Spirit is depicted as Water, Fire, Wind, Dove, Oil, Rain, Dew, and Seal, in many books in the scriptures. I will describe in turn what these emblems symbolise in our lives and how we can relate them to our everyday life.

WATER

Our world, the earth, is founded upon floods. Psalms 24:2 said that the earth was founded upon the seas and established upon the floods. Scientists have confirmed that the surface of the earth is made up of 70.8% water and 29.2% land. Water has a lot of significance in our life and world. Jesus, in John 7:38 said, *"He that believes[in] me… out of his belly* (innermost being) *shall flow rivers of living water."* Jesus made this clearer in verse 39, when He said the "living water" that He was referring to in verse 38 was the Holy Spirit, which those who believe in Him will receive. Likewise, in John 4:14, Jesus said that whosoever that drinks out of the water He came to provide shall not thirst again because the water shall in them be a well (fountain, spring) of living water springing up into everlasting life.

The Holy Spirit is portrayed as the living water that resides in our innermost being, as a constant stream of steady supply. If anyone thirsts, they can tap into that ever-flowing seamless reservoir and receive an unlimited supply, and unlimited power to do the work that we have been commissioned and placed to do here on planet earth.

In the natural context, I can draw an inference that the effect that water has in our natural bodies is the same that the Holy Spirit has in our spiritual life. They say the human body is made up of 70% water, so it goes without saying that water is vital for our very existence.

As ***water quenches our thirst*** in the natural, does the Holy Spirit satisfy our thirst in the spiritual?

Water also cleanses and the Holy Spirit cleanses us with the word. There is cleansing power in the word of God that we hear and read. As we read and meditate on the word of God, we are being cleansed and renewed and our spirits are also being regenerated. The church (the body of Christ) is also said to be washed and sanctified by the Spirit and the word.

The Spirit of God is constantly cleaning and purifying believers (the church) as we embrace, receive, and meditate on the word. Romans 12:1-2 tells us that we should present/yield our bodies (ourselves) daily before the Lord as a living sacrifice and that we should not conform or pattern our lives after the desires of the world but after the word of God. By doing this our hearts, minds, spirit, soul, bodies, and intellects are being transformed, cleansed, and renewed as we pray, study, and meditate on the word of God.

Water refreshes: communing with the Holy Spirit is refreshing and clears our minds of clutter and clogs.

Water cools: it gives us that calming effect, and so does reliance on the Holy Spirit. Where we would have thrown caution to the wind and behaved exactly as we wish, if we rely on the Holy Spirit during those times of rage, temper, and anger, He has His own way of calming us and bringing solutions that we could not have imagined. ***Water truly is the only drink that can satisfy and quench thirst***; any other kind of drink comes second. In the same, way the Holy Spirit quenches our spiritual thirst and provides all we need to live healthy, happy, productive, satisfying, rewarding, fulfilling, and Spirit-filled lives.

The main difference between natural water and spiritual water is that with natural water, we will always thirst again. We might be drinking from the fountain of fame, power, worldly pleasure, human knowledge, lust, and wealth. These pursuits in themselves are endless and are not satisfying because you can never have enough of them; the more you have, the more you want until it finally consumes us and leads to self-destruction. But with the spiritual water, our thirst is constantly being satisfied as we stay with the origin and source of the living water.

The well of living water inside us constantly clears out any dirt and debris from our minds when we allow Him to permeate our minds and have pre-eminence in our lives.

Jesus, in Revelation 22:13 said, *"I am the Alpha and the Omega, the beginning and the end…"* and in verse seventeen of the same book, said, *"…let him who thirsts come [to me]. Whoever desires, let him take the water of life freely* (without cost*)."* The cost for us, or the prerequisite for having the living water, is to ask if we thirst and the guaranteed answer is that we will be filled.

My question to you today is: ***are you thirsty for the living water?*** If you are, the Holy Spirit will fill you to overflowing and you will be effective for the work He wants to do through you.

FIRE

The Holy Spirit was also portrayed as fire. Fire gives light, burns, purifies, and consumes. In Matthew 3:11, John the Baptist said, *"I indeed baptise you with water unto repentance: but [the one that comes] after me… shall baptise you with the Holy Ghost and with fire."* This event took place in Acts chapter two, which relates how the Apostles, after the death, burial, and resurrection of Jesus, were in the upper room in one accord, waiting for the promised Holy Spirit. Acts 2:3 says, *"…there appeared onto them cloven tongues [resembling] fire, and it sat upon each of them. And they were all filled with the Holy Ghost…"*

The fire talked about here also means power, which is a Greek word known as '***Dunamis***', which literally translates into '***miraculous, wonder-working power***'. We can read about many demonstrations of this power in the book of Acts by the Apostles and indeed in the rest of the New Testament.

The fire-power changed the ministry of the disciples. After their master, Jesus Christ, had left, they were about to quit, and they were scattered; Peter went back to his old trade of fishing and even took some disciples along. Others went about doing their own things, the Shepherd had gone, and the sheep were scattered. Little did they know that all this was about to change. They got themselves together again after Jesus had appeared to them on several occasions and commanded them to wait in Jerusalem for the promise that He had told them about before His death on the cross. They went into the upper room, had several meetings, prayed and they were in one accord (united). At the appointed time, the Holy Spirit came as promised and their lives and ministries took on a whole new shape and dimension.

The fire of the Holy Spirit charges us up. He will empower us in the same way that He charged up the 120 disciples on the day of Pentecost and empowered them for service. Fire purifies, burns, and consumes any impurities that might hinder the work or the flow of the Holy Ghost in our lives. When we are baptised with the fire of the Holy Ghost, it cannot be business as usual; we are set apart to do the work of the Kingdom, as the Apostles did. Wherever we are (at work, school, business, church, home, etc.), we should not quench the fire of the Holy Spirit in us. We should follow His leading like the Apostles did and He will manifest his miraculous working power through us, to bless our generations.

Fire is a powerful symbol; ***it also signifies the light of the Holy Spirit burning in our hearts***. Light dispels darkness, so we can be certain that where there is light, darkness cannot have a foothold. Fire sheds light and brightens the dark areas in our life. The Holy Spirit comes as a search engine, searching our hearts and the intents of our hearts. He sheds light on our lives and helps us to adjust and align our ways and thinking to the way He has laid out for us.

We should constantly search ourselves and ask these questions, ***"Is the fire of the Holy Spirit burning in me? Am I filled with the fire of the Holy Spirit, the way the Apostles experienced and were filled with the Holy Ghost power?"*** If that is not the case, you need to renew your commitment and ask the Holy Spirit to fill you, use you, and help you to accomplish His will for your life.

WIND

Using the same text, Acts 2:2 says, *"And suddenly there came a sound from heaven as of a rushing mighty wind and it filled all the house where they were sitting."* The Holy Spirit comes like a mighty wind sometimes and ***saturates our entire being*** as He did with the disciples here. Have you noticed that sometimes when you are praying or waiting on the Lord, you can feel the breeze of His presence flowing? John 3:8 also has something to say about this aspect of the Holy Spirit. It tells us that the wind blows where it wishes, and we can hear the sound but cannot tell whether it is coming or going. So, it is with everyone that is born of the Spirit. As we hear the wind in the natural realm, in the same way, those who have surrendered their lives to Jesus, hear the voice of the Spirit in the spiritual realm. We do not dictate to the Holy Spirit when and where we want His breeze to blow; He is sovereign, and blows according to His wishes and not ours.

Wind can also bring life to dead situations, as we saw in Ezekiel 37:1-10. These verses outline another account of the working of the Holy Spirit. Ezekiel recorded that the hand of the Lord was upon him, and he was led by the Spirit to a valley full of dead, dry bones. Ezekiel was asked what seemed like an impossible question; the Spirit of the Lord said to him, "Can these bones live?" He was very selective with words in his response, saying, "Only you, God, know." He was instructed to prophesy to the dry bones, to make them hear the word of the Lord, and if he did as he was told then the Lord would breathe into the bones and they would live again. The Lord promised to lay sinews (give strength, tendon, ligament, and muscle to the bones) and bring flesh upon them to cover their skin, so they would live.

Ezekiel prophesied as he was commanded and there was so much noise, shaking, rattling, and crackling, as the bones began to come back together. Ligament, muscles, tendon, and flesh came upon them, and they were covered with flesh but there was no breath in them. Ezekiel was again instructed to prophesy unto the wind, and he said thus says the Lord God, "Come from the four winds, O breath, and breathe on these slain [dead bodies] that they may live." Ezekiel prophesied as he was commanded, '*and breath came into them, and they lived and stood upon their feet, an exceedingly great army.*'

I am sure that we have gone through phases or are going through a phase in our lives that looks or feels like dead, dry bones. In these instances, ***we will need the breeze of the Holy Spirit to blow and restore us, and breathe life back into those dead areas***, so that, through the workings of the Holy Spirit in us, we can receive strength and arise like mighty armies ready to do battle and hold captive anything that has weighed us down.

Have you ever had an idea that is bigger than you and you have said to yourself, I cannot see how this idea can come to fruition? It is comforting to know that you are not alone. Ezekiel felt the same way when he was confronted with the valley of dead bones. You can do the same thing that Ezekiel did. The idea came from God himself, so when you go to Him with big dreams, visions, and ideas, He will direct you through the Holy Spirit as He did with Ezekiel.

The wind of the Spirit was also instrumental in parting the Red Sea. The account of this story is in Exodus 14:21-31. There are many features in this story that really fascinate me because it is nothing short of a miracle. One moment, the children of Israel were being frantically pursued by their enemies, the Egyptians, and the next moment, in their attempt to flee from them, the Red Sea was confronting them. Talk about being caught between a rock and a hard place! This is the point at which many of us will give up the fight, throw in the towel, and even give up on life itself, saying we are as good as dead. When we get to this 'deadness' kind of situation in our life, it is vital to listen very carefully to the instructions of the Holy Spirit; He knows how to get us out of tight corners.

Let us see what Moses did; being the leader of the children of Israel, he listened carefully to the instructions of God, as if his life depended on it. As a matter of fact, it did, and it was not just his life but also the life of all the children of Israel fleeing Egypt. The Lord instructed Moses to stretch his hand over the sea; in obedience to the Lord, Moses stretched out his hand over the sea and as he did, the Lord caused the sea to be rolled back by a strong east wind. The east wind made the water form walls, like curtains on both sides, and the children of Israel, with all their families, their possessions, and livestock, walked through the midst of the sea throughout the night. What basically happened was that the sea created a dry land path for the Israelites to walk through safely. I am sure you will agree with me that this is not an ordinary occurrence. It is nothing other than a supernatural act of God, to show the Israelites that there is nothing impossible for Him to do.

I once heard a Minister of the gospel say that if God asks him to run through a brick wall, he would because when he gets to the wall, God will make a hole for him to pass through.

Carrying on with our Red Sea story, when everyone had walked through the divinely created pathway amid the high sea, Moses their leader, being the last person to walk through, turned back and saw the Egyptian armies still frantically trying to catch up with them, with all their might. The Lord instructed Moses again to stretch out his hand over the sea and the water came back together and returned to its usual strength and all the Egyptian armies and their horses and chariots were overthrown in the sea.

What fascinates me most about this story is that the whole scenario took place at night. When we are going through scenes and different scenarios in our lives, it feels like night. In our recount of the stories, we usually say something like, 'I wish it were a bad dream or a nightmare, I wish it would just go away when I wake up.' Can you imagine what was going through the minds of the Israelites? Some would have said, 'I wish this dream would stop and go away.' I am sure many things were going through their minds and around in their heads, just like they do in ours when faced with difficult circumstances. Well, they could not run back, so they just kept going and then, suddenly, in the dark of the night, they began to watch this panoramic scenery unfold before their very eyes. They witnessed the parting of the sea, watched how the waters turned into an iced wall, and formed a pathway with curtains of frozen water on each side, making way for a majestic passage. I do not know what you are going through now but what I do know is that if you trust the Lord, the ending of your story can be like this one.

I am sure the children of Israel watched with amazement and were blown away by this great and spectacular miracle when the Red Sea parted, and they walked on dry ground. The children of Israel did not play any part in the miraculous happening; all they did was follow the instructions of their leader, Moses. At the end of the scene, by this time it was daybreak, the dawn of a new day, and the children of Israel saw the reverse of what the enemy had intended to happen; all the enemies that were ready to attack and kill the children of Israel were drowned in the rage of the sea. As we allow the Holy Spirit to work on any issues that are bothering us, and as we experience the dawn of a new day, we will be filled with His Spirit, we will receive answers, solutions, guidance, clarity, and victory in those areas.

I am sure that the children of Israel would have replayed the scenes in their heads many times over and I am sure that they were forever giving God the glory, every time the thought crossed their minds. I am sure you will do the same too. When I think of what the Lord has done for me, I am forever giving thanks. I am sure you can think of many instances that will cause you to be lost in gratitude and praise when you remember the goodness of God. We can see the importance and victory of obedience from this account. The Bible, in Exodus 14:13 says that the Egyptians you see today, you shall see them no more. In effect, we can say that when we depend on the Holy Spirit to fill, lead, and direct our paths, the things we are going through today, by tomorrow, will be no more.

If we are going through any kind of situation, we need to decide to leave it in the hands of the Master, as He knows how to obtain the solutions; our part is just to obey. Partial obedience is tantamount to no obedience. Can you imagine if Moses were partial in his obedience? He would have been responsible for the life and blood of many people on his hands.

The wind blows wherever it pleases. We hear the sound but cannot see or tell where it comes from or where it is going. The Bible says that is how the Spirit of God operates in our lives (John 3:8). When the wind of the Spirit is at work, no one else can direct, dictate, or take credit for the work that is accomplished. The children of Israel did not tell the east wind which way to blow and certainly could not take credit for the victory accomplished. No one can foretell where, when, and how the Holy Spirit will display His mighty power. Ours is to trust and obey and He will carry out His mighty acts as He will.

We cannot see the wind with our naked eyes; in the same vein we cannot see the Holy Spirit with our naked eyes, except through the eyes of the Spirit, yet we can certainly see and attest to His workings in our lives. The wind is invisible, yet effective. The Holy Spirit moves the same way in our lives, invisible yet very effective, as He manifests and executes the plans of God in our lives.

The wind is independent and so is the sovereignty of the Holy Spirit over us. He moves in us as He wills, not according to our wishes but according to His supreme purpose and plan for our lives. Wind gives breeze and blows fresh air, and oxygen. As we breathe in oxygen for our very survival in the natural, by the same token, we need the Holy Spirit for our spiritual survival and sustenance.

The question here is: ***are you allowing the wind of the Holy Spirit to fill you, blow through you, blow away all those bad habits and debris, and use you as channels of blessings to yourself, your generations, and the world?***

DOVE

The Holy Spirit is also described as a dove. Doves are harmless creatures; they are gentle, and they have comforting power. The Holy Spirit was present at the baptism of Jesus, symbolized in the form of a dove. Matthew's account (in Matthew 3:16-17) and Luke's account (Luke 3:21-22) tells us that after Jesus was baptised, as He was coming out of the water, the heavens opened upon Him, and the Spirit of God descended like a dove and lighting shone upon Him. We can see on display here, the unified working of the Trinity. God the Son (Jesus Christ) was on the earth fulfilling all righteousness and as always, in constant communication with God the Father, went out to John the Baptist to be baptised like everybody else. After baptism, as Jesus was coming out of the water, God the Holy Spirit descended from heaven in the bodily form of a dove anointed, filled, sealed, and endured Jesus with power, and officially inaugurated His public ministry on earth. God the Father then spoke from heaven, saying, "This is my beloved Son, in whom I am well pleased."

Just as it was during the baptism of Jesus, so it is now. God the Father is saying to us, 'You are my children, I am pleased with you.' The Holy Spirit is spurring us on, supplying, and filling us with much-needed power. God the Son is saying, 'I have equipped you. I have given you all you need in life to fulfil your call, purpose, and potential in life.' Jesus answered the call and fulfilled His mission on earth. I would like to pose this question, we have been commissioned, anointed, sealed, and empowered as well, but are we going to fulfil our calls?

One of the fruit of the Spirit is gentleness; the Spirit of God is working on the inside of us, gently filling and empowering us to develop and exhibit the characteristics of the fruit of the Spirit in our daily lives. The Holy Spirit is described as a gentleman; He will not interfere where He is not invited. He is harmless, all He wants to do in our lives is to bring the goodness and godliness of heaven to us and help us to run our race here on earth, so that we can finish well.

I remember an incident that once happened in my life when I would have made a rash decision. Months before this occurrence took place, this scripture kept on coming to my mind, "Be wise as a serpent and harmless as a dove." At the time, I did not know what was about to happen, but the scripture prepared me for the eventuality. When the situation finally came up, I had to decide; the scripture came back to my mind, and I made the right decision. I was very gentle, calm and not abrasive or rash, and I made the right decision. The Holy Spirit, with His gentle dove-like qualities, helps us even when, sometimes, we do not realise the magnitude of what we are faced with, or the decisions we need to make. I had peace with the decision I made, with the help of the Holy Spirit, and everything worked out fine.

Doves also have comforting powers; the Holy Spirit is our Comforter, our Helper, and the true and ultimate Comforter in times of need and adversities. His dove-like abilities, qualities, and characteristics are still available for us here and now.

I would like to pose another question here: ***are you allowing the dove-like qualities of the Holy Spirit and the other fruit of the Spirit, to characterise your life? Also, are the fruit of the Spirit emanating through you to others, or are you just living any way you please?***

OIL

Oil, in the Bible, is mainly used for ***anointing and consecration***. In the Biblical context, oil carries consecration and anointing power. In Psalm twenty-three, the latter part of verse five says that our heads are anointed with oil. We are consecrated as children of God to do the will of the heavenly kingdom on earth, i.e., we are consecrated as kings and priests and ambassadors of heaven on planet earth. This is a huge task and can only be accomplished with the help of the Holy Spirit. Before Jesus started His public ministry, the Bible records, in Luke 4:18, that He went to the synagogue on the Sabbath day, as was customary for the Jewish people. On this occasion, He stood to read the book of the prophet Isaiah. He opened the book and found where it was written, pertaining to His ministry.

The verse reads, *"The Spirit of the Lord is upon me because He has anointed me to preach the gospel to the poor; He has sent me to heal the broken-hearted, to preach deliverance to the captives, and recovering of sight to the blind, to set at liberty them that are bruised, to preach the acceptable year of the Lord."* A cross-reference to this commission can be found in the book of Isaiah 61:1-3.

Jesus was anointed and consecrated to do the task listed in the paragraph above. The name Christ means anointed One. Jesus does not have a surname like us. Jesus means salvation (saviour); in other words, we can say He is the anointed saviour. Jesus was consecrated and set apart to carry out His earthly functions and similarly, today, the Holy Spirit consecrates and anoints us for the work we have been set apart to do.

In the natural context, oil lubricates and locks in moisture. In Hebrews 1:9 and Psalm 45:7, the Bible says because Jesus loves righteousness and hates lawlessness, God anointed Him with the oil of gladness above His fellows. As we delight and partake in the things of the Spirit and not in the lawlessness we see around us, the Holy Spirit will anoint us with the oil of gladness in our hearts, above our fellow men. ***Our joy, happiness, and gladness are locked in the things of the Spirit***. The Bible says, "In the presence of the Lord there is fullness of joy and at his left-hand, pleasures forevermore." As we keep our focus and gaze on the Holy Spirit, we are being anointed with the oil of gladness to help us see the full picture and carry out our assignments here on earth.

It is amazing, the rows and wide selection of oils you see when you go to the supermarket today. Gone are the days when there were just a few selected ranges. Some oils have healing properties, especially olive oil and other essential oils. In James 5:14, the Bible says, *"Is anyone among you sick? Let him call for the elders of the church; and let them pray over him, anointing him with oil in the name of the Lord…"* The anointing oil here is merely symbolic of the healing of God by the Holy Spirit.

Naturally, oil has a soothing and comforting effect. We can liken this to ***the comfort we receive from the Holy Spirit in times of need.*** Oil in its liquid state can reach places that we cannot; likewise, the soothing and the comforting of the Holy Spirit. He can get to the knots and cracks of our lives and soothe those heartaches and melt away pain. Before the days of electricity, oils were used in different vessels to give light, so, oil illuminates when used in certain vessels, such as lanterns and oil lamps. Some parts of the world still use oil for illumination. ***The Holy Spirit illuminates our lives with the radiance of His presence.***

Jesus was anointed for Service by the Holy Spirit, in the same way that ***the Holy Spirit fills us and anoints us for service*** today. If we are in tune and stay focused on the Holy Spirit, we will be anointed to do things we never imagined or thought possible. For the lubrication of the Holy Spirit to perform and work wonders in our lives, we ought to be willing and yielded vessels.

RAIN

Another symbol of the Holy Spirit is rain. Just as rain revives the earth and plants, so the Holy Spirit is sent as rain to revive areas that are dead and could do with a sprinkling of showers in our lives.

Rain is refreshing and has life-giving and quickening power. ***The Holy Spirit quickens us in our areas of shortcomings***. He also gives life in areas where we are dead and need awakening. Without rain in the natural, there would be no vegetation, no crops, no food, no water, trees will wither and die, and there would be drought and famine. We have all seen images in the media and read in the newspapers about areas where it has not rained for some time. Without the rain of the Holy Spirit in our lives, we would dry up and be lifeless on the inside.

There are many scriptures that talk about rain in the Bible, the latter and the former rain. Zechariah 10:1; Hosea 6:3, 10:12; James 5:7; Joel 2: 23-32. In the natural realm, the former or early rain falls at seedtime, which is when farmers plant their seeds. The latter rain usually falls six months after the early rain. The latter rain helps the seeds to grow, mature, and ripen. The early rain comes at the beginning and the latter rain comes at the end, just before the harvest.

In the spiritual realm, the early or former rain fell at the inception of the church during the time of the apostles. The latter rain will be poured out at the end of the age when the complete harvests of the church age will be gathered (Acts 2:16-21). Our work as Christians is to help till the ground, sow the seed of the word, help to increase the crops, and help to usher in the harvest. One of the

Ministries of the Holy Spirit is to help us to fulfil this great commission and assignment. The Holy Spirit lives in us and He is pouring out the rain of His presence in us. The Holy Spirit helps us spread the word, pray for the lost and dying and tell the world about the saving grace of Jesus. He helps us give whatever we can for the advancement of God's kingdom, use our time constructively and plant the seed of the word in the hearts of men, women and children of our generation.

The church age started at Pentecost when the Holy Spirit fell on the 120 people in the upper room. The church age will end when Christ comes for His church (the precious fruit of the earth). James 5:7 says, *"...the husbandman* (farmer) *waits for the precious fruit of the earth, and has long patience for it."* God is waiting patiently for His harvest, which are the many souls that need to be saved. We can say that is why He has not yet ended the world. The Bible says that God does not take pleasure in the death of sinners but in their repentance. Long-suffering is one of the attributes of the Holy Spirit and that is demonstrated in this patient wait. We are the ones on the frontline, participants to be and being used to rake in this harvest. We have no excuse; we are being enlisted, equipped, endowed, and empowered by the Holy Spirit to help reap this harvest of souls.

We are advised, as believers, to work while it is day because the night will come when we will not be able to work. ***One of our primary duties now, with the aid of the Holy Spirit, is to harvest souls for the kingdom of God***. The harvest is indeed many and ripe, but the labourers are few and we are asked to pray for the Lord of the harvest to send labourers into the field. The question for you and me today is: are we ready to be co-labours in this bountiful harvest?

In Joel 2:23-32, we are told to be glad and rejoice because the former or early rain was given to us moderately. In Zechariah 10:1, we are commanded to ask the Lord for rain in the time of the latter (spring) rain. The combination of former and latter rain is promised to us in abundance when we put these two scriptures together. It kind of puzzles me when I read Zechariah 10:1, which says we should ask for more rain in the time of the latter rain. When we ask for more rain, we are asking for the former and the latter rain put together; we are asking for enablement, we are asking for labourers, we are asking for a harvest of souls.

The promise is that the Lord who makes bright clouds in the sky will give showers of rain to every grass, and to every person in the harvest field. In effect, what the scripture is saying is that if we ask, we will receive. So, unless we ask, we will not receive the souls. We are instructed here to ask for more (abundant) rain in the rainy season, so souls can be harvested for the kingdom of God. We cannot take anything of ours to heaven from this earth; the only things that we can take with us to heaven are the souls that we win for the Lord. The Bible says that 'he that wins souls is wise'. To be wise children, we need to go about the Father's business and win souls for the Kingdom of God with the aid, help, and assistance of the Holy Spirit.

The Joel and Acts accounts symbolise the Holy Spirit like the rain that is poured out on all flesh, to the heirs of salvation. In Ezekiel 34:26-27, the scriptures said, "... *I will cause showers to come down in their season; and there shall be showers of blessing... the trees of the field shall yield their fruit, and the earth shall yield her increase."* Rain causes an increase to take place; farmers will understand this more than anybody else. Rain helps the word sown to germinate and take root in the hearts of the hearers. ***When we plant the seed of the word in the hearts of men, the duty of the Holy Spirit is to allow the word to take root in the heart of the hearers***. He gives them enlightenment and understanding and as they hear more of the word through different channels and avenues, the word will eventually begin to take root, germinate, and grow.

The rain in the Old Testament has now culminated in showers in the New Testament. During the official inauguration of the presence of the Holy Spirit, in the book of Acts chapter two, the Apostles were showered with the rain of the Spirit, and they were empowered for service. The same Holy Spirit is very much present in our lives today, to shower us with the same endowments, fill us with His presence and power, and empower us for His service here on earth.

My question to you after reading about the rain of the Spirit is this: ***are you allowing the rain of His presence to fall on you, so you can do the most important job we are placed on planet earth to do?*** I do not want to alarm you, but I just want you to know that the reason you are still here and not gone to eternity yet is to do this very assignment. How are you affecting souls for Christ in your neighbourhood, family, at work, places of social engagement, etc.? Here is a soul-searching question: ***are you soul-conscious?*** With the help of the Holy Spirit, you can be a soul winner and rake in the harvest, if that is your heart's desire. As children want to make their parents proud, your aim should also be to make your heavenly Father proud of you as well. Ask the Holy Spirit about how to get started and I am sure He has many strategies just for you.

DEW

Dew has been depicted in many places in the Bible as a symbol of God's providential blessings on the earth. Dew refers to little drops of rain that water the earth every morning. In the tranquillity of the night, even the desert places, barren regions, and wastelands are gently watered by the morning dew. Trees, grasses, shrubs, plains, mountains, rocky places, and valleys are generously covered and watered with dew.

Desert places are glad for the dew, and plants, trees, and solitary places are refreshed by the dew. Dew is one of the most wonderful experiences of grass and dry places because no one bothers to water them. Dew uplifts and gives assurance of existence in the most unlikely of places.

As dew is new every morning, so is the mercy and blessing of the Lord. Lamentations 3:22-23 puts it this way, *"[The mercies of the Lord] are new every morning; great is [His] faithfulness."* If we are barren in any area, feeling dejected, rejected, and isolated, as the morning dew refreshes the earth, so we should allow the mercies of the Lord and the filling of the Holy Spirit to overshadow us, drench our beings, and revitalise those areas. As we do this, we can wake up to a new day with optimism, ready to receive and embrace the plans the Lord has for us for each day. No matter what we are going through, we should allow the dew of the Holy Spirit to soothe, refresh, comfort, and bring life to the dead areas of our lives. As we allow this every day, we will experience brand-new mercy, filling, favour, and blessing of the Lord, awaiting us to help us accomplish the day's tasks.

Even whilst it does not rain every day, the Lord waters the earth with the dew. As we water our plants to prevent them from dehydrating and eventually dying, the Holy Spirit likewise waters us with dew; He gives us revelations, even when we are unaware or least expecting it. He gives us refreshing and uplifting ideas when they are most needed. As we co-operate and walk with the Holy Spirit, He sheds light on our ways and paths.

As insignificant as the dew might seem, some parts of the earth are glad for its functions. I once heard a story about the cloud and the desert, which ties in nicely with the dew. The story goes like this; the cloud and the desert were feeling so insignificant and sorry for themselves and were complaining about their lack of values. The desert said, "People say that I am too hot, and nobody wants to come near me," while the cloud said, "People complain that I flood the place when I give them rain." After a long time of moaning and complaining, the desert stopped and said to the cloud, "One thing that makes me really happy every morning is when the dew covers me." The cloud, now feeling particularly useful, said, "In that case, you will not mind if I rain on you." So, the cloud rained on the desert and the plains, hilly and rocky places were also watered and covered with life and vegetation.

No one is insignificant, and no situations that we are going through are insignificant; if it bothers us, it bothers God and we should let the blessing, the dew of heaven, the acts of grace, mercy, and favour, fall on those areas by not resisting and fighting the work of the Holy Spirit in our lives.

We are not alone when we feel so unimportant and insignificant like the cloud and the desert. Gideon had his moment in Judges 6:36-40 when he asked the Lord for a dew test. Before the dew test, Gideon felt he was small and could not achieve much. After the dew test, it was a different story; Gideon was now convinced that the Lord had called him to make a difference in his generation and to lead the children of Israel in battle. We do not have to put the Holy Spirit to a dew test, like Gideon did. All that we need to lead victorious and fruitful lives has already been made available to us.

I was told that the darkest part of the day is just before daybreak. One minute it is pitch black and then, the next minute, the day begins to break. So, no matter what we are going through today, tomorrow is another day, and we should allow the blessing of the new day to fall upon us. We are created for significance and purpose, just as the dew has its significance and purpose. Let the morning dew melt away the hardship we might have experienced the previous day or night. The Holy Spirit is depicted as dew, to bring life to what we term as lifeless and dead situations.

Are you feeling insignificant? ***As the Lord waters the earth every morning with the dew, ask the Holy Spirit to fill you with His power, so that you can perform your daily tasks.*** One prayer that is worth saying when you wake up is to ask the Holy Spirit to help you to fulfil His will for your life every day.

SEAL

The working of the Holy Spirit is vital to our salvation; we receive the Holy Spirit after we have repented and believe in the finished work of salvation. Salvation, as we know, needs to be received by faith. Upon believing, we were/are sealed, preserved, protected, and endorsed by the Holy Spirit. A seal in the natural is a sign to confirm ownership. A seal also authenticates, confirms genuineness, and validates that we belong to God. Ephesians 1:13 says, "*... ye were sealed with that Holy Spirit of promise...*" And Romans 8:9 also confirms that anyone that does not have the spirit of Christ does not belong to Him. ***The Holy Spirit Himself confers on us the right of adoption that we belong to Him***. We are approved, stamped, marked, and branded by the Holy Spirit.

I particularly like one of the definitions of seal, which says 'a seal of approval is put on letters to conceal its contents and can only be opened by authorised personnel'. We can put it this way: the Bible is a sealed letter to us, and, with the help and aid of the Holy Spirit, we can unravel and unscramble the words. As we open and read the contents of the Bible, the Holy Spirit gives us illumination, enlightenment, and understanding and translates it from a mere book to a blueprint for our everyday life.

The Bible says that the letter kills but the Spirit gives life. If we read the Bible without the help of the Holy Spirit, we will not gain or understand much, but when we enlist the assistance of the author of the Bible to read His sealed letter to us, then we get a real understanding and meaning, and He gives us revelations of how to appropriate the words. The Holy Spirit transforms these words and makes them living words, as we read them.

Ephesians 4:30 says, *"And grieve not the Holy Spirit of God, whereby you are sealed unto the day of redemption."* We are sealed with the Holy Spirit, to authenticate that we belong to the heavenly kingdom. He has sealed and kept us onto Himself until the day that we shall be redeemed from our mortal bodies. As a seal guarantees security, we are also secured by the Holy Spirit; He guarantees our security. Security acts as a down payment for a transaction. The Holy Spirit acts as our down payment; we are the investment, and He is our benefactor. By looking after us, He is looking after His investment and watching His transaction grow and yield. ***His vested interest in us runs throughout the course of our lives***.

It is a privilege to know that we are sealed with His presence and closely guarded with awesome power, so that we can run the course of our Christian race until the day of redemption (from this world) and ensure that we finish well and arrive home. The goal of any athlete who takes part in a race is to reach/arrive at the finish line. A colleague at work took part in one of the London Marathons and it took her just over four hours to complete the race. The person that came first completed the race in just less than two hours, and many of the other runners finished at different times. One year, someone completed the marathon in three days.

The race that is set before us, the Bible said, is not for the swift but for the diligent. The person that took three days to complete the race was diligent; he had a mission, focus, and faith, where many people would have given up. Can you begin to imagine how he felt when he got to the finish line? I bet it was the same way that the ones who came first, second, twentieth, and so on, must have felt.

The dream, desire, and goal of everyone should be to make heaven their home; we are sealed for this purpose. The sovereign ministry of the Holy Spirit in our lives is to make this a reality. Making heaven our home is the ultimate for everyone in life. We have not arrived until when we get to heaven.

In conclusion, the emblems (Water, Fire, Wind, Dove, Oil, Rain, Dew, and Seal) represent or can act as a reminder of the workings of the Holy Spirit in our lives. These emblems are day-to-day things that we see, feel, and can relate to. So, the next time you think, feel, or see the physical representatives of these emblems, try to relate them to the numerous ways in which the Holy Spirit moves and works in our lives.

Talking about emblems and symbols, the one that readily comes to my mind is the covenant God made with Noah in Genesis 9:11-16. God told Noah that He would let the rainbow be a symbol of His promise to him and every living creature, that He will not end the world again with a flood. The scripture says (in Genesis 9:16), *"...I will look upon [the rainbow], that I may remember the everlasting covenant..."* Let the emblems be a constant reminder of the significance of the Holy Spirit to us.

12

FRUIT OF THE SPIRIT

VINE AND BRANCH

Trees bear fruit. Jesus in John 15:4-5 tells us that He is the vine, we are the branches, and if we abide in Him and Him in us then we will bear much fruit. As a branch cannot bear fruit if it abides alone, so our lives cannot bear fruit except we abide in Him. When we anchor ourselves to the Holy Spirit, as trees bear fruit, so will our lives. We will bear fruit of the Spirit as we follow the leading and prompting of the Holy Spirit. Every tree will produce after its kind; a mango tree will not produce apples and an orange tree will not produce pears. If we are led by the Spirit of God, our lives should produce the fruit of the Spirit.

Except a grain of corn falls to the ground and dies, it abides alone. We believe that when a dead grain/seed falls on the earth, it multiplies itself and we are nourished by its multiplication. We cannot understand how it is done, we cannot tell how one grain becomes multiple grains and how the earth, air, water, and sunshine work together to create the new crop. We believe it not because we understand it but because it produces results. If that grain has not fallen, it will be alone. If all the conditions that it requires to develop and flourish are not present or given the opportunity, then it truly dies without reaching its full potential. So are we, when we cut our supplies from the real-life-giver and focus our attention on the second-best or on our limited human reasoning. Our lives will not yield the fruit they are supposed to bear if we do not abide in the vine.

On one of the days while I was writing this book, I went to the library. When I was taking a break, I picked up a book about an oak tree from one of the bookshelves. The book described the journey of how a mighty oak tree grew from a single acorn seed. The bit that fascinated me most, and that we can apply to our lives, was about what happens when a storm hit the forest.

A mighty wind whipped through the trees, which caused some of the branches to crack and some were blown away. The top of some trees broke off and crashed to the ground, but the rest of the tree was still standing, alive, and continued to grow. The tree never stopped growing, despite the storm damage. One of the interesting things about trees and plants is that they die from their roots. You might see some lifeless-looking trees and plants and conclude that the plant is dead. But give the plant and tree sometime, especially after some TLC (tender loving care), and in the right environment, they will begin to sprout and grow, and flourish again. The oak tree survived the storm and new wood started to grow underneath the bark, in place of the ones that fell to the ground. And every year, the trunk of the tree grew a little wider, until it became a gigantic mighty oak tree.

Our lives are like that, in many respects. From time to time, we will experience difficulties and frustrations like the branches that fell and crashed to the ground. If our roots are anchored in the Holy Spirit, we might feel the storm, but it will not consume us; we will continue to grow and survive as we put our faith, hope, and trust in the Holy Spirit, who is our root during stormy times. The secret of the branch is to remain in the tree. The secret to bearing fruit is to remain in the vine. For our lives to bear the fruit of the Spirit, we need to be firmly rooted in the tree of life.

FRUIT OF THE SPIRIT

The nine Fruit of the Spirit are grouped together in threes. ***The fruit of the Spirit build godly characters in us***. The Holy Spirit helps us in this character shaping, character moulding, and personal development. These fruits help us to improve our behaviour/responses, and help us to live lives that are increasingly pleasing to God and beneficial to others and ourselves. The first group is love, joy, and peace. The second is longsuffering, gentleness, and goodness and the third group is faithfulness, meekness, and self-control.

FRUIT OF THE SPIRIT - FIRST GROUP OF THREE

The first group of three focuses on our relationship with God. In our relationship with God, we should experience ***love***, ***joy***, and ***peace***, which in turn, is evident to others.

1. Love – ***our lives should radiate divine love.*** The dictionary defines love as strong ardent compassion or a devotion to the wellbeing of someone. There are different types of love; agape love is the God kind of love, and it is this kind of love that Christians should emulate and model their lives after. This kind of love is unconditional. God the Father demonstrated a perfect example of this kind of love in John 3:16, where the Bible tells us that God loves us so much that he gave His ONLY begotten son to die for us, in order to redeem us, re-direct our footsteps and give us eternal life.

Agape love is unconditional, and it's the kind of love God has for us; the kind of love parents have for their children. This is also the kind of love that God expects us to have toward our fellow human beings. Do you show acts of love to your neighbours, colleagues, friends, and family as you should? We have the capacity to love because love lives inside us in the person of the Holy Spirit. The distinguishing factor between Christians and the rest of the world is the love we display and share. Jesus himself said in John 13:35 that by the acts of love that we show to one another, people will know that we are indeed His disciples. One duty that we Christians owe to our fellow human beings more than anything else is the duty of love. In the book of Romans 13:8, the Bible says we should not owe anyone anything but a debt/duty of love. The love being referred to here is agape. The entire thirteenth chapter of the first book of Corinthians is also devoted to how we are to love.

Love is in action and not by mere words. Love is more than emotions and it is certainly not feelings. The Bible commands us to love, so love for us is not an option. God, Himself, is love and His love for us transcends our understanding. The kind of love described here is a product of the fruit of the Spirit and can only be produced in us when we abide in the vine. We do not have the natural capacity to love that way.

Love is not selfish; it is selfless, always putting others first. As we learn to give love with the power of the Holy Spirit working on the inside of us, we need to learn to receive love as well. The love God has for us surpasses all our knowledge put together. You might say, "How can God love me? I am so bad; I do not do things right; I am far from perfect; I have done too many wrong things; I find myself doing the wrong things even though I know I should not be doing them." The good news is that God loves us just as we are because He has the overall picture. He knows where He is leading us and has a plan for our lives. He knows what He has promised us and as we respond to His love, He will complete what He wants to do in our life. God loves us regardless of what we are going through or have done. If we have missed it in any area, we can go to God boldly in prayer and ask for forgiveness of our sins. With God, there is restitution and forgiveness. He is a God of many chances. If we still have breath and are alive, we can still make it right with God; it is never too late. God is waiting on you to respond to his love call.

Someone once asked the question, "How much does Jesus love us?" "***With outstretched arms***," came the answer. He died for our sins on the cross with his arms stretched out, showing His all-encompassing, all-embracing, and all-inclusive love. This kind of love is a demonstration of God doing for us what we cannot do for ourselves. God loves sinners but does not love their sins. If we love a person, we want to please and make them happy, so, if we love God, we will want to please Him. Love has responsibility; we cannot say we love God and not obey or listen to Him. If we love God, we ought to obey him and listen to the words He speaks to us. The Bible says, "If we do not love our neighbours that we see, how can we love God that we do not see?" We cannot love the way God wants us to love, using our own power, human effort, and human strength. This love walk can only be achieved with the power of the Holy Spirit working in us. He will help us to fulfil our love responsibilities towards God, and our neighbours, and help us to live pure and blameless lives before God.

2. Joy – joy is defined as an emotional excitement, gladness, and delight, over blessings received or expected for self and others. As we are talking about the fruit of the Spirit, I would like to define joy as;

Joy (J)

Of (O)

Yielding (Y)

The fruit of the Spirit can only be manifested in our lives when we yield to the giver of the fruit. Joy is different from happiness; happiness is a by-product of joy. Happiness is temperamental, we can be happy in the morning and by the afternoon we are not so happy or even sad. Joy is much deeper-rooted than happiness. ***Joy is what our lives should radiate, even in the face of difficulties and moments of unrest.*** We do not only have joy when everything is going well, we also experience joy in the face of difficult times. We yield fruit of joy during these times because we have placed our lives in the hands of the joy-giver. No matter what obstacles we go through in life, we know that He is there with us, so we have expectance of Joy when we go through tough times.

The Apostle John, quoting Jesus in John 15:11, said, *"These things I have spoken to you, that My joy may remain in you and that your joy may be full."* Mind the tense, Jesus said 'my joy'; the prerequisite for this type of joy is obedience. When students pass exams, they are so joyful; parents are filled with joy at the birth of a baby; when a businessperson is awarded a contract; when we get a new job or promotion; at any kind of happy occasion, we are filled with gladness. The fruit of joy surpasses these because it is felt in expectation of the occasions, during the occasions, and in adverse occasions.

If we look at this world the way it is and the way it is going, as they say, it is nothing to write home about, nor is it something to be joyful about. When we come up against obstacles in life, which we will, what will be our reaction? When we know that we should be upset, lamenting, angry, or full of fury but instead we have this unexplainable joy, bubbling on the inside of us. Where is the joy coming from? This sort of joy can only come from the Holy Spirit, and we need to learn to accept this joy rather than fight it. This kind of joy is often beyond our understanding.

Apostle Paul, in 2 Corinthians 8:4, described it as die-hard joy. He said you feel this joy regardless of the circumstances. This is because we know that when we are beaten or struck down, we are not knocked out or destroyed. When we are troubled, we are not distraught. When we are perplexed, we are not baffled, ruffled, or confused. When we are persecuted, we are not forsaken or abandoned, and when ***we have zeroed out on ourselves, He zeroes in on us***. When we live in the Spirit, the joy of the Lord sometimes so overwhelms us that it feels as if we have temporarily lost the ability to be sad, bitter, unhappy, grieve or we feel like the capacity to do those things have been suspended. The Bible said that our Lord Jesus Christ, for the joy that was set before Him, endured the death on the cross. Now this is supernatural joy. You are looking in the face of anguish, sorrow, and death and yet you are joyful; that is supernatural joy.

God wants our joy to be full; the joy of the Lord can be described as a state of rest, calm, and tranquillity when all hell is breaking loose around us. It can also be described as a confident assurance that the Lord is in control. Jesus said, "My joy I leave with you, not as the world gives." The joy of the world will not sustain us in challenging times. When the Holy Spirit is taking us to a place of joy, where our joy will be full, He gives us the supernatural ability to cope and face setbacks. He comforts us and spreads his wings around us and enables us to bear the fruit of joy amid the turbulence.

We experience the joy of yielding when we yield to the Holy Spirit and allow Him to take the reins and control of our lives. We will be amazed at how we react when tough times hit us, and surprised at our conduct. Outwardly, we might want to throw fits of anger and rage but on the inside, when we check our joy radar, we find that it is calm, not raging, peaceful, and joyful. I remember one time when I wanted a job so badly and I took my time to prepare for the interview. When I received the feedback that I was appointable but unsuccessful, my initial reaction was disappointment and sadness. Two days later, when I was relaying the story to a friend, she asked me how I felt about it in that moment and I said, "Funnily enough, I felt joy on the inside of me." It was like a river of joy flowing on the inside of me, which I said should not be. She looked at me, and said that it could only be the Holy Spirit. Jesus said, "My joy I give to you, not as the world gives." We should learn not to quench this supernatural outburst of the Holy Spirit when it bubbles inside of us, in the face of unseemly circumstances. You know that you are operating in this kind of supernatural joy when your natural reaction to adverse situations should be to the contrary but instead, you have this unshakable, unspeakable, unbroken joy.

3. Peace – is defined as the state of quietness, rest, repose, harmony, order, and security amidst turmoil, strife, and temptations. This kind of peace can be experienced by any believer if they abide in the vine.

I have experienced this kind of peace many times, amidst circumstances that are not peaceful. ***This peace surpasses all understanding and reasoning; it is supernatural, and it is being in a state of peace and tranquillity when other people are losing their heads.*** I can go as far as saying the ability to worry was supernaturally suspended and I just felt this reassuring peace. I am sure that you can give examples of this kind of peace in your life as well.

We are commanded by scripture to seek peace and pursue it; if peace is not important and a valuable commodity for our daily living, the Bible would not ask us to seek and pursue it. The connotation this gives to me is that peace is running, and we need to run after it, otherwise, we might lose it. The Bible also commands us to live peaceably with everyone. The Holy Spirit will help us to bear the fruit of peace in our lives and help us to live this kind of peaceful life.

Obedience, faith, and trust are key to bearing the fruit of the Spirit. Peace is not the absence of a problem but experiencing unbroken peace in the face and midst of trying moments and situations. When I gave my life to the Lord, amid unemployment, no money, not being sure about my direction in life, and negotiating with credit agencies on how to pay back my debts, I had this unshakable peace. I had to examine myself because the situation was really causing me a lot of concern before but a few days later after I gave my life to the Lord, it did not seem to matter that much or weigh me down like it used to. Instead, I had this peace that I could not understand or explain. What I did not realise at the time was that I was bearing the fruit of peace. It was much later, when I began to hear teachings about the fruit of the Spirit, that I realised what it was that I had experienced.

When we are plugged into the vine, we will, from time after time, enjoy the peace that surpasses all understanding, as promised in the Bible. It does not matter what the situation is, big or small. The Prince of Peace, living on the inside of us, is more than able to yield the fruit of peace in us at any given time and in any given situation, when the conditions are right.

Jesus said, in John 14:27, "*...my peace I give unto you: not as the world gives...Let not your heart be troubled, neither let it be afraid.*" Note again here, the Lord Jesus said 'My peace'; this is different from the normal peace or the world's definition of peace. We can reap this kind of peace in the face of turmoil and confusion. If we have the prince of peace living in us, our life can only yield and bear this peace when people all around us are losing their peace and cool. The situation you are facing right now might not go away just like that but instead of worrying, you can tap into the peace that gives clarity and will enable you to work things out and overcome any given situation.

I have, not too long ago, learned about ***the peace check***. I will explain what I mean by that. I once heard someone say before deciding or doing something; check your peace status. Your peace check will let you know if you are making the right or wrong decision. If you are confused, not at ease, worried, anxious, doubtful, fretful, and lacking peace, then you will know that God is not in the decision you are about to make. God is not the author of confusion but peace (1Corinthians 14:33). The peace check can be conducted by simply checking the peace status of your heart; if it is peaceful then go ahead with the decision, if not, do not make any decision, but pray about the situation until you get that peace. We can also experience peace during chaotic situations and make the right decisions.

Sometimes, before we make decisions, we find ourselves waiting for God to speak first, either to us audibly, through someone else, or any other way. I have learned that we can be guided by the deep unshakable peace we feel on the inside, if God has not chosen to speak to us in any other way. Be guided and led by the peace of God that garrisons our hearts. A friend once asked me how she would know if her prayers have been answered. She'd received news that her grandmother, who brought her up, was unwell, and she wanted to go and visit her. But she said that she had prayed about the situation and had not received any direction about whether to travel, or if her grandmother would get better or be alive when she arrived. In fact, she was confused. I told her that I had learned one thing and that is to be led and guided by the peace of God. I said if she has prayed about the issue and she feels the peace of God on the inside of her, then she should believe that all is well and put her plans into motion. She took my advice, and guided and led by the peace, travelled to Nigeria with her children and saw her grandmother. She came back to testify that she was so fulfilled and happy that she got to see her grandma again alive, after so many years.

The gospel that we preach is a gospel of peace that brings good news to the world (Romans 10:15). When we are evangelising, we do not have to fight the people; the gospel we proclaim and bring to people's attention is that of peace, it carries power if delivered under the directive of the Holy Spirit. When we follow the peace agenda and are led and directed by the Holy Spirit, we reach the people He wants us to reach. ***Are you guided and led by the peace of God in every area of your life?***

Love, joy, and peace are fruits that we produce and experience in our relationship with God. The outcome of these fruit radiates out of us, and people around us will notice and see the evidence.

FRUIT OF THE SPIRIT - SECOND GROUP OF THREE

The second group of three focuses on our outward relationships with others. In our relationship with others, our lives should generate fruit of ***longsuffering*** (forbearance), ***kindness***, and ***goodness***.

1. Longsuffering – this is patient endurance; the ability to bear frailties, offence, injuries, and provocation by others, without murmuring, complaining, or feeling resentment. God is described as longsuffering because He forbears with us; His desire is that no one should perish but come to know the saving grace of our Lord Jesus Christ. We get so many chances with God; when we blow it, He makes room for restitution so we can come boldly to Him and ask for forgiveness. If God were to be like us, the world would have ended a long time ago. God is a God of order and a God of many chances. He does not give up on us, and that is one of the reasons why the world has not yet ended.

As children of God, bearing the fruit of the Spirit, our lives should radiate the longsuffering nature. When people offend us, we should be ready to forgive and bear along with them, because this is how the world, we are trying to reach will know that we are the children of God. We are God's representatives on earth and are the God or Jesus that some people would only ever see. So, we should be mindful that we occupy this position here on earth. If we profess that we are children of God, our lives should be proof of this. The Holy Spirit will help us to bear this fruit if asked.

Are you believing God for something, and the answer does not seem to be forthcoming? Let patience run its course and in due season, you will be rewarded if you do not faint and give up.

Are you patient with people that are naturally slower than you, or do you judge the faults of others too readily, and are you easily provoked or irritated? Then you need the help of the Holy Spirit to help you bear this fruit, so you can be Christ-like in all ramifications.

Longsuffering patience is a good quality to possess; it makes us better, rational, and those who people want to relate with. If you know you are going to see an impatient person, you are sometimes hesitant because they can be so irrational, and their behaviour is highly unpredictable. So, you prepare yourself, ensuring that you tread gently because you do not know what will trigger an outburst, a quick temper, or a snappy reaction. Most times, you do not know where you stand with people that exhibit such traits; they are not fun to be around, and people mostly try to avoid them because they feel uncomfortable with them. With the fruit of patience working in us, by the power of the Holy Spirit, we can overcome this in-built habit. As we yield to the Holy Spirit, He will give us the ability to become better husbands, wives, fathers, mothers, children, employees, employers, friends, colleagues, sisters, and brothers; in short, better people, when we allow this fruit to develop, flourish and have a place in our lives.

The Bible in James 1:2-4 says that we should consider it joyful whenever we are enveloped in or encounter trials of any sort or fall into various temptations. We should be assured and understand that the trial and proving of our faith produces and develops endurance, steadfastness, and patience in us. Verse four says to let patience, longsuffering, and endurance run their courses and do their thorough work in us, so that we may be mature, complete, and fully developed in that area of our lives. You will find that adversities often make us stronger people. It helps us to develop the character that we need and helps us to overcome that problem. Joseph had his fair share of this character formation when he was sold by his brothers into slavery, and he later became the prime minister of Egypt. He developed and showed attributes of patience, longsuffering, forgiveness, wisdom, integrity, and credibility, and did not show offense or retaliate when he had the perfect opportunity to do so.

Job experienced a similar fate and developed character formation and transformation when he went through rigorous and strenuously trying times. The Bible recalls, in James: 5-11, that we should remember the patience of Job. When we go through affliction, persecution, discipline, or chastisement, patience is borne and worked out in us, and the character that we need to go through that situation is borne in us as well. We all experience this from time-to-time and moment-to-moment when we move from one height to the other and from one level to another.

The small daily battles of patience that we go through prepare and equip us to endure greater ones. On an amusing note, someone was praying for patience, and they said, 'I want patience and I want it *now*.' They say patience is a virtue. Patience is indeed a good asset, a good quality to possess because it makes us better and more tolerant people. The Holy Spirit will help us to bear this fruit, as we remain in the vine.

2. Gentleness – this is a disposition to be gentle, soft-spoken, kind, even-tempered, cultured, and refined in character and conduct. We are to be gentle but firm. As has been emphasized several times in this book, the Holy Spirit is described as a Gentleman. He will not force His way into our lives, and he only operates when He is invited. When we yield our lives to Him, we will surely bear this fruit of gentleness, kindness, even-temperedness, and not harsh and brash behaviours. He will also help to refine our character and conduct in areas where that refinement is needed.

We should be kind, even-tempered, not giving fire for fire, jungle justice, an eye for an eye, and a tooth for a tooth. God is multi-faceted and one of His facets is gentleness. This quality needs to be evident in the life of a believer. I know that we are not all gentle by disposition or at the best of times, but by being conscious of this defect, we can allow the Holy Spirit to work out and radiate more of these qualities in our lives. To bear this fruit, we should continually learn to bridle our flesh. The only person that can help us to change and sustain the bearing of this fruit is the Holy Spirit.

The Bible commands us, in Ephesians 4:32, to be kind, compassionate, understanding, loving, tender and gentle-hearted, and forgiving of one another, as we have seen in the examples of Jesus. The Bible recorded that during Jesus' earthly ministries, He went about doing good and carried out acts of kindness. I was thinking not too long ago about the acts of kindness that the early church exhibited in the book of Acts. The book is called the Acts of the Apostles, showing us how they operated the examples that Jesus exhibited and left for them. The question for us today is: ***are we following the same outstanding examples recorded for us to read in the Bible?***

Sometimes, I just cannot help but sit back and reflect on how Christianity has really helped to shape our society as we know it today. Hospitals, orphanages, places of refuge, places of study (schools), and the criminal justice system were all initiated and started by Christians and Christian organisations. There are many more Christian pioneers like that in our world today, showing and doing various acts of kindness. Are we one of them, or are you supporting these people? I take my hat off and thank God for the lives of these people who have given themselves to carry out various acts of kindness to help meet people's needs, serve humanity, make notable difference, and provide a better today and tomorrow for the underprivileged and underrepresented. I also appreciate the efforts of people that support them as well.

This is what we are meant to do as Christians; to be salt in the world. If the salt loses its savouriness, then it is not useful anymore and therefore worthless. It is my sincere prayer that we as believers stand up and begin to show these acts of gentleness and kindness in our world. The world is not interested in how much we know until they begin to see how much we care. We have a lot to give, so let us start giving and caring for the needy, the lost, the dying, and those that require our help. The Bible, in Luke 6:36 says we should be merciful, just as our heavenly Father is merciful. Mathew 5:7 says, *"Blessed* (happy) *are the merciful: for they shall obtain mercy."* The Holy Spirit will give us grace and the ability that enables us to exhibit attributes of mercy and compassion, if we are interested in helping others. I would like to sound a note of caution here; in all our acts of kindness, mercy and gentleness, and compassion, we should be led by the inner witness of the Holy Spirit. The reason for this is so that our time and resources are targeted and aligned with the will, plan, and purpose of God. Jesus, Himself, said that He did everything the Father told Him to do, and did not do anything of His own. He was directed and instructed to do the good works.

We should be kind to those who seem less deserving of our kindness; if we are only kind to those who are kind to us, then we are not true imitators of Christ. Luke 6:31-35 shows us that 'as you would prefer people to treat you, treat them the same'. If we only love those who love us, if we only do good to those who do good to us, and if we only love our friends, how are we different from the people of the world? ***What characterises us as Christians, as children of God, is to be imitators of Christ and that is why we are called Christians.*** Christian means Christ-like. Verse 35 tells us to love our enemies, be kind, be gentle, and do good so that someone derives benefit from it. It encourages us to lend our time and resources, expecting and hoping for nothing back in return, and then our reward will be great; by so doing we are affirming we are children of God, for He is kind to the ungrateful, selfish, wicked, and less deserving.

According to 1 Corinthians 13:4, love is kind and gentle. Kindness has a role to play in every area of our lives and especially if we are Christians. If we lack kindness and we want our lives to radiate the God-type of kindness, we should ask the giver of the fruit – the Holy Spirit – to help us to bear the fruit of kindness and gentleness in our relationships with others.

We should not confuse gentleness or kindness for weakness, the reverse is the case; it is a great strength of character, and it exhibits and shows that we can operate in wisdom and understanding.

3. Goodness – this is the state of being good, kind, virtuous, benevolent, generous, and God-like in life and conduct. How will the world know that we belong to God if we only do good to those that do good to us? Anyone can do that but as children of God, we are called to be different. We are called to go the extra mile.

We cannot achieve goodness in our power, strength, and might. Goodness is a fruit of the Spirit and can only be achieved with the giver of the fruit if we remain in Him. Ephesians 5:9-10 says that the fruit of the Spirit, consists of goodness, kindness, righteousness, uprightness of heart and truth, and to learn what is pleasing and acceptable to the Lord. If we want our lives to be acceptable to the Lord, then we have no excuse other than to allow the Holy Spirit to bear this fruit in us. Goodness that stands the test of time can only be produced by the help and leadership of the Holy Spirit. We should be good for goodness' sake and our goodness should have direction and bearing. This bearing comes from the Holy Spirit, and not from any other source. Goodness can be misguided, given for personal gain or hidden agenda.

Goodness does not exist alone; you can see that the fruit of the Spirit co-exist, and they overlap. One of them cannot work in isolation; they are mixed and work dynamically well with our faith. 2 Peter 1:5-7 lists the eight spiritual virtues we need to add to our faith, which I will call ***the fruit and faith mix***. We should add to our faith virtue (excellence, goodness), knowledge, temperance (self-control), patience, godliness, kindness, and love. It is a fruitful and worthwhile exercise, to strive for excellence, but not necessarily for perfection in all that we do. We should be diligent and constantly strive to improve and better ourselves, so that our lives will constantly bear fruit and be a testimony to others. It is frustrating to strive for perfection in all that we do, as it cannot be attained on this side of eternity. We are not perfect, and we make mistakes; God is the only person that is perfectly good. Through the power of the Holy Ghost, our Christian walk is b-e-i-n-g perfected daily; this is a journey, and we never arrive until we get to heaven.

When we seek the giver of the fruit of goodness, our lives will begin to bear the fruit, it will be evident, and we take it wherever we go. We will be like goodness waiting to happen. Goodness is the nature of God; the Bible called Jesus the Good Shepherd. The Bible recorded, in Acts 10:38, how God anointed Jesus of Nazareth with the Holy Ghost and with power, and how He went about doing good. If Jesus Christ, God the Son, was dependent on the power of the Holy Spirit during His earthly ministry to do good, how much more would we need the power of goodness to be endowed upon us, by the same Spirit? The goodness of God is being lived and walked out in us by the person of the Holy Spirit, who brings about the manifestations of the fruit of the Spirit and God's promises working in us and through us.

Every act of Goodness is always accompanied by love, patience, and kindness; they all go hand in hand. Acts of goodness is love personified, love in action, on show, and on display. It is merely doing good out of a good heart to please God, with no hidden agenda. We Christians should be a show-piece, God's workmanship, demonstrating the goodness of God in our generation.

The Bible says that if your neighbour is hungry and you have the means to meet their needs but withhold doing that good, of what good is that? The Christian virtues we should demonstrate to the world are wisdom, knowledge, peace, justice, truth, faith, patience, kindness, holiness, love, joy, peace, grace, mercy, goodness, and other attributes of the Trinity.

If we are rooted in the Vine, we will produce the attributes listed in the paragraph above. All trees produce leaves but not all trees produce fruit. We have been called to produce fruit – fruit that will abound/are worthy of emulation – or else we will be cut down. We need pruning to produce good fruit and the Holy Spirit does that work of pruning when allowed to move freely in our lives.

Longsuffering (patience), gentleness (kindness), and goodness are mainly exercised and demonstrated in our outward relationship with others. If we are quick tempered, easily provoked, unkind or selfish, we will be failing in our Christian duties to God, our neighbours, and ourselves. The Holy Spirit works in us to transform us so that we produce fruit of patience, kindness, and goodness.

FRUIT OF THE SPIRIT - THIRD GROUP OF THREE

The third group of three focuses on God working in us and through us, developing personal qualities in us to bless us and to make us a blessing. These are namely ***faithfulness***, ***meekness*** and ***temperance***.

1. Faithfulness – this refers to a loyal, acquired and created principle, which is inward and wholehearted, divinely implanted confidence, assurance, trust, and reliance on God and all that He says. This fruit of faithfulness is referred to in the King James Version of the bible as faith. This fruit talks about the ***faith of character*** (faithfulness), not the believing definition of faith.

We say ***someone is faithful when they are consistently trustworthy and loyal, especially to a person, promise, or duty***. The Bible says God is Faithful and great is His Faithfulness towards us, and He watches over His words and promises to perform them in our lives. The Bible is full of promises that we know God is performing and can perform in our lives. When we say God is Faithful, we are referring to the character of God, and of how He does not fail us because if He says something, He stands by His word and accomplishes it. The Holy Spirit wants to develop this similar trait and character in us, if we let Him. The book of Hebrews, in chapter eleven, lists the heroes of faith, who obtained the promises that God had for them with their faithful conducts.

The Bible talks about us standing before the judgement seat of Christ someday, when we will be judged according to our faithfulness and obedience to the call. In our Christian lives, the Lord will lay, and lays, many things in our hearts that He wants us to accomplish. ***Are you aware and paying attention to those things? Are you faithful in little things?*** The level of your faithfulness will grow when you consciously take your time to develop it with the leading of the Holy Spirit.

Apostle Paul, when he was about to be executed, said in 2 Timothy 4:6-8, "*...I am now ready to be offered, and the time of my departure is at hand. I have fought a good fight, I have finished my course, I have kept the faith. Henceforth, there [awaits]for me a crown of righteousness, which the Lord, the righteous judge, [will award to me] on that day, and not to me only, but also [to those who love and look forward to] his[returning].*" Do you know your calling in life? Apostle Paul knew His call and was faithful to fulfil it. Do you know what the Lord wants you to do? Has he laid it on your heart? Or are you following your own agenda? It is not too late; you can ask the Holy Spirit to help you go back and re-visit the plans that have been ear-marked for you to achieve in life. Notice one thing; Apostle Paul called it the 'good fight of faith'. ***It is called good because we know the outcome***, as we follow the master planner, by remaining in the vine.

Our Lord Jesus Christ, in the book of John 17:4 said, "*...I have finished the work which you have given me to do.*" And on the cross of Calvary (John 19:30), He said, "It is finished." I have heard stories of people, who wrote their own obituaries, order of service, picked the songs to be sung at their funerals, put things in order, wrote their wills, and explained how they wanted things to be at their departure, before they died. One thing that came to my mind is that these people believed that they have done what they have been sent to the earth to do, and felt confident, which led to writing the epilogue of their lives. I think this is remarkable. I do not know about you; I would like to exit this world like that as well, someday.

It starts from now if we want such a testimony, legacy, and exit. Would it not be good to know that we are pursuing God's agenda for our lives and not just our own? If we want to be faithful, and to fulfil our God-given purpose and call-in life, we need to enlist the help of the Holy Spirit. If we are rooted in the vine, this will be our testimony as well. We should be God-pleasers, not people-pleasers, to run our race and finish our course with joy in life.

Faithfulness and fidelity are signs of spiritual maturity; it basically means that we have accepted the responsibilities that God has given to us. The Bible says the just (the man with right standing with God) shall live by faith. Are we reading our Bibles and praying every day? ***Are we praying for the will of God or for our will***? These soul-searching questions reveal a heart of faithfulness. The Bible says that if we are faithful in little things, more will be entrusted to us. A good example of this is the parable of the talent found in the book of Matthew 25:14-30. The Lord wants to accomplish so much through us, and it starts with daily acts of obedience and faithfulness in little and big things.

As the fruit of faithfulness is being developed in us, we will notice increased faithfulness in our daily lives and conduct. We need to be people of integrity; when we say something, we should keep to our word and promises. We should be people that can be trusted and relied upon, if not how can we say that we are imitators of Christ, and who will we be likened to? If we cannot be truthful, faithful, and honest to people we see every day, how can we be faithful to our call and to God, who we do not see? We Christians have a tall order and a reputation to live up to; how can we win the world over to Christ if there is no difference in their lives and ours? You are not alone in this battle; the Holy Spirit will help us to fight this good fight of faith and we know the outcome if we are rooted firmly in Him.

2. Meekness – this is the disposition to be gentle, kind, indulgent, evenly balanced in tempers and passions, and patient in suffering injuries without feeling a spirit of revenge. It is power under control, and strength under discipline.

It took God forty years to develop meekness in Moses; he was brought up in a privileged background, was a Prince in

Egypt, and was influential, rich, high-minded, mighty, power-drunk, and overzealous. He learned submissiveness through what he went through. Can you imagine a Prince, brought up with a silver spoon, being in the desert for forty years? When his days of grooming in the desert were over, he was re-launched and came back to Pharaoh's palace, this time with meekness and not arrogance.

When the Children of Israel were disobedient in the wilderness, God said to Moses, "I will wipe them out and start a new generation under you from your loins." Moses pleaded with God not to destroy them and that earned him the title of the meekest man on earth.

It took that long to break Moses and bring his will under God. So, you see, God needs our will to accomplish what He wants to do in our lives. Without our consent and cooperation, it will be impossible for the Holy Spirit to accomplish God's plans and purpose in our lives.

Peter was harsh, brash, and very implosive, reacting spontaneously without giving much thought to his actions. It took the taming of the Holy Spirit to change him. Peter, by not resisting the transforming power of the Holy Spirit in his life, went through some shifting and adjusting experiences that changed him and made him the leader of the disciples after the death of Jesus

What should we say about Joseph, Abraham, Apostle Paul, and others? They had their fair share of waiting and humbling as well. When we go through this process, God is birthing something in us. He is shaping us into the way He wants us to be, so that we will not be high-minded but sober and considerate.

Matthew 5:5 says, *"Blessed* (happy and spiritually prosperous) *are the meek* (the mild hearted people), *for they shall inherit the earth."* The Bible talks about God waiting patiently for the harvest, for the precious fruit of the earth in James 5:7. With meek attitudes, we can begin to make this prophecy a reality.

We should not confuse meekness for weakness; in fact, the opposite is true because meek people are very strong people. Meekness is a great character of strength. It is power under control. Most meek people have the power to do things but choose not to do them. They look at the long-term consequences and not the immediate gratification, and for them, the end is what justifies the means.

Sometimes, when we are awaiting a promise from God and it is taking longer than we expect, we should take it as a learning experience; the Lord is birthing, moulding, and shaping character in us. It took Joseph 13 years from his dreams to the pit, prison, and finally the palace. If Joseph had not gone through those experiences, do you think that he would have been the competent, effective, and wise Prime Minister that we read and learn from today?

It took Moses 40 years from the palace to the desert and back to the palace again as a leader who delivered the Children of Israel from the oppression in Egypt. It took Abraham 15 years from when he was promised Isaac, to the actual manifestation when his wife Sarah was past the age of childbearing.

Meekness is one of the fruit that focuses on our self-development internally, with outward manifestation. When the Holy Spirit wants to birth something in us, He takes us through this process of dying to self and helps us to focus and build reliance and dependency on Him. If we are patient through this process, we will come out better than when we went in and there are many lessons to be learned through this process. Not everything with God is spontaneous; sometimes we need to go through a process of refining and re-firing. The fruit of the Spirit is certainly character forming and does not happen overnight, as we know. It takes remaining in the vine to form, mould and shape this character and attitude in us.

Jesus was described as the Lion and the Lamb; He is the ultimate example and embodiment of meekness. Meekness means knowing when to draw the line, knowing when to be a leader, and knowing when to be subservient. Jesus was also described as the servant King. Being the servant King shows great power under control. Meekness is also knowing when to apply the brakes by using the carrot and stick approach. Jesus knew when to take His rightful place and act as the Lion of the tribe of Judah and when to act as a Lamb, caring and loving. Meekness is being able to demonstrate these attributes.

This kind of meekness, inward strength, and character moulding does not drop on us like ripe cherries; it is usually borne out of adversity, spiritual battlefields, and battlegrounds. The Bible says that Jesus learned obedience through the things He suffered. When He was being taken through the route of the cross, He opened not His mouth. Jesus displayed great love and power under discipline, at Calvary. He demonstrated the love He has for us by laying down His life for the sins of the world. He also demonstrated power under control, by not stopping those who taunted Him or the process that led to the cross.

As the Lord has developed meekness in the life of the people we have mentioned under this heading, so does the Holy Spirit want to develop the same strength, discipline, character, attitude, and control of power in us, called meekness.

3. Temperance – this is self-control, a moderation in the indulgence of appetites and passions. It also means knowing when to stop and not overdo things. Some people will say they cannot control themselves but with the help of the Holy Spirit, we can. I cannot over emphasise that He is our Helper, sent to dwell in us to help our frailties and limitations.

We all have a measure of self-control in us. A good example is when someone is asked to put their hand in a fire. We refrain from doing it because we know that fire burns. That is self-control in practice. We sometimes claim or hide under the cloak of saying, "I cannot control myself." This excuse will not work all the time because we have help at hand. Self-control can be exercised in every area of our lives, and we cannot be using excuses such as, "It just happens," "I was not thinking," or "it is a reflex action." We are all creatures of habit, but we can break bad habits and learn new ones. It might take time for our minds to get used to the new way of behaving, but if we persevere, the newly acquired good habits will soon become a lifestyle. We cannot achieve self-control by our own power; we have the Almighty power of the Holy Spirit to help us.

Apostle Paul's popular sermon on self-control is found in 1 Corinthians 9:24, when he said that everyone takes part in a race, but only one person wins the prize. He said we should not just run for running's sake but run to win the prize. To achieve this, certain things should take place; we need to get into a strict regime of training and we need to know what to forsake and what to sacrifice, all for the sake of winning the prize.

I was told that sports people begin to practice for the next Olympics as soon as one is finished, and there are four years between each Olympic event. Most sports people, to win, spend more time practicing than doing any other thing. The ability to be able to say no to some things and yes to certain things is called self-control.

If we want to make heaven our home, we will have to exercise an element of self-control. Paul, in the same verse of scripture, said that runners who get into this strict regime of training do so to win a crown prize that will perish. When we exercise self-control in every area of our lives with the help of the Holy Spirit, we obtain a crown, a reward, and a prize that will last forever and will not perish.

Paul urges us to embark on this plan of self-control and self-development, so that we do not run aimlessly but have a goal and a plan. In this way, we would not be like fighters beating the air. ***We should run the race to win and knock out any obstacles to our progress***. We should be able to exercise self-control, with the help of the Holy Spirit in all areas.

In verse 27, Paul says that he keeps his body under and brings it into subjection; in other words, he will not teach others how to apply self-control if he cannot apply it himself, and, in the end, lose the reward if self-control is not applied. It is easy for us to see the wrong in others and not in ourselves. That is why it is important to have a goal, to have check and balance plans, and to have the Holy Spirit act as our umpire, so we can run and finish the race that is set before us.

We need to exercise self-control in dealing with others and ourselves. Overdoing anything which is bad for you indicates a lack of self-control. Even in our thinking, we can exercise self-control because it affects people mentally if self-control is not applied in this area. ***We should be able to control our thoughts and actions.*** We need to be temperate, not blowing hot and cold at the same time, such that people do not know where they stand with us. Temperance and self-control mean being even-tempered.

The self-control, and temperance, that we need to guard our lives, spiritually, physically, emotionally, financially, and mentally, can only be found in the Person of the Holy Spirit when our lives stay rooted in the vine.

Faithfulness, meekness, and self-control are about self-development, unlike the first group of three or the second group of three, which looks at our relationship with others. This third group of three focuses on ourselves and what we need to do to develop ourselves inwardly. This process can be described as the Holy Spirit working in us, so He can work through us.

FRUIT OF THE SPIRIT RULE

There is no law that prohibits or is against the fruit of the Spirit. No law can condemn one that exhibits the fruit of the Spirit because the fruit of the Spirit is not a state of lawlessness, but a state of lawfulness and the law only condemns sin, not righteousness. To manifest the fruit, there should be dying to self. When seeds fall to the ground, they die and are buried in the ground. The seeds die before they begin to grow and produce fruit. If we are not dead to the things of this world, our lives will merely produce works of the flesh, which are opposite to the fruit of the Spirit. Fruitlessness is a result of us not being crucified and not yielding to the Holy Spirit. The purpose of our existence after salvation is to bear fruit.

After salvation comes the Christian life to lead and the fruit of the Spirit to bear. Shallow Christians will not enjoy the better part of their Christian race. What happens when things do not go according to our plan after salvation? Do we quit, run away, and hide and forever remain a babe in the Lord, or do we use the opportunity to gain experience as we grow and develop our faith?

When we are going through tough times, which we all do, the Holy Spirit will supply the strength and courage that we need to go on. When we learn to surrender the adverse times and situations to Him, in the long/short run, we will be able to testify to the fact that He is the very help in time of need.

The Bible calls Him our Helper and that is what He is and does at the point of our needs. Turn the need over to Him and He will help you to cope better in the situation, you will have joy and peace of mind, knowing that He is in control. The Bible, in Romans 14:17, says, "*...the kingdom of God is not meat and drink.*" In other words, it is not just about food and outward religion but righteousness (right living), peace, and joy in the Holy Ghost. On the one hand, we have the lust of the flesh and on the other hand, we have the fruit of the Spirit. The only way to overcome the lust of the flesh and bear the fruit of the Spirit is when our ways of life are sold-out to the Holy Spirit.

We need to take time to critically examine and take an inventory of the fruit that our lives are yielding. ***Is your life yielding the fruit of the Spirit or the fruit of the flesh (disobedience)?***

13

DAILY LIVING AND THE HOLY SPIRIT

OUR ULTIMATE LEADER

The title of this book came to me on my way to work one morning. I thought about it for some minutes and after a while, I began to reason my way out of it. Over time, it seemed to me that I have become an expert at reasoning my way out of things, especially if it does not make logical sense at the time, or if I do not fully understand it. Most times, when I receive promptings or an urge from the Holy Spirit, my human-reasoning gear always comes alive, and I will try to use my limited human reasoning to analyse what has just been deposited in my spirit. So, when it came to the book title, I discounted it straight away as it did not make sense or had any bearing on my situation or circumstances at the time. This kind of approach does not work because when we receive a message in our spirit, our minds cannot fully comprehend it straightaway. It takes some time for our minds to catch up with our spirit.

The Lord knows our tomorrow better than we know our past. When our tomorrow is dropped into our spirit, we cannot figure it out just like that and we find ourselves saying things like, "This is just out of the blue. Where did this thought come from?"

We have two choices when we receive 'out of the blue' promptings. We can either discount it or pray about it and ask the Lord for further light. Have you ever wondered sometimes, when just minding your own business, how a thought just drops into your mind saying to do something? Sometimes, you find yourself rehearsing answers or solutions to a problem that has not yet arisen. The solution or scenario will just come to your mind, and you will be wondering where this came from; then after a while, the situation will present itself in real life and you will say, "No wonder I was thinking about this the other day." It is the Lord's way of preparing us for what lies ahead. We can also call it the sovereign act of God.

I had one of these sovereign acts on my way to work that morning. I was prompted to write a book about the Ministry of the Holy Spirit. Straightaway, my mind went into reasoning mode, and I said to myself, "There are many books about the Holy Spirit in the bookshops, so why should I write another one? I am not qualified to write about the Holy Spirit. I do not know enough about the subject. Who will read the book anyway? I do not know what to write!" and the list went on and on like that. This was my way of making excuses and talking myself out of the assignment. I do not know about you, but I think I am a world champion at this sort of thing, or does your record beat mine? All these excuses and more kept going round and round, like a broken record in my head. It almost became like torture, carrying the vision and not doing anything. Believe me, it takes a lot of energy and strength to just be thinking about something and then do nothing about it. It is better to utilise that energy to carry out the assignment than just contemplate it. Someone said worrying is a waste of nervous energy. I can concur with that and I'm sure that you can too.

What I did not realise at the time, was that it takes time to develop an idea and that once I set my mind to it, the materials would come and of course, there is always help available from the Holy Spirit. I was looking at the negatives and focusing on the impossibilities instead of the positives and the power of the Holy Spirit. Even when I embarked on carrying out the vision, I will not say it was the easiest of things to do, as I was still being bombarded with thoughts. From time to time, the thoughts would come into my head, "Do you know what you are doing? Are you not just wasting your time? Should this time not be spent doing something more worthwhile? Who will read the book anyway? Do you think anyone is interested in what you have to say?" I was just being bombarded left, right and centre. One thing that helped me during this time was the strong conviction that I had on the inside. I have had many moments when I would stop writing for weeks and then I would go back again and resume my writing.

What cemented my thoughts about starting to write this book was that during that period, I was believing the Lord for so many things in my life. I would religiously pray on most mornings and commit my day to His hands. So, when the thought came to write this book, I knew it was from the Holy Spirit. At this stage, the notion of writing a book was not new to me anymore as I knew I would write a book/s someday. Up until then, I had been carrying the vision of writing for seventeen years. I had many topics and titles come to my mind, but I was not really committed to following through. They were just ideas in my head, which I knew I should be doing something about but did very little. When the impression came to me on the way to work that day, to make this book my very first one to be published, I struggled with the idea because I had kind of started writing and gathering materials for other titles at that time. I would slot in one hour here, two hours there, mainly in the early hours of the morning. So, I was not thinking about making this book my first, as I was still collating materials for the one that I thought would be my first book.

I had learned at that time to distinguish the voice of the Holy Spirit from my 'head voice'. So, I was pretty sure it was not my head, and it was the idea of the Holy Spirit to make this my first book. I decided not to struggle with the thoughts anymore and just settle for obedience. As soon as I got to my office desk that morning, I grabbed a pen and paper and wrote down the title, and asked the Holy Spirit for guidance, help, and direction. I said, "Lord, if you have impressed this on my heart, you have a way to bring it to pass." With total reliance on His ability, I embarked on the mission to put pencil to paper. If I tell you it was easy and all the materials that I needed were at my beck and call, then I would be lying to you. It was a very challenging venture and involved a lot of hard work.

If you find yourself struggling with what the Lord has placed on your heart, even if you do not know it is the Lord that placed it there at the time, but you have a burning passion to do something, my advice to you would be not to waste another second thinking about it. Please start straight away, and as you obey the call, you will find a route; an opening will emerge as you embark on the project, and please make sure you enlist the help and direction of the Holy Spirit. I tried to reason my way out of writing for too long. I was like Gideon, asking for one sign or the other before I ventured (read this story in Judges 6:17-21, 36-40). I would say, "Lord, if you want me to write, give me signs and let people make reference to my writing." The Lord must have really felt sorry for me because true to my prayer request, when I attended church and other services, read a book, listened to Christian radio shows, or watched television programmes, seeking confirmation, the Lord would speak through the various channels. The Lord was so kind to me that not even one person I spoke to discouraged me; the Lord must have known that I was waiting for someone to do that. I thought my husband would say for me to concentrate on my career but when I told him about my plans, he just said for me to 'go for it' and that 'if the Lord lays it on my heart, it is not my problem to bring it to pass'. During this same period, the pastor of the church I was attending then called me one day out of the blue and said, "What has happened to the book you said you were going to write?" I told him I was working on it; I did not tell him about the struggles.

Part of my problem was my job. I did not realise that my job provided a haven; I felt so secure and comfortable in the job. The income was coming in, and there was enough to spend, give and save, so I was complacent, and I could not really be bothered to venture into becoming an author. Well, the job ended one day when my employment contract was not renewed, and I was made redundant. That was when reality dawned on me, and I saw it as a sign. Even though I started to look for alternative employment straightaway, I decided to prioritise my writing. If you are reading this book and you can relate to looking for cues everywhere, the time is now. You have had enough cues, and it is time to start.

Most of my employment was either a temporary or a fixed-term contract. At this time, I was working on a fixed-term contract, and what I would usually do was secure another before one contract ended but, on this occasion, it did not happen that way. When the contract was ending, I was told that they might call me back in a few weeks' time but in the meantime, I could take the period of inactivity as an unpaid holiday. I decided to register with recruitment agencies and at the same time, started to apply for other jobs, just in case I was not called back. I saw the break as a window of opportunity, so I made up my mind to go to the library as if I were going to work (9:00 a.m. to 5:00 p.m.) and concentrate on writing the book. I gathered all pads and pieces of paper I had been jotting things on and went to work on my writing.

I did one thing that even surprised me; as I became engrossed in my writing, I prayed that the recruitment agencies I had registered with and the jobs I had applied for should not call me for the next two weeks, so that I could make significant headway with this book. I can only say God was faithful in answering my prayer request. I was not called to start any job until three weeks later and the temporary job I started afterward was not onerous, so I had enough time to devote to the writing of this book and developing other ideas. In case you are wondering if my old employer called me back, they did not.

The Holy Spirit becomes our ultimate leader when we allow Him to lead, stir and direct our life commitments, ambitions, affairs, cares, and worries into His capable hands. Obedience is the key to walking with Him. It is in obedience that we tend to see the bigger picture, as we take one step at a time. It is in taking these steps that the doors that we never imagined begin to emerge.

You might say, "Why do I need the Holy Spirit? I can do all this by myself, without someone directing and dictating to me from the inside." That is true, we have our natural abilities. The abilities given by the Holy Spirit are supernatural abilities and cannot be compared to our natural abilities. With supernatural abilities, we can accomplish far more beyond what we can ever imagine or think. This is not to say that the Holy Spirit encourages laziness; He requires reliance on Him. Believe me, that is hard work because the natural tendency of us humans is to depend on ourselves and our abilities, skills, and talent, and not acknowledge the giver.

Walking with the Holy Spirit is a partnership-building relationship. It involves God using the gifts and talents he gave us and Him working them in us and through us. In addition to that, there is a deep-rooted and rewarding satisfaction in living this way because you know that you are doing what you are created for and living out the will, purpose, and plan of God, for your lives. People are forever looking for satisfaction, approval, and acceptance; this can only truly and genuinely be achieved when we live in a manner that acknowledges the author of creation and the giver of talents and gifts. It does not matter if we are rich or poor, successful, or unsuccessful, famous, or notorious, down, and out, up and flying, or have ideas or no ideas, what really matters is that every person wants to fill the void they feel inside. This void has been put in us from creation when God breathed into us, and we became living souls. The void cannot be filled any old way nor be found in anything or anybody other than in the presence of our creator, who lives in us in the person of the Holy Spirit.

HOW DO WE HEAR HIS VOICE?

When we have a relationship with someone and get to know them well, we can distinguish their voice among a crowd of people. This also applies to the person of the Holy Spirit; when we have taken the time to develop and build a relationship with Him, when He speaks, we will know. I once sat with a group of people at a party having a lovely conversation. One woman stood up, went out and came back in to retake her seat, and re-joined the conversation. Our conversation drifted to talking about how to know when the Holy Spirit is speaking to us. The woman who got up and later came back said, "Whilst we were talking, I heard my son crying, so I went up to find out why he was crying." She added that she did not see anybody else's head turn or even flinch even though she knew that she was not the only mother here. The point she was making is that if you know a person so well, when you hear their voice, you will know.

If we are amid a crowd and someone that we know calls us, we will be able to identify their voice and say so-and-so is calling me, without even seeing their faces. The reason why we can distinguish their voice is that we know them, and we have been around them enough times to discern their voices.

There was an occasion when a friend came to visit me, at a time when there was another friend staying with us, as our guest. My husband and our guest were chatting in the corridor and had left the front door slightly ajar, as they were about to go out. My friend was about to leave as well, so she stood by the sitting-room door, and I was in the sitting room. I heard another person's voice, so I said to my friend to see if there was somebody else with my husband, but she said, "No, it is the same person he has been talking to." I heard the voice again and questioned if she was sure it was the same person. She said, "You can come and take a look yourself; it is the same person he had been talking to all the while." As I got up to prove to my friend that it was another person, we saw my guest coming down the stairs; my friend screamed and said she thought it was the same person all along. You see, the two of them are brothers and they look so much alike. She could not tell the difference in looks and obviously could not tell the difference in their voices because she does not know them nor has she built enough of a relationship with them to be able to tell the little things that set them apart.

The only way that we can discern the voice of the Holy Spirit is by spending time with Him. How do we spend time with the Holy Spirit? We spend time with the Holy Spirit when we communicate with Him about anything and everything, when we allow His indwelling presence to take a foothold in our life, by allowing Him to captivate our thoughts and attention, when we take time to build a strong lasting relationship with Him, and by communing and fellowshipping constantly with Him. When we make this a deliberate habit and pattern for our lives, believe me, when He speaks, we will be able to discern His voice. There are many voices all around us, competing for our attention. Which one are we listening to and allowing to shape our thoughts and directions in life?

AUDIBLE OR STILL VOICE

This reminds me of the story of Elijah in the 1 Kings 20, when Elijah was fleeing from Jezebel. Elijah was a prophet that God used mightily and when Jezebel heard that Elijah had eliminated the false prophets, she promised to avenge their death. Elijah ran away and desperately wanted to hear the next instructions from the Lord. The word of the Lord then came to Elijah and told him to go to the mountain and the Lord will pass by. When Elijah got to the mountain, he experienced a great strong wind that broke the rock into pieces, but the Lord was not in the wind. After that, an earthquake engulfed the mountain, but the Lord was not in the earthquake either. After the earthquake, there was fire, but the Lord was not in the fire. Finally, after the fire, came a still small voice, and the Lord spoke to him through the small, still voice.

There are other instances; for example in Exodus 20:18-21, when the voice of the Lord was revealed in thundering, lightning, trumpet noise, and through the smoky mountain. We cannot choose the mode, medium, and method through which we want the Holy Spirit to speak to us. Sometimes it might be a small, still, inner witness, a knowing, or an impression on our hearts. At other times, it might be an audible voice.

The Lord has spoken to me in many ways, as He chooses, and I am sure He has to you as well. To my recollection, I have encountered only one vivid audible voice and numerous inward witnesses, knowing, promptings, small still voices, etc. I would like to relay a story of the audible voice experience.

I have had many roles and worked with many organisations. At one particular place of employment, we were informed of staff redundancies. Posts were being deleted and some roles were restructured and we were informed that it would involve everyone's contract. In a bid to beat the restructuring and redundancy process, I decided to apply for other jobs out of panic, which I believed was a reasonable thing to do in the circumstance. I was on my way to work one day and had parked my car in the parking lot, got out of the car, and as I was about to shut the door, I heard an audible voice that said to me to stop applying for jobs. I quickly turned around to see if there was anyone behind me but there was no one there. I immediately knew that it was the Holy Spirit because this matter had really been bothering me and had consumed most of my thought-time. For all I know, the Holy Spirit may have been trying to communicate to me through different channels, but I was too preoccupied to hear or listen. For one, maybe He had been trying to impress it on my heart, or secondly, had sent people to advise me but due to the cares of life and anxiety about the job situation, I was too busy and worked up to listen. Sometimes, we can block the channel of communication with the Holy Spirit for different reasons, like:

1. We are angry about the unpleasant situation happening to us.
2. We do not want to listen.
3. We think God has gone away on vacation and left us hanging dry.

4. We want to be left alone to wallow in self-pity (the 'why me, why me?' syndrome).
5. We want God to speak in a certain way that we are used to, and he has not chosen that medium; for example, through dreams.

I tell you something; it was good that I hearkened to the voice. I did not quite understand it, but I decided to quit applying for jobs. There is always a master plan that we do not know. I was not made redundant; the restructuring took place and I was given more responsibility. I also did not have to be re-interviewed for my post and it was handed to me on a silver platter. Additionally, I gained a lot more experience that helped me afterward in my career progression.

In my experience, the Holy Spirit does not give us goose-bumps when He speaks or causes the hair to rise on our body or induces an eerie feeling; often, He speaks to our spirit in a small, still voice, and sometimes you might mistake Him for your own thought. ***He speaks to our spirit because He wants us to own 'the' thoughts***. His voice is gentle and firm, as He stirs us in the right direction. Sometimes, we might find ourselves saying, "Where does this thought come from?" Sometimes, it might just be a knowing, and we know without any doubt, what to do or say. When we are in tune, we will pick up the signal.

In Elijah's case, conveyed earlier, He spoke in a small, still voice. In my case, He spoke in an audible voice from my mind, loud enough for me to hear it with my ears. As mentioned before, we cannot dictate the mode and way that we want the Holy Spirit to speak to us. He will speak to us in a way that He chooses and prefers; we must remember that He is our sovereign leader.

YIELDING TO HIS DIRECTIONS

I am sure that many of us will find that when we are driving or even walking, sometimes the Holy Spirit will say stop, turn right, turn left, go this way, go that way and we find ourselves struggling to yield. We have an inner toss of will because, to the logical mind, we do not see any reason to follow the promptings or go in a different direction. It can happen if we are a student studying for an examination, or a worker or businessperson preparing a report for a business venture. It might even happen when we need to take or make a major or minor decision in life. If we take our time to respond accordingly, even when our mind is fighting against it, we will always reap the reward. From my experience, if I do not see any logical reason to follow the promptings, I have learned to follow the strong sense of peace that I feel deep within me.

When we yield to the promptings of the Holy Spirit, the rewards are not always apparent. As human beings, our tendencies are to get the full picture or see the benefits before we embark. But the faith walk is that of not knowing or seeing the full picture and as we move, the Lord will reveal more and more. Abraham was told to lead his kindred to a land that God would show him. He obeyed and the rest, as they say, is history; the account of this story is recorded in the book of Genesis.

An example of someone that springs to mind, in connection with obedience and yielding to His directions, is a certain clergyman. This minister, by the inward witness of the Holy Spirit, was instructed to buy a wasteland that nobody wanted. He paid some ridiculously small amount of money for the land because it was in a swampy region, and nobody wanted anything to do with it. Years later, crude oil was found on the site and the clergyman later sold the land for a handsome sum.

Writing this book was because of listening to the leading and promptings of the Holy Spirit. I have been carrying this vision of writing with me for seventeen years before I put pen to paper, as narrated earlier. I will never forget that it was sometime around December 1990; I had just given my life to the LORD properly, a few months before. I was on a platform at New Cross station going to Charing Cross and it was as if I had (from nowhere) an impression in my heart that said, "I would like you to write a book." It was an inward witness, and I knew that it was not my imagination. I had just given my life to the LORD and the fire and zeal that accompanied my experience was something else. I knew, without a shadow of a doubt, that it was the LORD talking because I had been spending so much time in His presence daily. Naturally speaking, knowing myself, I will shy away from anything like writing a book of any description. The first thing that came to my mind was, "What will I write about?" And here I am seventeen years later, obeying the call. Publishing the book was another matter, as narrated in the Preface section of this book.

Has the Holy Spirit impressed something on your heart, and you have not yet yielded? Let this act as a challenge for you. I had to ask myself a critical question: What if I were to meet the LORD face to face and He says to me, "Why did you not do what I ask you to do?" I will have no excuse. I am mindful of that because we are blessed to be a blessing and when the LORD has endowed us with a gift, it is not just for us, but to benefit humanity. So please, do what the Lord has laid upon your heart and follow the passion in your spirit.

If you find yourself reading this book and you are a non-believer, with a burning passion in your heart, especially for something that will be of benefit to humanity, I will say embark on it and ask the Holy Spirit to come into your life and into your heart to help you to accomplish the venture.

I once heard a story of a man that wanted to do the will of God so badly. He woke up one morning and said, "LORD, help me to do your will, wherever you say I will go." After praying, he was quickened in his spirit to go to the supermarket and without question, he got dressed, grabbed his car keys and off he went. He followed the promptings of the Holy Spirit as to what to buy, paid for the goods, and got back into his car. Still following the Holy Spirit's direction, he drove downtown, parked the car, walked down an alleyway, stopped in front of a house, and knocked on the door.

As he was knocking on the door, he could hear the voices of people roaring inside the house. When they opened the door, they were still quarrelling and yelling at themselves. He handed the shopping to them and said, "The LORD said to give this to you." It so transpired that the family had a baby and young child in the house, and they could not even afford to buy milk for the baby. The husband and wife were arguing about the lack of money for groceries when he knocked on the door. At times, when we receive promptings, we cannot make head or tail of it. It can be for something that might seem so insignificant to us. If we ignore the voice, we might later pay for the consequences or deprive someone of being blessed. On the other hand, it might be for something so significant that we do not know what to do or where to turn. The Bible says, "He that searches the heart knows what is in heart of the spirit." **When we do not know, the Holy Spirit knows;** it is an act of obedience to follow and yield to His promptings.

HOLY SPIRIT AT OUR DISPOSAL

The Holy Spirit is at our disposal at any time, all the time, to help us to find our way in life. As I said before, it might be for something that we see as insignificant, or it can be for something significant that we will run to Him for help and directions. Examples of these might be when we are about to make major decisions in life like marriage, career, business ventures, raising children, general help, and guidance. I have learned to consult the Holy Spirit regarding my career path and other issues in life. Earlier on in my Christian life, I would not say my prayers were targeted or patterned after the will of God. When I believed God for a job, for instance, I would just say, "God please give me a job." I have learned to be more specific and to incorporate 'if it is thy will' into my prayers. I do not want to get it wrong or waste my time on unfruitful ventures. I will say, "LORD, is this your plan for me at this point in time, I do not want to run ahead of you. Please hold me by the hand and lead me, I so desperately need your promptings, leading, and directions."

When you say prayers like this, you should mean it and be prepared because sometimes, it will be tested. The Lord leaves things, sometimes up to the last minute, before He answers. Have you ever had that experience? You have prayed beforehand and waited for leading and direction and the answer comes when your patience has been thoroughly tested, stretched, and worn out.

This reminds me of the case of a friend and a lost file. A friend was handed a file by his boss to keep during an office move. This was in the days when files were not stored on computers and every office had filing cabinets. After the move, his boss needed to prepare for a meeting and asked for the file. They still had not unpacked everything yet, so they had crates everywhere. Among the many crates, it was impossible to know in what crate the file was located. The boss would ask for the file every day as my friend searched and prayed to find the file. On the day of the meeting, the boss requested for the file by a certain time. My friend prayed and said to the Holy Spirit, "I need your help right now because I will be in big trouble if I cannot find the file."

My friend then went into the room where all the crates were and carried on searching, as in previous days. The Holy Spirit impressed on his heart to put his hand in a crate. Without hesitation, my friend obeyed, and **bingo** pulled out the file. Nobody could have had that foreknowledge among all the crates, to know exactly where the file was. The most amazing thing was that my friend did not even rummage through the crate; it was a simple act of obedience; he put his hand in without even looking and pulled out the right file. The Holy Spirit is at our beck and call to help us. When we do not obey His promptings, we underestimate and limit His working and leading in our lives.

HE WANTS TO COMMUNE AND COMMUNICATE WITH US

Can you imagine two people living in the same house, sharing the same room and still having little or no communication between them? We sometimes live like this with the Holy Spirit. Some of us do not even know that He resides inside us, let alone acknowledge His presence. He wants to commune and communicate with us; He longs for our relationship.

He is God living in us; we need to know, understand, and acknowledge this fact. He wants that dialogue, acknowledgment and to be close to us. Believe me, if we consult Him as we should, we will not take the wrong steps or make the wrong decisions. I challenge you today to take this step of acknowledging and consulting Him about everything in your life and I promise that you will see how He will respond with love, care, and deep compassion.

This is one relationship that we cannot afford to do without; we need Him as much as we breathe in the fresh air. Yet, we give ourselves heartaches and headaches by not communing with Him. We suffer because of ignorance. Even the law court says ignorance is not an excuse. Please do not be ignorant or suffer in silence. Hand over every detail of your life to Him; He cares like you never know and longs to be involved in your life.

TRIALS AND CHALLENGES

You might ask the question, "Why do I have trials and challenges?" You see, we are overcomers, and we are born to overcome. John 16:33 says that in this life, we will have trials, but we should not worry because He has already overcome the world. We have the power within us, in the person of the Holy Spirit, to help us overcome challenges, and trying times. The Bible says, in 1 John 4:4, that, "Greater is He that is in us than he that is in the world." To grow in our Christian faith, there are bound to be challenges, adversities, and trials; the Bible even says so. But our consolation is that He has obligated Himself to meet and take care of all our needs. He said He will not give us challenges that we cannot bear and that He has already made a way of escape for every trying and challenging time (1Corinthians 10:13). When we ask the Holy Spirit for help, we can be assured that He is there to rescue, encourage, support, and comfort us. He has the appropriate strategies and rescue packages.

I can give many instances when this has happened in my life, and I am sure that you can think of many more yourself. There was an instance in the book of 1 Samuel 30:6, where the Bible recorded that David encouraged himself in the Lord. The background to this story is found in the preceding chapters; David was fleeing from Saul, the then King of Israel. David fled Israel with his family and six hundred men and their families. He found favour with the Philistines and was given a city, called Ziklag.

Historically, the Philistines and Israel were always at loggerheads and constantly waging wars against one another. So, David found himself stuck between a rock and a hard place on one of the occasions when the Philistines were about to wage yet another war on the Israelites. In a bid to show appreciation and allegiance to the Philistines, David gathered his men that fled with him to join the armies of the Philistines, and to fight against Israel. When the roll call was made, David and his men were spotted amongst the armies for the battle. The Philistines called David and advised him and his men not to take part in the fight, as they were not too sure of the side that they would take in the heat of the battle, when it came down to fighting against their fellow Israelites.

The captain thanked David and his men for their loyalty and told them to go back home. This whole event took three days from when David and his men left to prepare for the war, to when they were told not to bother. When David arrived back home with his men, to the city of Ziklag that was given to him by the Philistines, they discovered that their enemies had invaded their city and burnt it down with fire and taken all their families captive. David's men were so upset that they thought of stoning David.

David was devastated and deserted, and he was by himself, thinking about what to do. He did not know what to do as the men would not reason with him and blamed him for the mishap. The Bible recorded here that David sat down alone, thinking of the next strategy and that he encouraged himself in the Lord. He took time out to seek the face of the Lord and he was encouraged and was given the next line of command that led to victory and all that was lost, was recovered.

What fascinates me about this story is that when the chips are down, and we are stuck and don't know what to do, it is not the end of the matter. We have the *paraclete*, in the person of the Holy Spirit inside us, to comfort, lead, help, direct and guide us.

Paraclete, as previously explained, is a Greek word that translates as helper, standby, encourager, counsellor, advocate, friend, defender, guide, and one who takes us by the hand and walks with us side by side. David sat down and encouraged himself in the Lord. Those were the times when the Holy Spirit would come upon the people, as opposed to living in them as He does now. The Holy Spirit came upon David, and he was encouraged; he received comfort and solace and the next strategy was revealed to him in a quiet place that led to victory. He inquired of the Lord, and he was told to pursue the invaders. He did and he gained the victory and retrieved all that was stolen from them and more.

When we seek the face and the help of the Divine *paraclete*, in times of trials and challenges, He will always pull through for us, show us the way out, and give us comfort, encouragement, peace, and rest of mind.

Trouble and trying times will come; but when they come, they will surely go, because we have the greater one living inside us. The Bible said that we are overcomers and we have already overcome.

14

THE HOLY SPIRIT AND US

In life, we experience good and bad moments. The strongest moments are the ones that live in our memories forever; other moments are forgotten as soon as they happen. Life is lived on a moment-by-moment basis; we should follow the leading of the Holy Spirit moment-by-moment, as we cannot live more than one moment at a time. Trying to live more than one moment at a time causes confusion, frustration, and misery. We need to make moment-by-moment decisions to yield to the Holy Spirit, to avoid this pitfall. You can say it this way: to be led by the Holy Spirit requires second-by-second, minute-by-minute, hour-by-hour, and day-by-day decision, trust, and obedience.

OUR PLAN VS. HIS PLAN

We cannot instruct the Holy Spirit; our ways are not His ways, and our plans are not His plan, and we cannot put Him inside a box. We need to decide to follow His leading.

He is sovereign; He moves as He wants in our lives according to His will for us. We should always remember that He is God living inside us.

At one of my first attempts at getting started, I woke up one morning and decided that, today, I would make a start at writing this book. I embarked on a plan for the day. I planned to have a two-hour early evening nap when I come back from work, go to a prayer meeting, and when I got back at about 11:00 p.m., I would start to write until about 5:00 a.m. the next morning. I went to the prayer meeting with my husband and when we got back home, my husband went to bed. I put on the television and watched a programme on the Christian channel. One of the presenters (a male minister) on the show prayed and then began prophesying. At that time, I was still welcoming every bit of confirmation and re-confirmation that I could get. As he was prophesying, he said, "Do whatever the Lord has laid on your heart to do, ask Him for help and direction," and he went on to list the things. He said it might be to write a book, a song, etc. You can imagine how I felt and what went through my mind. I said to myself, 'I have chosen the right day to watch this channel,' and I knew that I could not go wrong with the prophecy. Just before the Minister began the prophecy on the programme, I had said a quick prayer. I said, "Holy Spirit, minister to me through him." So, when he mentioned the book, I was excited, elated, and encouraged, and I said to myself, 'Wow, tonight is the night.'

The programme finished at about 12:00 midnight, and I brought out my laptop with the intention of writing until about 5:00 a.m. However, I am talking about my plan here, and not His. As the Holy Spirit would have it, I only wrote two pages with much struggle; there was no inspiration, and the two pages looked so disjointed. It was hard work to finish one sentence, let alone string two coherent sentences in a row. At about 2:00 a.m., I abandoned the effort. I put it down to mental block, being too uptight, and being overexcited about my plan and the sequence of events that evening/night. I was disappointed that my plan did not work. The thought of the Holy Spirit not sanctioning my plans for writing or having a different plan for me for that night did not cross my mind. In disappointment, I shut down the laptop, went to bed, and dozed off.

Two days later, on a Sunday, during my quiet time with the Lord, I kept it short as I was struggling to string two words together. I was fighting and binding the spirit of distraction; I could not concentrate, not for any reason that I could think of, but I am sure you know what I mean if you have been there before. I was just struggling to concentrate and kept on asking myself why. Amidst this toss for concentration, the inspiration started to flow.

Every Sunday morning, for so many years now, I always prepare our Sunday lunch before we go to church. On this Sunday morning, I woke up late and the natural inclination for me would be to start the Sunday lunch. As the inspiration was flowing, I made up my mind not to disturb the flow, especially going on the experience I had two days previously, when I was struggling for words to write. What I am trying to say is that the Holy Spirit moves when He wants. His timing is not our timing. He wants us to recognise and discern the time and the seasons, and decide to yield and flow with Him.

Have you noticed that sometimes the Holy Spirit moves at times that are not so convenient? Sometimes you might be in the bath, driving, cooking, in places that I would deem awkward or even cause awkward moments. Then, you begin to get inspiration and you are saying wait, wait, I need to get pen and paper. I have learned to take my pen and paper with me wherever I go, and I am forever jotting down notes.

To return to my story; going back to that Sunday morning, I was so appreciative and grateful, and I just kept on saying, "Holy Spirit, thank you. I say thank you. Holy Spirit, thank you; I say thank you," because the inspiration was just flowing effortlessly, and I wrote so much.

Another bit of detail about the story that I would like to chip in here is that usually, every Sunday, I wake up around 6:00 a.m., pray for about an hour, and then begin my Sunday chores. On that Sunday, I woke up at about 7:45 a.m. I called two of my children early risers, because sometimes, as early as 6:45 a.m. on a Sunday morning, they are up. One will just come and sit in my lap, saying they are hungry, while the other one will be pulling me in every direction, causing maximum distraction.

On this particular Sunday, these early risers were still in bed by 9:30 a.m., by which time everyone in my household would usually be up. So, it was an unusual Sunday morning for me. The Holy Spirit was showing me how He can change the sequence of events to suit our needs.

I am still talking about our plan versus His plan. If we trust Him, He can do the unusual and make the usual unusual, and vice versa, when we handover the reins of our life to Him. What are the problems, issues, or cares that you are grappling with today? Decide to hand them over to the Holy Spirit; I can assure you that you will be glad you did.

After this experience, which I can only describe as a miracle and an unusual course of events in my household, I asked the Holy Spirit to turn on the tap whenever He wants and help me to yield. We cannot turn Him off and on like a tap or at our own will and leisure; He moves when He wants, and we should learn to tap into the flow and enjoy the benefits. His time is not our time. He has a way and time of doing His things. His timing is perfect, and He is always right on time. I have had similar experiences like this while writing this book and in other areas of my life in general.

It is a good habit to ask the Holy Spirit for help in everything that we do, even if we know how to do it. Do not say, "I can handle this on my own, it does not concern you." What we are forgetting is that He can help us do it faster and better. Look at the athletes; some of them are forever beating their personal best. Product manufacturers develop improved versions, and people are coming up with new inventions and new ways of doing things every day. ***The Holy Spirit can help us to beat our personal best in any area.*** In the service industry, they call it service improvement, transformation, and innovation; people are forever and constantly looking for better, more efficient and most cost-effective ways of doing things. This rule applies in every area and every endeavour of our lives. The Holy Spirit wants to be involved in our everyday finite details. He wants to be involved in what we call significant or insignificant details, and He wants to build a relationship with us; He wants to be our friend and our buddy.

HELP WITH WEAKNESS

There are many things that we like to do but do not think we are able or capable of doing. Formerly, I did not like speaking in public but with the help of the Holy Spirit, and with practice, I am now confident to speak in public. I would avoid any opportunity to speak in public and would become so frightened that my voice would shake and begin to tremble. At other times, I just find myself shedding tears, all because I dreaded the whole ordeal of speaking in front of people. I have attended many job interviews and believe me, interviews are ordeals in themselves for people who do not like them. I tell you; I have come a long way. I am not where I want to be yet, but I am well on my way. I admire many great speakers; Billy Graham is one of them. As you can see, I have set myself a high target and I have some way to go yet. I will ask the Holy Spirit to show me books to read to help me overcome this fear and shyness. Believe me, He has really helped me and is still helping me.

He has led me to workshops where these very issues are being addressed; how to make a personal impact when addressing the public, etc. I have come from not liking public speaking to running group training sessions, delivering presentations, and taking the lead role in other areas. We cannot underestimate the power of the Holy Spirit. He will teach us all things and I mean *all* things if we let him. He wants to be involved in every minute detail of our lives. What is bothering you today? It is not too big or too small for the Holy Spirit to help you resolve.

On a personal level, the Holy Spirit will help us to become better people, better children, better parents, better wives, husbands, students, brothers, sisters, in-laws, mothers, fathers, uncles, aunties, grandparents, friends, colleagues, employers, or employees.

As I was writing this book, I would stop and pray, and say, "Lord you know the target audience, you know the people that will read this book, help me to write what will minister to them, teach them what you want them to know." I knew that I wanted the book to be practical but in terms of how the content would flow, I was not sure. I asked the Holy Spirit to help, as He knows those who this book will bless, such as believers, church people that do not know His ministry, backsliders and those yet to be saved. I pray that the Holy Spirit will minister to you through the pages of this book. I have tried not to write what I think will be a good read but allowed the Holy Spirit to lead and at the same time allowed Him to search my heart, intentions, and motives.

You must think by now that I am an expert at consulting the Holy Spirit. Believe me, I am just like anybody else; I have flaws too. I have my down days and my up days. I wish I could tell you that I always remember to consult the Holy Spirit before I do or say anything, but the truth is that I do not. Sometimes I remember and at other times, I forget. Sometimes it is when things are going or have gone pear-shaped, that I remember. We all know that it is a very good idea and good practice to build into our daily routine, the consciousness of the Holy Spirit in all that we do, say, or think. But, why do we find ourselves struggling in this area? The answer is simple: we cannot do this in our own power and strength. We need to ask the Holy Spirit to help us to remember to consult Him, and to build His consciousness in us and help us not to forget that He is in us, and He is our helper.

FILLING VS. FEELING

The Bible says that the just shall live by faith. We are to respond to the leadings and instructions of the Holy Spirit by faith, not by feelings. We are commanded to walk by faith, not by feelings. We cannot relate to God with our emotions or feelings because our emotions, intellect, and feelings lie within our souls and our souls are not equipped to commune with God. God is a Spirit and those that worship God must worship Him in spirit and in truth. God communicates with our spirit through the Holy Spirit living inside of us. God came down to earth to show us the way to heaven. The Holy Spirit has also come down from Heaven to fill us with Himself and to help us live the Christian life. God has gone to such a great extent to show us His love, and reducing this to mere feeling before we believe, means that we do not really understand.

I would like to give an account of a man who was led by his feelings. Isaac, before he died, was going to bless his children (Esau and Jacob). At this time, his eyes had grown dim, and he felt and blessed the wrong son first (you can read the whole account of this story in Genesis chapters 27 and 28). We can see that his feelings affected his sense of judgement and consequently, let him down on this occasion. Our feelings can also let us down. God does not dwell in the realm of feelings; He is longing and yearning to fill us with His Spirit and not feelings. There are records of many instances when the apostles were filled with the Holy Spirit in the Book of Acts and they did many outstanding things to propagate the gospel of our Lord Jesus in their generation, which are now examples for us to follow. They walked by faith and not by feelings.

I am sure that some of us, from time to time, would have experienced moments like this; you pray, and still it seems as if nothing is happening at all. It is as if your prayers have not hit your ceiling, let alone get to God. At other times, when you pray, the atmosphere is filled and charged up with the Spirit of God; you can literally touch it, even feel it in your bones and you do not want to leave that environment or atmosphere. We thank God for such experiences. I would like to inform you that the Lord will not allow us to have such experiences all the time, otherwise, we will be waiting for a repeat of the experience to know our prayers are heard and answered. The Holy Spirit is with us in instances when we feel or do not feel His presence. If He comes and goes like in the days of the Old Testament, then He will not be abiding with us.

In a discussion with someone some time ago, the person asked me if I thought they were saved because they do not feel saved. I said the prerequisite for salvation is to say the sinners' prayer (which is to believe and confess that Jesus came in the flesh, He died for our sins, and He has risen from the dead), which I knew that this person had done many moons ago. I told them that feeling has nothing to do with our salvation, as it is not based on feelings; it is based on confessing and believing in the finished work at Calvary. What is evident to us after our salvation experience is that our outlook on life is different. We might still have the same circumstances, habits, addictions, problems, etc., but after the transforming power of salvation, we begin to see them in a different light. We know beyond a shadow of a doubt that something has happened inside of us. Some lyrics from a popular song that somewhat encapsulates this occurrence are, "I can see clearly now, the rain is gone. I can see all obstacles in my way." 2 Corinthians 5:17 puts it this way: *"If anyone is in Christ, he is a new creature, the old [ways of life] have [passed away]; [from now on everything has become new]."* Just like my friend, we probably forget or sometimes do not realise that we are children of God. When we are in doubt and do not feel saved, we should take time to listen to our inward witness. The Holy Spirit testifies to us that we are the children of God, by the inward witness.

The salvation experience is a filling rather than a feeling. God fills us with His Spirit, teaches us all things, and we will know all things. Salvation is received consciously and intelligently, so we are aware of our actions when we accept the offer. As a result of the salvation decision, the flow of the Holy Spirit is activated in our lives, as we turn over the control and ownership of our lives to Him. As creatures of emotion, we are used to 'feelings' before we do things, but when it comes to the things of the Spirit, our emotions play a less important role.

As we fellowship with the Holy Spirit, He will fill us to the degree that we yield to Him. We can be guaranteed the infilling of the Holy Spirit when we ask and do things that are pleasing in His sight. We should be assured that the presence of the Holy Spirit is with us, whether we feel Him or not.

STIR VS. LEAVE DORMANT

We have responsibilities as believers and are commanded to do certain things in the Word of God. If we do not fulfil our part, then the equation is not balanced. As mentioned in an earlier chapter, someone once said, God and humans (us) make an explosive force. God wants us to work with

Him to make things happen for ourselves and for others, and that's where our responsibility comes in. If we are dormant and just wait for things to happen by chance, the odds are that they will not, and we might be waiting till thy kingdom come. One thing we need to know is that we will have to give an account to God of how we spent our time here on planet earth. I am not writing this to scare us but for us to know that we have designated duties and responsibilities as children of God, on planet earth.

Paul admonished Timothy in 2 Timothy 1:6, saying, "*...I remind you to stir up the gift of God which is in you...*" The gift here can be symbolised as fire. Before the invention of stoves, gas, and electric cookers, people used to cook on open fires with wood or coal. If the wood or coal is not frequently stirred up, the fire will go out. It is clear from this verse and in 1Tim 4:14, that gifts can be ignored, neglected, ***or left dormant. If this happens, it means that they are not properly used or replenished. If we do not stir up our gifts, they become powerless, ineffective, unproductive and dormant.*** The book of Acts talks about many fillings of the Holy Spirit. This filling can be obtained through obedience, desire, and seeking after the Holy Spirit. It may sometimes involve fasting and prayer, and studying and reading the Bible. Jesus, during His earthly ministry, lived a prayerful and obedient life, and He received a constant supply of power from the Holy Spirit.

We are commanded to stir up the gift of God in us and not to leave it dormant. The fire and the anointing of the Holy Spirit abide within us; it is up to me and you to do something about it. Praying in the Spirit, and being attentive to the Holy Spirit's promptings, will keep the fire glowing and stir up our inner fire. The Lord wants to accomplish many things through us; are you going to let Him use you, or are you going to let the gift lay fallow?

OUR TIME VS. APPOINTED TIME AND SEASON

Time is a major factor between believing and receiving; sometimes we do not want to wait for the Holy Spirit's manifestation because of our biological clock. God has an appointed time for everything under the sun; if we ask the Holy Spirit for patience, He will help us to wait for God's divine timing and help us to stay cool and enjoy the process He is taking us through, instead of being anxious and worried whilst waiting for the appointed time and season. God does not have a 24-hour clock tied to His wrist, a calendar stuck on the wall, or other electrical gadgets that tell the time. We operate in time on this side of eternity. God does not work by our time and clock but by His appointed time and season.

Understanding divine timing and seasons requires patience, and as we know, patience is one of the fruit of the Spirit. The Bible says in Isaiah 40:30 that those who wait upon the Lord shall renew their strength. When we are waiting on the Lord, we should feed our spirit with the word of God, spend time reading and meditating on the word, and as we do so and do not focus on problems, our strength will be renewed. Problems have a way of sapping us of strength. We should not grow weary, lose hope, and lose our strength while waiting for the manifestation of God's promise or answers to prayers. The above passage from the Bible promised us a renewed strength while waiting for the appointed time and season. God does not arrive early, and

He does not arrive late; He always arrives on time, all the time.

OUR WAYS VS. HIS WAYS

The Bible says His ways are not our ways. We might have our own set pattern, which are set ways figured out of how we want our prayers to be answered or how we want things to be done. We might have rehearsed it in our heads and refused to consider it any other way; we just want it our own way. If you are inclined this way on certain issues, it will be difficult to give the Holy Spirit an in-road. In fact, when He is speaking, you will not hear because you are stuck in your ways and not open to suggestions, other ways, or other ideas. In essence, our minds are like umbrellas, they work better when opened. Our Christian lives will be more effective and yield more fruit when we are open and remain open to the Holy Spirit.

If I have just described you in certain areas, I have good news for you; you will have to let down your guard, let go and let God. Do not hinder the move of the Holy Spirit because believe me, He knows everything and knows what is best for you and the plans He has for you. All He wants to do is help you to achieve them in His own way, on His terms, and not through your human, limited ways. Read the story of Gideon in the book of Judges, chapter Seven, on how he defeated the Midianite army of over 100,000 with just 300 men. If Gideon had wanted his own way, from the human standpoint, he would have said the instructions he received were absurd, rubbish, and impossible, but in obedience, he was victorious.

Another relevant story is that of Joshua, the children of Israel, and the wall of Jericho, (Joshua 6:1-24). Who would have believed that by marching around the wall seven times and blaring loud trumpets, the fortified great wall of Jericho would just collapse like a pack of cards? If Joshua had stopped and asked himself how possible it could be, to engage in no fight to capture a city, he would think that surely, this would not work. He did not reason it out, he decided to obey, and the victory was won.

It is our duty and responsibility to seek and give the Holy Spirit the go-ahead to do His goodwill through us. Isaiah 55:8-12 says that His ways are not our ways, and His thoughts are not our thoughts. Could you begin to imagine the thoughts that must have gone through the heads of the 30,000 men that were told to go back or the thoughts that went through the heads of the remaining 300 men that went to the battle to fight in chapter 7 of the book of Judges? What about Joshua and his men, what must have been going through their minds? If He can defeat an army of over 100,000 men with just 300 men, or cause a great wall to collapse just by marching, do you not think that He knows something that we do not know. God can do the unthinkable through us, if we let His Spirit have His way in our lives.

STRUGGLE VS. REST

At the beginning of this book, we looked at how the Holy Spirit was very instrumental in creation. On day seven of creation, the Bible said God rested. Hebrews 4:9-11 says: *"There remains therefore a rest for the people of God. For he who has entered His rest has himself also ceased from his works, as God did from His. Let us, therefore, be diligent to enter that rest, lest anyone fall according to* [by following] *the same example of* [unbelief and] *disobedience."* The example of unbelief here and disobedience relates to the children of Israel when they were in the wilderness. God has ceased from creation and has already planned everything for our lives and given us all that we need for life and godliness (living godly lives). All has already been created; He is not creating anything anymore. The labour we are asked to do is to enter His rest. It is called labour because we need to work at it every day. When an expectant mother goes into labour, she relies on the instruction given by the midwife to push the baby out. We need to rely on the instructions of the Holy Spirit to remain in the rest.

I would like to ask this question: do you want to enter His rest with the situation and circumstances in your life or do you just want to figure it out yourself, or wallow in self-pity? ***God knows the end from the beginning***; when you enter His rest, He begins to unfold His plans for your life. Entering His rest requires a high level of trust from our human perspective. If you know someone has the solutions to your problems, answers to your questions, and rest for your weary soul, it makes perfect sense to draw closer to that person, so you can find direction, solace, and solutions to life's uncertainties that we all experience from time to time. It makes sense, doesn't it? There is a saying that goes: "let common sense prevail." Apparently, common sense is not common. We need the help of the Holy Spirit to enter this rest that has been procured for us. I will suggest that, daily, one of your prayers should be along these lines, "Holy Spirit, help me to enter into your rest today."

They say it is the simple things in life that often work best. I am sure that you will agree with me that making up our minds to enter His rest daily is a simple thing, but we humans love to complicate simple instructions because our minds cannot comprehend the simplicity. It is called paralysis by analysis. We over-analyse things with our limited minds and wonder why things are not happening for us. We tend to complicate simple matters. We are called to obedience, not to disobedience; when we do not follow the example of disobedience, we will enter His rest. Logic and too much reasoning get us in trouble, and we twist a straightforward matter. Do not even think for one moment that I am innocent of this matter; I am equally as guilty as you or anyone else. One thing I try to do is to make amends when I notice that I do not have peace in certain areas of my life. I will let you into a little secret; we cannot carry out this simple instruction of entering His rest without the daily help of the Holy Spirit. The key to entering the rest is obedience, which gives us peace.

Anytime you find yourself worrying about a particular issue and it is affecting your peace, you need to carry out a rest self-check. Say to yourself: "Have I entered into the rest of the Holy Spirit with this issue?" The chances are high that you have not surrendered the issue and entered His rest. Do not forget that with the help of the Holy Spirit, we can enter His rest with any ailment, condition, problem, issue, etc. When you have entered His rest with the issue, you will feel a sense of peace guiding your mind. Sometimes, it is peace you cannot explain. You might even say to yourself that the problem is not resolved, yet you are not worried about it anymore: "I am at peace within myself." When you get to this stage, then you are in a state of rest and just waiting to see how things will pan out. Do not be tempted to say it is taking too long, renew your rest commitment, and refuse to lose your peace or sleep on the issue again; the whole of heaven's artillery is at work on the issue or issues, and on your behalf.

WISE VS. FOOLISH

1 Corinthians 3:19 says, *"For the wisdom of this world is foolishness with God."* Our beliefs, truth, and knowledge should not rest in the wisdom of this world because people have limited knowledge, and are puffed up by it, but true divine wisdom comes from God. If you want or lack wisdom, approach God who promised that He will give it to those that ask liberally. James 1:5 says if anyone lacks wisdom, let him ask God that gives, to everyone who asks, liberally and without holding back. As God does not hold back wisdom for those that ask, it will be in your best interest to ask, and the result is that it shall be given to you. The Bible describes a fool as a person who says in their heart that there is no God. Wisdom, on the other hand, is described as the application of knowledge. There are two kinds of wisdom; the ***God kind of wisdom*** and ***wisdom of the world***. God's wisdom surpasses worldly wisdom. If you acknowledge your limited wisdom and go to God for His all-encompassing wisdom, you will have much greater success and peace of mind in life.

In the bible, there is a story/parable told by Jesus about a rich man, who was very successful and lived a comfortable life. Because of his sheer hard work, he stored up much wealth and many good things for himself. After years of working, he decided to retire and said to himself, "Even if I do not work another day in my life, I will not go without. I will be comfortable from now on. I will take things easy, eat, drink, be merry and enjoy myself."

In all his thoughts and planning, he left out one vital detail, he failed to factor in and acknowledge the giver of life, wealth, and health. Our possessions are given to us, not for selfish consumption but for our needs and to help others. Everything we do in life should have eternal value and significance to God, otherwise, all our good and hard work will be lost forever. Read the story for yourself in Luke 12:16-21. In verse 20, God said to the rich man, "*...You fool! This night, your [life] is required of you, and the things you have prepared, whose will they be?*"

Jesus went on to say in verse 21, that this is how it will be for anyone who hoards up possessions for themselves and does not acknowledge what God can do through them with their time, skills, talents and abilities. The Bible called this man a fool because all he thought about was celebrating his possessions without realising that his life consists of more than the abundance of his possessions. To live truly fulfilled lives, we need to acknowledge God as the giver of materials, and spiritual and physical blessings. The Bible, in Psalms 53:1, defines a fool as a person that says in his heart there is no God. Believe it or not, accept it or not, The Intelligent Being (God) that designed the world will one day ask you to give an account of how you spent your days and your stewardship on earth.

We should acknowledge God in all that we do and ask for his wisdom to live godly lives. This wisdom we are talking about is available in the person of the Holy Spirit. The Spirit of God is the Spirit of wisdom. 1 Corinthians 1:18-

25 talks about human wisdom and the preaching of the cross. The wisdom that underpins Christ's death on the cross is foolishness to those who do not know Him but to us that are saved, it is the power of God. If the enemy had known that Christ dying on the cross would bring many people to know God, believe me, he would not have been party to it. Verse 25 is awesome, it says, *"For the foolishness of God is wiser than [the wisdom of men put together] and the weakness of God is stronger than [all the strength of men put together]."* If I were you, I would know on which side of the fence to be and what camp to choose.

RELIGION VS. RELATIONSHIP

Religion, by definition, is a set of rules, laws, instructions, and creeds that people follow to attain right-standing or be convinced that they are doing something worthwhile and right to please God. It was hard for the people in the Old Testament to keep the law because it is difficult to fulfil all the demands of the Law. No one can follow the law to the latter without wavering.

After the death, burial, and resurrection of Jesus, the promised Holy Spirit came to help us live a happy, content, productive and acceptable life that pleases God. The word Christian means 'Christ like' i.e. to be like Christ in our ways, conduct, and manners. Christianity is therefore not a religion but a personal relationship with the person of our Lord and Saviour, Jesus Christ, and who better equips us to live this kind of life, other than the Holy Spirit?

I once had a conversation about religion with a work colleague, in which she grouped Christianity in the same category as the otherworld religions. I pointed out that what she said about religion is true, but Christianity is not a religion per se. I explained that it is a personal one-on-one relationship with the person of our Lord Jesus Christ. She said she had not seen it that way before. I also explained that the Ten Commandments were given to draw people's attention to God, not to help us attain a one-on-one relationship with God, let alone save us.

The Holy Spirit came to enable us to have that personal relationship with Jesus because He lives inside of us. This is what distinguishes Christianity from all other religions. Religion is man-based, in the sense that we are trying to achieve what is not achievable within our grasp and power. Christianity, on the other hand, is reliant on the Holy Spirit's help to live right before God.

Being born into a Christian family, attending church, and giving your life to Jesus Christ are all separate issues. I was born into a Christian family and a time came when I started to search the scriptures for myself. I told myself that if I can fulfil the Ten Commandments, I will feel very satisfied with myself, however, little did I know at the time that no one can fulfil the Ten Commandments in their own power and strength. Thank God for the Holy Spirit because during that process of attempting right-standing with God in my own limited abilities, I was saved. The Holy Spirit supernaturally energised and enabled me to experience the saving grace of God. God's grace, through the power of the Holy Spirit, enables us to do what we cannot attain with our human power, intellect, or abilities. We simply cannot live right and please God in our human strength, so we need a supernatural power in the person of the Holy Spirit, to help us live this kind of life.

Religion is full of legalism; the law was given in the days of the Old Testament to help people live right. Jesus came to fulfil the law, and by putting our faith in Him, we will be free from the law. One of Apostle Paul's writings in the Bible says that 'the law kills but the Spirit gives life.' Anything that we do in the legal mindset, and out of obligation, is in the flesh and not of the Spirit. They are dead works. For example, praying, reading the bible, giving, and doing good deeds should not be done out of obligation or reprisals (dead works), but should be done with spiritual knowledge and understanding.

The Holy Spirit helps our relationship with Jesus to come alive. He gives us the unction to live above the law. He helps us to live a successful Christian life, as opposed to being bogged down with self-righteous, dead works, sets of rules, regulations, and traditions. It's more profitable to be led by the Holy Spirit in all we do in life than by religion.

ACCOMPLISHMENT VS. FULFILMENT

Anyone can accomplish anything they desire or want in life. Accomplishment does not necessarily mean fulfilment. We might all have experienced it in one way or another, and I'm sure you know that the more we accomplish, the more we want. Typical examples are, "When I get married, all my problems will be over, I will find satisfaction and be fulfilled." Others might say, 'When I have children,' 'get that job,' 'buy or build a house,' 'get a car,' 'complete this business deal or transaction', and the list goes on. We find out that after achieving the set goals, we still feel empty inside. Anything we achieve outside the power of the Holy

Spirit does not really satisfy. The more you accomplish, the more you want.

Anything we achieve through the help of the Holy Spirit has a sense of fulfilment, because it relates to our purpose in life. We have heard, seen, or read of great inventions, attainments, and success stories, yet the authors of these achievements still feel unfulfilled inside. On the outside, they appear, confident, cool, calm, calculated, composed, and appreciative. Some even love the accolades and attention. Yet, after a while, they want more conquests. ***There is a God vacuum on the inside of every one of us, and our achievements and accomplishments will seem futile until we make that connection with the Holy Spirit who helps us to fill the vacuum.*** Do not get me wrong; the Holy Spirit is not against our success and progress. The point I am making is that anything that we accomplish without the Holy Spirit just leaves us empty after a while. We will be wondering and saying to ourselves, "Is that all?", which leads to desiring more and more, eventually ending in a vicious circle.

True satisfaction and fulfilment are only found when we follow God's plan for our lives. We know or have read of people that have risen to the top of their careers and we will count them as being very successful, yet they are not fulfilled. Fulfilment comes when you allow the Holy Spirit to run the show and you know it is not in your own power or position. Consult Him every inch of the way and when you accomplish that task or venture, you will experience true satisfaction.

The system of this world sets people up to fail, and we have seen or heard examples of this in the rise and fall of people and empires, kingdoms, countries, regimes, reigns, rulers, etc. The blessing of God, the Bible says, "*makes us rich, satisfies and does not add any sorrow* (Proverbs 10:22)." There are many people, past and present, whose riches have added enormous sorrows to their lives, instead of blessings. The Holy Spirit will not set us up to let us down; He does not operate that way. Sometimes, we might not fully comprehend the way that He is leading us, but if we have built a trusting relationship with Him, we can rest assured that the end will always work out for our good.

You might argue that, 'I have accomplished many things and I feel satisfied, and I did not or cannot remember asking for the help of the Holy Spirit.' That might be true, but in these instances, they are not one of the endless pursuits in life. Searching for money, power and fame are endless pursuits and without the help of the Holy Spirit guiding these activities in our lives, we will end up wanting more and more, until it eventually leads to destruction. There is a cautionary note in the latter part of Psalm 62:10, which says that if riches increase, we should not set our hearts upon them as the end all or be all. These things in themselves do not really satisfy for long and they are very uncertain and temporal.

Having said all that, there is satisfaction and fulfilment when we ask the Holy Spirit for guidance and direction in all that we do in life, either in what I call the endless pursuits or in day-to-day living for major or minor issues, decisions, and endeavours.

DAILY REGIME

Consult with the Holy Spirit daily and not on a sporadic basis. Our attitude toward the Holy Spirit cannot be wishy-washy, i.e. whenever we feel like it or whenever we think it is necessary or convenient. He is our consultant and expert in any subject. A friend who was completing a life coaching accreditation course asked me to be her client. In the first session, she explained the process and we looked at my expectations. We looked at different areas of my life on a life wheel; I had to plot where I was then on the wheel and where I would like to be. We brainstormed my goals, set goals, and put deadlines on the goals.

I can equate this experience to how we can communicate with the Holy Spirit in a way; plotting where we are now and setting targets of how we can get closer to Him. My advice would be to consult the Holy Ghost if you are thinking of setting life goals. He will not only help you to set the goals but also help you to accomplish them. It is a partnership working agreement. He knows how and when to provide the resources to enable you to achieve the goals. At the beginning of a year, many people set New Year goals and resolutions. Enlist the help of the Holy Spirit for this task and, together, you will make a greater impact and finish the year well. Believe me when I say that you will not be sorry that you did. They say a trial will convince you, so try it; ask the Holy Spirit for help daily, listen to His leading and directions, and act on them. Don't just converse with the Holy Spirit and do nothing. People say, "talk is cheap," "it's easier said than done." Do not be a talking shop, show me your actions and by your deeds, and I will show you a serious person.

You might ask, 'If the Holy Spirit can help us to this extent, why do we have failing Christians, and why are we not all living in victory?' The long and short answer to that question is that not all Christians will always enlist or solicit the help of the Holy Spirit. Either consciously or subconsciously, we assign to ourselves certain things we can do without the intervention of the Holy Spirit. The truth of the matter is that the Holy Spirit helps us with everything, even things we already know how to do. He helps us to do them better.

I would like to refer to the Holy Spirit as our Senior Partner, Consultant, and Life Coach. I met with my coach every six weeks to review my goals and monitor progress. The sessions lasted twelve months, and, at the end, I achieved the set goals. After that, I had the option to continue with the coaching, which will involve setting new goals or expanding on the old ones.

A friend once said to me, "Do you know, I still do not know what profession I want to choose, or what I would like to be in life?" I can tell you that there are many adults in that category. My take on this is that you are good at something, so search within yourself and follow your natural flare: it will lead you to the right profession. This same advice can be given to children and young people. Don't forget that we cannot leave the Holy Spirit out of this equation; He knows all things, He knows what he has prepared for you, and He will lead you into the Promised Land. Consulting Him is essential for daily direction, decision-making, and important things such as choosing a career or profession, who to marry, where to live, and where to study, as well as for our spiritual, social, emotional, physical, or psychological needs.

GIVING GOD THE GLORY

All the glory, honour, and praise must be given to God. Everything that the Holy Spirit helps us to accomplish is not by our power, and we must be very careful not to take the praise, accolade, and credit. For God is a jealous God, **Glory is reserved for God and God alone**. No one on earth should honour himself other than he should, for all the glory must be given to God. We have examples of people in the Bible that ascribed glory to themselves and their lives were disasters until they repented. We also have examples of people in our today, past, and present, who thought that they are untouchables, and we have seen their disastrous ends.

We need to acknowledge the role of the Holy Spirit in making things happen in our lives and we should give Him the full honour and credit. We should not say it's by our power, might, knowledge and wisdom.

As humans, we tend to take credit for our success. When it comes to Christendom, all the Glory must go to the one that really deserves it. Many times, God sometimes allows us to exhaust our natural abilities, knowhow, and expertise until it dawns on us that we need to acknowledge our limitations and run to Him for help. I particularly like to watch the American Oscar Awards ceremony on TV, especially the bit where the celebrities that win the Oscars will often say, 'first and foremost, I thank God'. Some of their deeds, behaviours, and actions are far removed from what God would approve. But the fact remains that many of them recognise and have the belief that God gave them their abilities and has enabled them to achieve and excel. Personally speaking, I think this is a very good habit to covet in our chosen endeavours and in life, in general.

We need to acknowledge our frailties and approach God in times of hopelessness, helplessness, sheer despair, wit's end, or crossroads. When the Holy Spirit is invited at times like this, He will give us beauty for ashes, joy instead of sadness, hope instead of despair, and He will rescue us and energise us to accomplish what we can only imagine was possible in our dreams. At times like this, we must not misappropriate all the honour, praise, recognition, appreciation, and adoration. ***All the glory MUST be given to the Lord.***

I have tried to explain some aspects of our relationship with the Holy Spirit and how it works. Those times when we feel most discouraged and most vulnerable are times when we have released our faith and are waiting for something extraordinary to happen, and nothing happens. Some people call this ***the silent times*** while others call it ***the wilderness experience***. When it happens, it feels like we are out there in the wilderness and God is not talking; nothing seems to be happening naturally. But once we have handed the situation to the Holy Spirit, believe me, in the spiritual realm, plenty is happening. If we persist, hold on to our faith, and confession, and do not give up, we will yield the fruit of obedience. Our patience and obedience are vital; patience is one of the attributes of the Holy Spirit. The Bible says that ***if we do not give up, in due season, we will reap***.

The applications you are reading in this book will only work if they are applied and put into practice; it does not end at the reading stage. We have a responsibility and duty to put into practice what we have learned, because it's only then that we will reap the benefits. It's no good buying a bicycle and not learning how to ride it. When you start to learn how to ride a bike, you are a bit unsteady on your feet and lack focus. You fall, and you do a little adjustment here and there. Practice riding often, and finally you are on your way. Sometimes, this happens when we are learning to flow and walk with the Holy Spirit. We will have to learn and exercise flowing with the Holy Spirit in different areas and aspects of our lives continually. It's one long, lifetime learning curve; you can find that you win the victory today but tomorrow, you are struggling. The secret is in not giving up.

We need the Holy Spirit to renew our strength daily. The Bible says it's not by power, nor by might, strength, or intellect, but it's by the Spirit of the living God that we do the supernatural and extraordinary things in life.

15

HOLY SPIRIT MINISTRY TO NON-CHRISTIANS

REPROOF THE WORLD OF SIN

As I said in earlier chapters, the Holy Spirit is a gift to the church, the body of Christ. You might be an unbeliever reading this book; I would like to assure you that the Holy Spirit has been sent for you as well. If you say the Salvation prayer at the end of this book (on Pages 281 and 282), you will receive the baptism of the Holy Spirit and you will be saved. You will be able to access all the benefits I have mentioned in this book when you allow the Holy Spirit to reside and preside in your life.

The Holy Spirit has a threefold ministry in the life of unbelievers (unsaved people). This threefold work is highlighted in the book of John 16:8-11. Jesus, speaking here, said that when the Holy Spirit comes (He came on the day of Pentecost), He will convince and convict the world (1) of sin, (2) of righteousness, and (3) of judgement. Most believers have already been convicted of these three things, hence their salvation experience and qualification to be called Christians. Unbelievers are convicted of:

1. Sin, because they do not believe in Jesus. They do not believe that Jesus came to the world and died on the cross to pay for their sins (past, present, and future) with His shed blood, at Calvary. The Holy Spirit will convince and convict unbelievers of this fact but if they refuse and remain in unbelief, then they will face the damning consequences of unrepented sins.

2. Righteousness, because Jesus has gone back to heaven, and He is no longer on earth. We only have access to heaven through the shed blood on the cross. The Bible says flesh and blood cannot glory in His presence. In other words, to be able to stand before the Holy God of Heaven, we need the blood of Jesus. To have the blood, we need to believe that Jesus came to the world to restore and save us from our sins. The blood of Jesus is our righteousness, and our access to God. Righteousness means the ability to have right-standing with God, without the sense of inferiority complex. We have access and the ability to stand before God because of the blood of Jesus. Unbelievers without the blood do not have this access that believers have. Here is where the Holy Spirit comes in; He will reprove, convince, and convict the world/unbelievers of unrighteous living. Unbelievers have two choices after this conviction, a) to believe and do what is necessary to get right with God or b) to refuse and face the consequences.

Jesus is no longer on the earth and cannot be approached like when He was physically here, so the Holy Spirit does that work now. Jesus has gone to the Father, and both the access rights and channel are open through the Holy Spirit.

We cannot produce righteousness in our own power, nor can we achieve this status by good works The Bible says our righteousness is like filthy rags before God; ***only the blood of Jesus Christ can produce right-standing before God***.

3. Judgement, because the prince of this world, the enemy, the devil, Satan, has already been judged. Those who refused the gift of salvation will face the judgement of damnation. The Bible said in Hebrews 9:27, "*...it is appointed unto men once to die, but after this the judgement.*" The message here is not to follow the enemy because he is already judged, and he knows his destination. The enemy's goal is to try to take as many people as he can with him. One of the jobs of the Holy Spirit is to convince and convict the unbelievers of this reality.

I would urge you to please make peace with God, if you have not already done so, by accepting what Christ has done for us on the cross. Proverbs 15:32 said, "*He that refuses* (rejects) *instruction despises* (hates) *his own soul: but [the person] that hears reproof [will gain] understanding* (wisdom, enlightenment)."

The Holy Spirit has only one ministry in the life of the unbelievers and that contract is to draw them to Christ. The Holy Spirit is given to everyone who repents of their sins and accepts Christ. John 14:17 says the world cannot receive the Spirit of truth because they do not know Him. Our duty as believers is to let the world see the Spirit of truth operating and dwelling in our lives, by our conduct, our presentation, and the way we carry ourselves. This will attract the unsaved people to us; they will want to know more about the God inside of us. You might think people are not watching but they are, they know there is something different about you, and some of them want to know more about this difference.

Believers are God's workmanship, showcasing and modelling the truth and the reality of the gospel to the lost and dying world. So, the lost people can come to the saving grace and saving knowledge of the finished work at Calvary. As believers, we have this as part of our brief and responsibilities.

If you are a non-believer, it is worth giving God a trial; the Bible says come, taste, and see that the Lord is good. The Holy Spirit is a gift to the church primarily, but this gift can be extended to whosoever desires it. In Acts 2:38-39, Peter addressed the crowd in Jerusalem on the day of Pentecost, saying to the onlookers, "*...Repent, and be baptised every one of you in the name of Jesus Christ for the remission of sins, and you shall receive the gift of the Holy Ghost. For this promise is [for] you and to your children, and to all that are [faraway], even as many as the Lord our God shall call.*" 'As many as the Lord shall call', as referred to in verse thirty-nine, includes you. ***The invitation is still open today, as Peter gave it on the day of Pentecost.***

16

HOW DOES THIS ALL FIT TOGETHER?

PERSONAL APPLICATION

I cannot overemphasise the power of personal application because it helps us to apply what we have learned to our lives. It is like testing the waters; they say the proof of the pudding is in the eating, so you will not know how beneficial the Holy Spirit is to your life until you begin to put what you have learned into practice. You might have questions and concerns like these; 'How does it work for me?', 'How does it benefit me and make my life better?', 'How can I get from A to B?', 'I have a plan, but I don't know how to go about it,' 'I don't have a plan,' etc.

The Holy Spirit will not bless ignorance, but He will lead you to acquire the wisdom and knowledge that you need. The Ministry of the Holy Spirit will work for you when you:

1. Make up your mind to follow the leadings and promptings of the Holy Spirit.
2. Acknowledge Him every day and in every way. A minister of God once said that every morning when he wakes up, he says, 'Good morning, Holy Spirit'. He wrote a book called 'Good Morning Holy Spirit' and another book titled, 'Holy Spirit, my Senior Partner.' This is a habit worth emulating. We need to acknowledge His person and His presence, and ask Him to help us get through the day.
3. If you can pray in tongues, pray in tongues every day. The Bible (Romans 8:26) says that we do not know how to pray as we ought, but the Holy Spirit makes intercessions for us with groans that cannot be uttered in articulate speech. You can pray in your understanding if you have not received the gift of praying in tongues yet.
4. Commit every day to His hands; say, "Holy Spirit, help me to fulfil all your plans and purpose for my life today." I cannot emphasise this enough, when you do this constantly, you know that whatever comes your way, the Lord has allowed for a reason, and it will work out for your good.
5. Wholly and solely dedicate every day of your life to Him. As the day breaks daily, in the same way, dedicate your life to Him daily. When you dedicate your life to Him, He will lead you step-by-step, moment-by-moment, day-by-day, and navigate you through the course of the day and, indeed, life. Jeremiah 33:3 says, "Call onto me, I will answer you and I will show you great and mighty things that you do not know you."

6. Form a long-lasting trusting relationship with the Holy Spirit, as you learn to walk with Him.
7. Be patient. You do not direct the Holy Spirit; He does the leading and directing, so do not run ahead of Him. Always stay with Him and you will not go wrong. Trust me, it will be the best thing you have ever done or experienced in a long time.

MINISTER TO HEIRS OF SALVATION

The Holy Spirit ministers to us, who are heirs of salvation. I have mentioned earlier that the Holy Spirit is a gift to the Church, the body of Christ. He dwells, resides, abides, reigns, and rules in the lives of those that permit him to do so. If you are not already an heir of salvation, which means you have not yet given your life to Jesus to be your Lord and Saviour, it is not the end of the story. By saying the salvation prayer (also known as sinners' prayer) further down this chapter, you will automatically invite Jesus into your life, become an heir of salvation, and be on your way to living a victorious Christian life. You need to grow in your faith walk and there are guidance points under the heading of 'Growing in your Christian Walk' below, to help you do just that.

Prior to my salvation experience, I was just a Christian attending church, and I had not made a formal commitment to the Lordship of Jesus Christ over my life. I did not even know, and was not taught at the church I was attending then, that I had to make a formal commitment to accepting the gift of salvation. A friend of mine travelled to Nigeria and came back with some books. She said someone gave them to her and two of them were not of any particular interest to her, and so she gave them to me. It so happened that during that period, I had developed a serious hunger for the things of God. I had come to a crossroads in my life, and I was asking the Lord for direction. Reading the books further whet my appetite and created more hunger for the things of God. One was written by T.L. Osborne and the other by Kenneth E. Hagin. I read both books, said the salvation prayers at the end of both books, and gave my life to the Lord twice within the space of one day. I signed and dated both books.

These two occasions were the first of many times that I gave my life to the Lord. A friend invited me to her church, of which I later became a member. When the altar call was made, I found myself going forward to give my life again to the Lord. When anyone invites me to their church, I would give my life again to the Lord. Any time I listen to any video cassettes and the minister gives an altar call at the end, you have guessed it, I would give my life again to the Lord. DVDs were just coming out in those days; the Christian TV channels, radio stations and other media outlets that we have today, were not common back then in the United Kingdom. God helped me; I would have just been giving my life every time I heard an altar call. Looking back now, I am not sure if it was ignorance or zeal without knowledge but whatever the case, I thought then, it was now or never.

I did not know that a friend had been observing me, and after I had responded to yet another altar call, she called me aside and said that she was really concerned about the number of times she was seeing me respond to the calls for salvation. "Tell me what sin you have committed that is making you respond to so many salvation calls," she asked.

I told her that I had not committed any grievous sin, but it was the way the ministers phrased their sentences. They would say if you die today and you are not sure you will go to heaven, come out now, and genuinely, I was not sure at that time. She then told me that you only 'give' your life once and that the Christian journey is a lifetime of commitment, growth, communing, developing, building a relationship, and walking with God. Believe me, I needed to hear those words because they really set me free. I stopped responding to salvation calls at any given opportunity after that and concentrated on growing in my newly found faith. I later came to realise that Christianity is a process of growing and walking with the LORD and the Holy Spirit helps us in this faith walk.

You do not have to give your life as many times as I did; just the once will do, if you do it wholeheartedly. Make a firm commitment to invite the Lord into your life, mean it from the depths of your being and you too can become an heir of salvation. After salvation, commence on a growth plan, which will keep you rooted in your faith walk. As you begin to develop in the things of the Spirit, you will see God's plan begin to emerge and unfold in your personal life and circumstances.

If you are in a position where you have already made this commitment and you now feel like a prodigal son, because you have drifted away from the Lord, say the prayer of restitution below and ask the Holy Spirit for help to sustain your faith walk, so that you will not fall again into the temptation of straying away from the Lord.

PRAYER OF RESTITUTION

Heavenly Father, you said if I come to you, I will not be cast out. Father, I have strayed from your commandments, your precepts, and your unfailing love. I now come to you like the prodigal son, to make restitution and to commit the rest of my life into your capable hands. I acknowledge all my faults and mistakes. You said if I draw closer to you, you will draw closer to me. Holy Spirit, I ask you to help me to draw closer to God and help me to keep this commitment. I thank you, Lord, for forgiving me and restoring me, in Jesus' name. Amen.

The fact is that God never stopped loving you, He was waiting for you to realise your mistake and turn back to Him.

1 John 1:9 says that if we confess our sins, He is faithful and just, to forgive us our sins and to cleanse us from all unrighteousness. The only way back for us to fellowship with God is for us to acknowledge, confess our sins, and believe that God is faithful and just, to forgive us. We should also recognise that our forgiveness is obtained in the death of Christ when He died for the remission of our sins at Calvary.

When we sincerely confess our sins, we must desire restoration and return to an intimate fellowship with God the Father, God the Son, and God the Holy Spirit. 1 John 1:9 is clear that God will forgive and remove any barrier that has stopped or kept us from living right.

After saying the prayer of restitution above, find a church where you can continue to grow in your Christian faith. This choice should be made prayerfully, on your knees. I personally believe that we go to a church out of conviction and not out of convenience. Pray and let the Holy Spirit direct you to the right church for you.

SALVATION PACKAGE

The word, 'salvation' is translated from a Greek word called, '*Soteria*'. It does not just refer to God saving us from our sins (wrongdoing, failure to follow God's commandments) and translating us from the Kingdom of darkness (this world), into the kingdom of light (heaven), assuring us that we are heirs to all the promises in the word of God. Salvation is a package; it comprises being saved (the salvation experience). It also means preservation, wholeness, wellbeing, safety, security, deliverance, health, wealth, prosperity, etc. We are constantly being saved from one thing or another, being delivered from one situation or another, and being rescued from one issue or another as we go from glory to glory and from strength to strength, throughout our Christian life and walk. Salvation can be used to describe our whole Christian journey and experience. It is a generic term, but at the same time, it covers specific areas and aspects of our lives.

An open invitation is given to the whole world, in John 3:16. There, the Bible says, *"For God so loved the world that He gave His only begotten son, that whosoever believes in Him will not die but have everlasting life."* If you are ever in doubt that this invitation is not for you, let me assure you that ***God loves the sinner and hates the sin.*** You are invited; you only need to confess your sins to Jesus. No sin is too great or too small that He cannot forgive.

This question about open invitations reminds me of a discussion that I had with a colleague at work some time ago. She said to me, "I would like to be a Christian, but my lifestyle will not permit me." I then told her about the open invitation in John 3:16. I said the Bible says **who-so-ever**. That is three words rolled into one. The **Who** means anyone and everybody, '**So**' means I decide if I want to, and **Ever** means whatever the circumstance, condition, past lifestyle, age, colour, belief, background, religion, etc. Whosoever is an all-encompassing, inclusive, and generic term that includes anybody and everybody, regardless of lifestyle or whatever we are accustomed to. I told her that God loves the sinner and not the sin. Once we confess the sin/s, God will fulfil His part of the bargain.

HOW TO RECEIVE SALVATION (GOD'S RIGHTEOUSNESS)

To receive God's gift of salvation, the steps are very easy, and it involves believing and confessing. Romans 10:9-10 says that if you confess with your mouth that the Lord Jesus died for your sins and you believe in your heart that God raised Him from the dead, then you shall be saved. It is that simple. Verse 10 says, "*...with the heart one believes unto righteousness and with the mouth confession is made unto salvation.*" As we believe that we have a right-standing with God and as we confess with our mouths, we are saved. What happens in the spiritual realm at that moment is awesome; we may not see it nor feel it, but we are automatically translated, converted from the kingdom of darkness to the Kingdom of God. Our spirit is regenerated, old things are passed away and everything becomes new. We are passed from death into life, passed from living in darkness, and into living in the light.

Salvation is a gift, and no man should boast or brag about it; it is an open invitation to the whole world. Let's reflect again on John 3:16, *"For God so loved the world that He gave His only begotten Son, that whosoever believes in Him would not perish* [be lost] *but have an everlasting life."* The everlasting life here means that after our lives are spent on earth, we will reign with Him forever and ever. Jesus is indeed a gift to the whole world. Salvation starts here on earth, and we enjoy the benefits when we make that confession into all eternity.

In the first chapter of the book of John, verse twelve said as many as receive Him (Jesus), He gave them the power to become the children of God. This power will change our lives for the better. We first receive, and then we are given delegated power to live and reign in life, taking our rightful place and authority as children of God. Note that this is an individual benefit. The passage said 'as many as received Him', which means that it is a choice situation. We can either choose to receive or not to receive; the choice is ours. Christianity is an individual race. Just as we are all individuals, we are called to run the race and our course in life as individuals. It is an individual race but not a solo race because we have the help and support of the Holy Spirit, steering us all the way.

If you would like to receive the gift of salvation, say this prayer.

SALVATION PRAYER (ALSO KNOWN AS THE SINNERS' PRAYER)

Heavenly Father, I come to You in the Name of Jesus.

Your Word says whosoever that calls upon the name of the Lord shall be saved (Acts 2:21).

You said if I confess with my mouth and believe in my heart that God raised Jesus Christ from the dead, then I am saved (Romans 10:9).

You also said that my salvation would be the result of Your Holy Spirit giving me new birth by coming to live in me (John 3:5-6, 15-16 and Romans 8: 9-11).

You said if I ask, You will fill me with Your Spirit (Luke 11:13), and everything will become new in my life (2 Corinthians 5:17).

I take You at Your Word. I confess that Jesus is Lord and I believe in my heart that You raised Him from the dead.

Thank You, Lord, for coming into my heart, for giving me Your Holy Spirit as You have promised, and for being Lord over my life, in Jesus' name. Amen.

By way of reminder, sign, and date the day you made this commitment.

Signature: ....

Date: ....

Read 'Growing in your Christian Walk' section below for pointers on how to grow in your faith walk.

OUR COMMISSION AND RESPONSIBILITIES AS CHRISTIANS

We are commissioned by Jesus in Mathew 28:19 and Mark 16:15, to go into the world and tell others of His great love and forgiveness, teaching them to obey and observe the commandments and be a witness. One of the chief reasons why I believe that I was led to write this book is because it partly helps me to fulfil a share of the great commission; to be a witness to you, and to remind you of your own duties. The commission can be summarised as going into the world, presenting, and telling them about the love of God, His saving grace, redemption plan, and eternal (everlasting) life.

PROFESSION AFTER SALVATION

I have been privileged to teach some children and young people the word of God. I call it a privilege because it gives me another avenue for fulfilling the great commission. I can recollect an occasion when I was teaching a group of children. I said to them that it is best to ask the Lord what He would like them to be when they grow up and by doing so, they will not pick the wrong career. I said trying one course after the other to find the right one is time-consuming and can be a real waste of time, so consulting the Holy Spirit, beforehand, will save them precious time.

One of the boys came to me afterward (he was only 9 years old at the time) and said to me, "You know what? I do not think I want to ask God for what He wants me to be in life," and when asked why he continued, "Suppose He wants me to be a Pastor and I do not want to be one, that is why I would not ask Him." The thought that occurred to me, at that point, is the deceit of the enemy and how he wants to rob us of God's best for our lives. He will try his uttermost for us to not talk to God; he will even go as far as trying to abort our call-in life, our hopes, ambitions, and drive in life, by using any means possible. This boy, at only the age of 9, had already concluded that he will not ask the Holy Spirit for career direction, just in case He says something contrary to his wishes. This is not faith in operation; this is fear, which the enemy also uses to stop us from fulfilling the great commission.

I said to myself that I would not let this opportunity go without correcting his thinking and helping him to balance things and to see things from a different perspective. To allay his fears and give him some assurance, I told him that everyone will not be called to be a pulpit minister, but we are called to preach the gospel and spread the word of God in different ways. I said to him that God will not call everybody to be Pastors because if we are all Pastors, who will be the engineers and people in the construction industry? Who will be accountants and people in the financial sector, cooks, chefs, and people in the catering industry? What about the doctors, nurses, therapists, and people in medical healthcare, social workers, and people in social care? Not to mention the entertainers and people in the media, lecturers, and people in education, lawyers, and people in the legal profession? Or the pilots, drivers and people in transportation, government officials, lawmakers, politicians, plumbers, people in arts, and crafts, sportspeople, electricians, businesspeople, homemakers, directors, office workers, and people in other walks of life? I told him that the reason to consult God before choosing a profession is for the Holy Spirit's direction - to avoid confusion when that time comes, and that the Holy Spirit will also help him in that profession.

The enemy will try everything and anything to prevent us from approaching the Holy Spirit about our future, our goals, our vision, our careers, and aspirations. If the thought that went through that boy's mind was not corrected, he probably will not want to talk to God for fear that God will say that he will be a Pastor, which he did not particularly want to be. But he eventually saw the reason why he should approach God; so that God can make him a better version of the person whom He already wants him to be.

Like the boy, I have had many thoughts like that go through my mind and I said the same thing (that I do not want to be a preacher), but the truth of the matter is that we are all ministers in our own right, within our sphere of influence. Whether in our neighbourhood, places of learning, secular work, corporate arena, or leisure activities, they are all platforms and avenues for us to minister to our friends, loved ones, neighbours, colleagues, or even strangers. Everyone cannot be called to be a Reverend, a Pastor, or a Pulpit Minister.

When we trust and depend on the Holy Spirit, He will lead us and direct us in the profession that He has chosen for us. As mentioned earlier, I can say that writing this book is fulfilling one of my ministerial roles. Your gifting might be in the same or different areas. We are all called to serve in one capacity or another within or outside of (secular jobs) the church. Our secular jobs are just an extension of what God has earmarked for us to do in life; they are by no means the ultimate. If you are in-between jobs, changing careers, or looking for fresh ideas or business ventures, ask the Holy Spirit for direction, as He knows best. As we yield ourselves, our services, and our availabilities to the Holy Spirit, He will use us in many ways and help us to fulfil our part of the great commission.

God has great plans for your life; ***His plan and purpose for your life are called His Will for you.*** He wants you to approach Him for them, so that He can guide, lead, and direct you on how to fulfil them. Although giving our life to the Lord does not automatically qualify us for a Pastoral call; it is a gateway to fulfilling God's best and chosen professions for our lives.

RELUCTANCE IN SUBMITTING TO THE HOLY SPIRIT

I found myself thinking one day about the likely reason why it is so hard for us to submit to the Holy Spirit. Why the reluctance, and why the excuses? I have tentatively come up with the following points:

1. We are creatures of habit and when we are used to a certain way or behaviour, it is hard to change or learn a new one.
2. We feel like when we give the Holy Spirit control of our lives, we are no longer in control. We feel vulnerable and our human instinct does not like and indeed protects us from vulnerabilities.
3. We are created and born to be in charge and to have dominion, and we will fight anything or anyone who wants to take that place or threatens to take the territory away from us.
4. Fear of the unknown; as rational human beings we want to know, reason, analyse and calculate. The fear of the unknown holds us back from following the leadings and prompting of the Holy Spirit. The fear of what would He ask me to do? What if I cannot do it? What if I do not want to do it?

5. Question of trust; do I trust the Holy Spirit enough to let Him run the show in my life? (Answer - I do not think so). I do not know this person enough to entrust my life to His hand.
6. Fear of submitting all. As human beings, we like to test the water first. We first submit one aspect or area where the risk and stakes are low. We check the result and if it took too long or the answer is not favourable, then we tend to withdraw or be more cautious.

These and other practical things can hold us back. We should commit all these doubts, fear, inhibitions, worries, and anxieties to the Holy Spirit. Commit a bit at a time if you cannot commit to everything and every area of your life at once. Like wine, we will mature with time and as our trust level increases, we begin to commit more aspects of our life into His capable hands. The Holy Spirit delivers; at the beginning of this book, we talked about His tried and tested, excellent, supernatural track record, that guarantees 100% result.

RECEIVING THE HOLY SPIRIT AS A GIFT

We all like to receive gifts and this gift that I am writing about is essential for our everyday life. We should bear in mind that these gifts come in order, as already mentioned in earlier chapters. Gift number one is the gift of salvation, gift number two is the gift of the Holy Spirit, and as you have read so far, there are many more gifts that we can receive from the Holy Spirit. Receiving salvation and, subsequently, the Holy Spirit, opens the door for the resources of heaven to be made available to us. If you have said the salvation prayer wholeheartedly, then you have received both gifts. To maintain your newly found faith, you will need to prayerfully look for a good church where the word of God is taught, and you can begin to grow in your Christian walk.

GROWING IN YOUR CHRISTIAN WALK

If you have said the salvation prayer sincerely, this is what you need to do to grow and flourish in your newly acquired faith.

1. Prayerfully look for a Bible-believing church, where the word of God is taught, and where you can go to worship and fellowship with other believers.
2. Read your Bible every day to develop your relationship with God (and if you do not already have a Bible, buy one). A good starting point for new believers is the Book of John. The book of John tells us about the love of God.
3. Pray every day and set a time aside to commune with your heavenly father. He wants to communicate with you.
4. Ask for the in-filling of the Holy Spirit, daily. As you read the Bible and have your daily devotions with God, He will expound the scriptures to you (being the author) and He will help you to pray for the Will of God.
5. Lastly, I would advise you to be mindful of the company of friends you keep. Your old friends will notice the change in you, and they will begin to feel uncomfortable around you, as you proclaim and profess your newly found faith.

You are now a new creature (person), your life is being transformed from the inside out, by the Holy Ghost; old things are gone, passed away and everything in your life will take a whole new perspective. That is the joy of salvation, that is the good news Jesus came to proclaim, and that is why the Holy Spirit has been sent to help us fulfil our assignments here on earth.

To be fully effective daily, we all need to be constantly filled with the Holy Ghost. You will be astonished at how the day will pan out and the joy, inner peace, and inner strength you will experience when you start your day with the in-filling presence of the Holy Spirit. What has been deposited on the inside of you will eventually work its way out. That is why it is important to ask for the in-filling of the Holy Spirit daily. You will be glad you asked, and you will be amazed at how your heart and your day will be filled with sheer joy, containment, and contentment, and you will find yourself intermittently breaking out in praises. You will be a daily living testament of the scripture in Ephesians 5:19, as you burst out in an ecstasy of unspeakable joy, speaking to yourself in psalms and hymns and spiritual songs, giving thanks, singing, and making melodies in your heart to the Lord. You will have this sort of experience when you start your day with a prayer along these lines.

SUGGESTED DAILY PRAYER

> *Father God, I thank You for sending your Son, Jesus Christ, to die for my sins, so I could be saved. I thank You for giving me your presence in the person of the Holy Spirit; I ask You to fill me with the Holy Spirit anew today. I now commit everything I will do, by way of actions, thoughts, words, and deeds into Your hands today. I*

give You the utter pre-eminence, I yield myself to You, have Your way in my life today, help me to fulfil Your will, plans, and purpose for my life today, in Jesus' name I pray. Amen.

When you start your day like this, there will be a spring in your step wherever you go or whatever you do. You will know that you are not alone. You will be a true Apostle and Ambassador for the Kingdom of God. Apostle means 'sent one' and Ambassador means 'a representative'. You will not go to your place of work as usual, but you will be sent there, and you will not go to your place of study as usual but are sent there. Whether you are in the house or outside of the house, you are sent on an errand, and are fulfilling the ambassadorial call. You will be aware that you are on an assignment and mandate to impact and influence people that you meet, see, or think about. This type of living is called experiencing heaven on earth. That is what eternal life is all about and the Holy Spirit has been sent to help us fulfil our individual calls and assignments in life.

AFTERWORD

I hope this book has answered some of the questions you might have about the Holy Spirit, and you have learned more about His role in our lives.

My hope is that your walk with the Holy Spirit gets stronger.

ABOUT THE AUTHOR

Stella has been a Christian for over three decades. She has a passion for God and loves to share her faith with others. The Holy Spirit is an integral part of her life, helping to shape her desire to encourage, empower and inspire those around her to live to their full potential.

This is her debut book.

She is a wife, mother, and health care professional. A hard-working, passionate individual, who enjoys finding new ways to pour into others, whether it's through offering advice, physically supporting people's visions, or lending a listening ear.

Find Stella online at: www.stellanbabudoh.com
Email Stella at: info@stellanbabudoh.com

REFERENCES

Dake's annotated Reference Bible
God's Answers to Man's Questions by Alban Douglas
I believe in Miracles by Kathryn Kuhlman
Major Bible Themes by Lewis Sperry Chafer
Amplified Version Classic Edition
English Standard Version
King James Version
New International Version
New King James Version
New American Standard Bible Version

NOTES

NOTES

NOTES

NOTES

NOTES

NOTES

NOTES

NOTES

NOTES

NOTES

NOTES

NOTES

NOTES

NOTES

NOTES

Printed in Great Britain
by Amazon

20852639R00183